Women and
Culture Series

*The Women and Culture Series is dedicated to books that illuminate the lives,
roles, achievements, and status of women, past or present.*

Fran Leeper Buss
Dignity: Lower Income Women Tell of Their Lives and Struggles
La Partera: Story of a Midwife

Valerie Kossew Pichanick
Harriet Martineau: The Woman and Her Work, 1802–76

Sandra Baxter and Marjorie Lansing
Women and Politics: The Visible Majority

Estelle B. Freedman
Their Sisters' Keepers: Women's Prison Reform in America, 1830–1930

Susan C. Bourque and Kay Barbara Warren
*Women of the Andes: Patriarchy and Social Change in
Two Peruvian Towns*

Marion S. Goldman
*Gold Diggers and Silver Miners: Prostitution and Social Life on the
Comstock Lode*

Page duBois
*Centaurs and Amazons: Women and the Pre-History of the Great Chain
of Being*

Mary Kinnear
Daughters of Time: Women in the Western Tradition

Lynda K. Bundtzen
Plath's Incarnations: Woman and the Creative Process

Violet B. Haas and Carolyn C. Perrucci, editors
Women in Scientific and Engineering Professions

Sally Price
Co-wives and Calabashes

Patricia R. Hill
*The World Their Household: The American Woman's Foreign Mission
Movement and Cultural Transformation, 1870–1920*

Diane Wood Middlebrook and Marilyn Yalom, editors
Coming to Light: American Women Poets in the Twentieth Century

Leslie W. Rabine
Reading the Romantic Heroine: Text, History, Ideology

Joanne S. Frye
*Living Stories, Telling Lives: Women and the Novel in Contemporary
Experience*

Coming to Light

Coming to Light
American Women Poets
in the Twentieth Century

Edited by Diane Wood Middlebrook
and Marilyn Yalom

Prepared under the auspices of the
Center for Research on Women,
Stanford University

ANN ARBOR
THE UNIVERSITY OF MICHIGAN PRESS

Copyright © by The University of Michigan 1985
All rights reserved
Published in the United States of America by
The University of Michigan Press and simultaneously
in Rexdale, Canada, by John Wiley & Sons Canada, Limited
Manufactured in the United States of America

1988   1987   1986   4   3

Library of Congress Cataloging in Publication Data

Main entry under title:

Coming to light.

(Women and culture series)
"Prepared under the auspices of the Center for Research
on Women, Stanford University."
Includes bibliographies.
  1. American poetry—Women authors—History and
criticism—Addresses, essays, lectures.   2. American
poetry—20th century—History and criticism—Addresses,
essays, lectures.   3. Women in literature—Addresses,
essays, lectures.   I. Middlebrook, Diane Wood.
II. Yalom, Marilyn.   III. Stanford University.   Center
for Research on Women.   IV. Series.
PS151.C65   1985   811'.5'099287   85-1145
ISBN 0-472-10066-1 (alk. paper)
ISBN 0-472-08061-X (pbk. : alk. paper)

Acknowledgments

It seems appropriate that gifts in honor of a mother and a daughter, women whose birthdates were separated by a century, made possible the 1982 Stanford University conference on women's poetry for which most of the essays in this book were written. We wish to thank Pauline and Sidney Newcomer for their gift in memory of Rebecca Kosier Newcomer, and Norma Lundholm Djerassi for her gift in memory of Pamela Djerassi Bush.

The conference was sponsored by Stanford University's Center for Research on Women, The Humanities Center, and the Division of Graduate Studies. Supplemental funding was received from the Ford Foundation and B. Dalton Books. We are grateful for their support.

Some members of the original conference planning committee—Professors Albert Gelpi, John Felstiner, Diane Middlebrook, and Marilyn Yalom—appear as contributors to this book; other members who gave equally of their time and energies include Professor Anne Mellor and graduate students Doree Allen, Joanne Kliejunas, Rebecca Mark, Valerie Matsumoto, and Loren Rusk (who proposed the title *Coming to Light*.)

Fifteen poets participated in the conference: Chana Bloch, Lorna Dee Cervantes, Kathleen Fraser, Judy Grahn, Louise Glück, Carolyn Kizer, Denise Levertov, Janet Lewis, Audre Lorde, Frances Mayes, Colleen McElroy, Josephine Miles, Kitty Tsui, Alma Villanueva, and Bernice Zamora. Sixteen professional women printers prepared the portfolio cover and one broadside each for the participating poets. Kathleen Walkup from Matrix Press coordinated the broadside project; participating printers included Christine Bertelson, Bonnie Bernstein, Frances Butler, Eileen Callahan, Betsy Davids, Carol Denison, Georgianna Greenwood, Mary Ann Hayden, Robin Heyeck, Shelley Hoyt-Koch, Susan King, Leigh McLellan, Cheryl Miller, Felicia Rice, Jaime Robles, and Kathleen Walkup.

Grateful acknowledgment is made to the following authors, publishers, and journals for permission to reprint previously published materials:

American Indian Culture and Research Journal for an earlier version of "Answering the Deer" which appeared in June 1983. Originally written under partial support of a fellowship from the University of California at Los Angeles.

Ulla E. Dydo for "To Have the Winning Language: Texts and Contexts of Gertrude Stein," © 1984 by Ulla E. Dydo.

Farrar, Straus and Giroux Inc. for excerpts from *The Blue Estuaries: Poems 1923–1968*, © 1968 by Louise Bogan.

Grand Street for "Trial Balances" from *Grand Street* 3, no. 1

G. K. Hall for "In Yeats's House" from *Sylvia Plath: Critical Essays*, 1984.

New England Quarterly for 'I Tapped My Own Head': The Apprenticeship of Anne Sexton" which appeared in an earlier version entitled "Housewife into Poet," *New England Quarterly,* December 1983. Previously unpublished materials by Anne Sexton printed by permission of Linda Grey Sexton and the Humanities Center, University of Texas, Austin. Previously unpublished passages from letters by John Holmes printed by permission of Doris Eyges.

Southern Review for "Hilda in Egypt," which appeared in an earlier version in *Southern Review* 18, no. 2 (Spring 1983).

Stanford Literature Review for "Philomela's Loom," portions of which appeared in "The Voice of the Shuttle Is Ours" in *Stanford Literature Review* 1, no. 1 (Spring 1984).

University of Chicago Press for "'I Go where I Love': An Intertextual Study of H.D. and Adrienne Rich" in *Signs* 9, no. 2 (Winter 1983); and "The Thieves of Language" in *Signs* 8, no. 1 (Autumn 1982).

Every effort has been made to trace the ownership of all copyrighted material and to secure permission for its use.

Contents

The open question with which I began was: what did it matter that many of the great writers of modern times have been women? What did it matter to literature?

—Ellen Moers, *Literary Women*

Prologue: Coming to Light

Diane Wood Middlebrook

> Thinking of the sea I think of light
> lacing, lancing the water
> the blue knife of a radiant consciousness
> bent by the waves of vision as it pierces
> to the deepest grotto
>
> And I think of those lives we tried to live
> in our globed helmets, self-enclosed
> bodies self-illumined gliding
> safe from the turbulence
>
> and how, miraculously, we failed
> —Adrienne Rich, "The Wave" (1973)

In 1971, Adrienne Rich read at the annual meeting of the Modern Language Association a paper titled "When We Dead Awaken: Writing as Re-Vision." Elegant, personal, and polemical, the paper described the situation of a mature talented woman who had received her education and her recognition in a realm of mastery where the work of women had been viewed as relatively insignificant. Rich held that studying the traditional literary curriculum inhibited women's drive for self-knowledge because that canon contained so little trace of women's consciousness of themselves. She urged a revisionary look at ignored women writers, and asserted that literature needed to be confronted with women's questions. "We need to know the writing of the past, and know it differently than we have ever known it," she argued; "not to pass on a tradition but to break its hold over us."[1] Breaking the hold of tradition was the theme also of many poems Rich was writing during that period, such as "The Wave." "Self-illumined," "safe," the diver—helmeted by both a technology and an education—brings into the sea's deep grottos the lamp of objectifying consciousness but not the full range of the senses, the naked person. Moreover in diving gear women look the same as men and everybody is the same color. Yet the voice in a piece of writing can never actually be without social identity:

it is always attached to a writer. So in a single metaphor does Rich condense a major theme of her essay: that the values of a seemingly "impersonal" criticism, shielded from the turbulence of the actual social contexts in which art is produced and circulated, circumscribe our access to the writer's vision.

"When We Dead Awaken" was not a highly original piece of thinking—Virginia Woolf had made much the same argument in *A Room of One's Own* (1928), among other texts acknowledged by Rich. But it was a thesis whose time had come—it is frequently cited in the notes of the essays that appear in this book. In her influential double role as poet and critic, Rich exemplifies the spirit of revisionary consciousness that integrates this collection of sixteen essays we have entitled *Coming to Light*. The essays are quite diverse in approach. But collectively they bring into focus two questions central to the feminist criticism of modern poetry, questions implicit in poetry by women and adumbrated in Rich's essay.

The first is: How have distinguished women poets solved the conundrum of receiving an education in a tradition scarce in exemplary women? The modern poetic tradition, right through the Second World War, acknowledges no influence comparable to the importance accorded Sappho by succeeding centuries of Greek and Roman poets, to whom Sapphics were a challenging stanza form. The desire to be a "great" poet in the sense that Shakespeare, Milton, and Whitman are acknowledged great is usefully delusional in both sexes, but like the desire to be president of the United States, a slightly less ridiculous ambition in a young man. Women writers have always had to rationalize imaginatively their efforts to achieve recognition within a system that overlooks them. Some of their solutions to the problem are explored here in Alicia Ostriker's introductory chapter, and in the following essays on Mina Loy, Gertrude Stein, H.D., Louise Bogan, Elizabeth Bishop, Denise Levertov, Anne Sexton, Sylvia Plath, Lucille Clifton, Adrienne Rich, and a contingent of Native American poets including Leslie Marmon Silko, Mary Randle Tallmountain, Wendy Rose, Elizabeth Cook-Lynn, Joy Harjo, Roberta Hill, Linda Hogan.

Of course, a book like this one is also an expression of an era that has come to challenge the very category of "greatness" as a social construct. The challenge itself now carries the academic label "postmodern": meaning, succinctly, the attitudes of a generation of artists that has flourished since the Second World War, inheritors of modernist formal experimentation and disillusion. The poetry of such influential modernists as Yeats, Eliot, and Pound reflects the devastation of a unified European culture; the characteristic work of each is an ironic individual fusion of a shattered great tradition. The postmodernist poet is one indifferent to or suspicious of the very idea of a "unified culture." Evolving contemporaneously with emancipatory political movements such as black nationalism, women's liberation, and gay consciousness, literary postmodernism licenses virtually any form of resistance to hierarchy and hegemony.

The second question explored in *Coming to Light* is based in the postmodernist perspective; it asks: How have women tapped for poetry the resources of specifically female experience in our polarized gender system, unexamined in criticism until very recently? For modernist poets such as H.D., Gertrude Stein, and Marianne Moore have previously been discussed, according to the modernist valuing of "impersonality," almost exclusively in terms of their contributions to poetic form and not at all as insinuators of female difference into the poetic tradition. It seems that on the whole this gender-blind acceptance was agreeable to them. But once the question is asked—What difference does it make that the poet was a woman?—fascinating new critical terrain opens immediately.

Coming to Light takes its place in this terrain, ground that has now been worked productively for over a decade. A few titles will help to clarify where we place our book. Suzanne Juhasz's *Naked and Fiery Forms: Modern American Poetry by Women, a New Tradition* (1976) was an early contribution to understanding the ways certain American women poets assimilated the modernist tradition. It was followed by the collection *Shakespeare's Sisters: Feminist Essays on Woman Poets* (1979) edited by Sandra Gilbert and Susan Gubar, which demonstrated in a wide range of critical approaches the value of considering a poet's sex and race as categories of significance in understanding the work. More recently, books such as *The Third Woman: Minority Women Writers of the United States* (1980), edited by Dexter Fisher, and Alicia Ostriker's *Writing Like a Woman* (1983) illuminate the influence of the new cultural climate on the way women read and write poetry today. These also testify to the enormous importance of women's poetry to the political evolution of contemporary women's movements.

Feminist thinking has also begun to trickle into critical anthologies not devoted exclusively to women poets. Two significant examples are

The Harvard Guide to Contemporary American Writing (1979), edited by
Daniel Hoffman, and *Claims for Poetry* (1982), edited by Donald Hall.
Hoffman devotes many thoughtful pages, mildly inflected by feminist
insights, to most of the poets discussed in *Coming to Light,* while Hall
inserts among the forty-three well-chosen pieces in his anthology
important claims for women's poetry by Sandra Gilbert, Alicia Os-
triker, Adrienne Rich, Audre Lorde, and Alice Walker; and important
general discussions of poetics by Tess Gallagher and Denise Levertov.
The wave, to recall Rich's metaphor, has swelled.

   Coming to Light is not offered as an overview or as a last word
about the place of feminist thinking in this sea of criticism, but as a
contribution to the wave. The book originated in a conference held at
Stanford University in 1982 to commemorate Sylvia Plath's fiftieth
birthday. Selected scholarly papers written for the conference form the
core of this book on the relation of women poets to the American liter-
ary tradition as it stands in the mid-1980s. Several of the papers are
biographical; others focus on symbols, on style, on single texts. But all
of the critics assume that uniquely valuable readings flow from asking
about the differences it makes that the poet is a woman. What the crit-
ics find, however, is never simply an untold "woman's side" to the
story. Since the subjectivity of literary texts is authoritative, appropria-
tion of a textual voice can be viewed as the appropriation of power.
This recognition leads to the questions raised in all of these essays re-
garding the contradiction embedded in culture between the category
"woman" and the category "writer," cross-grained by tenacious as-
sumptions that the writer is both heterosexual and white.

   Alicia Ostriker's essay "The Thieves of Language: Women Poets
and Revisionist Mythmaking" furnishes *Coming to Light* with its intro-
duction. Ostriker's essay presents an overview of the ways in which
twentieth-century American women poets have invaded "the sanctu-
aries of existing language, the treasuries where our meanings for 'male'
and 'female' are themselves preserved." Ostriker surveys a range of
revisionary strategies in contemporary short poems by Alta, Jong, Le-
vertov, Atwood, and others, then turns her attention to book-length
mythological poems: H.D.'s *Helen in Egypt,* Susan Griffin's *Woman and
Nature: The Roaring Inside Her,* and Anne Sexton's *Transformations.* In
the work of all these mythmakers, Ostriker observes, "the old stories
are changed, changed utterly by female knowledge of female experi-
ence. . . .they are representations of what women find divine and de-

monic in themselves; they are retrieved images of what women have collectively and historically suffered; in some cases they are instructions for survival."

After "Thieves of Language," the essays in *Coming to Light* discuss the poets in roughly chronological order, beginning with the modernists.

In "The New Poetry and the New Woman," Carolyn Burke writes about Mina Loy's contribution to major experimental modes developed in the twentieth century. Remarking that although Mina Loy's name is no longer familiar, "in 1916 it was synonymous with the most daring experiments in modern poetry," Burke goes on to draw explicit connections between the "politics of the new woman and the principles of the new poetry" appearing in the little magazines where the modernist revolution was influentially under way in the years of Mina Loy's flourishing (1914–19). "Now that we are revising our understanding of feminism in this period," Burke writes, "we need also to revise our literary histories, especially in relation to the woman question."

As Burke indicates, an important model for Mina Loy's radicalism was the work of Gertrude Stein. However, Stein's writing experiments proved so daring as to be virtually unpublishable, according to Ulla Dydo in "To Have the Winning Language: Texts and Contexts of Gertrude Stein." Working with both printed and archival materials, Dydo discusses the evolution of Stein's literary aesthetic, and proposes readings of specific works by Stein, describing connections between experience and design in Stein's poetry.

The next two contributions amplify themes initiated in Ostriker's discussion of revisionary mythmaking. Myths and archetypes characterizing the poet's power—a frequent subject in the criticism of Romantic and High Modern poetry—are the concern of essays on H.D. and Louise Bogan. Albert Gelpi's discussion of *Helen in Egypt* focuses on the evolution and completion of the "feminine archetype" who is heroine of H.D.'s poem, arguing that "the woman's myth it evolves posits the supremacy of the mother: Helen self-born in Thetis, Hilda self-born in Helen." Mary DeShazer, writing on Louise Bogan, observes that Bogan mythologizes the poet's power or Muse as "a powerful alternate 'self' rather than an externalized, objectified 'other'"; but this self takes shape in a "perverse" or "demonic" language and voice, Bogan's expression of anxiety regarding the embodiment of the poet's power in a female body. Bogan resolves the contradiction, DeShazer argues, in the imagery of self-confrontation that characterizes some of her strongest work.

The poetry of Elizabeth Bishop elicits from critics David Kalstone and Joanne Diehl different questions about the sources of poetic authority. David Kalstone explores the elusive influences on Bishop of Marianne Moore. Working largely from unpublished letters and journals, Kalstone speculates on the ways their respectful intimacy guided Bishop into uses of a personal history she tended to repress and deny: Bishop's "blithe strengths were the product of tensions and fears," Kalstone observes. "Moore's secure bravado in dealing with the physical world was something Bishop instinctively valued though she only gradually absorbed it into her writing."

In her essay on Bishop, Joanne Diehl summarizes the tradition of the American sublime as expressed in Emerson, whose "sweeping gesture of inclusiveness. . . incorporates both male and female identities." Rejecting the tradition of Emerson and Whitman, which identifies poetic power with an Adamic self, Bishop—like Emily Dickinson—makes herself "at home with loss." Through strategic use of irony and self-effacement, "Bishop breaks the confines of a sexually determined tradition to discover an authorizing voice that moves beyond gender."

Denise Levertov has for many years been a political activist, one particularly identified with human rights and with antiwar and antinuclear movements. John Felstiner discusses the presence of political consciousness in her poetry, associating Levertov's social conscience with her belief in the power of precisely named feeling to arouse the reverence for life which lies behind much commitment to social change. Personal and communal *witness* are the actions urged in Levertov's poetry, Felstiner observes.

Felstiner remarks on Levertov's unwillingness to be categorized politically as a feminist. Few of the other contemporary poets discussed in *Coming to Light* are self-styled feminists either. But a poet need not be a feminist (or a woman) to elicit feminist readings, as is demonstrated in the essays that follow on Sylvia Plath, Anne Sexton, Lucille Clifton, and the Native American poets discussed by Paula Gunn Allen.

The name of Sylvia Plath dominates this section of *Coming to Light,* reflecting the great interest stirred by the recent publications of both Plath's journals and the newly edited *Collected Poems,* which received a posthumous Pulitzer Prize. Like Rich and Sexton, Plath formed her early style in the intellectual environment of the poetics of

Yeats, Eliot, Tate, and Ransom. The most admired, and most marketable, poetry of the period was ornately formal, allusive, academic: what Robert Lowell called "cooked."[2] Achieving a distinctive voice in this artistic milieu meant, for the women, finding a way to admit into poetry not only the "raw"—social oppression, personal crisis, ordinary pain—but the female. Plath's poetry, most of it published after her suicide, gave enormous impetus to this movement in women's poetry.

The three new essays on Plath published here build on recently available biographical materials. Sandra Gilbert's wide-ranging commentary discusses Plath's rivalrous readings of modernist texts, exploring the conflicts internalized by Plath "between male authority and female identity, or, to be more specific, between male creation and female creativity." Gilbert proposes that Plath "had to 'lay down' her body. . . because, encouraged as she was by history and prophecy, she had to suffer in her own person the sexual battle that marked a turning point in time. . . . We who are Sylvia Plath's contemporaries and descendants must still listen to the questions she hammered out." Marilyn Yalom and Barbara Mossberg examine psychological issues significant in Plath's poetry. Plath's obsessions with death and childbirth are the focus of Yalom's reading of *The Bell Jar* and related poems. Exploring both existential and gendered dimensions of Plath's disequilibrium, Yalom gleans "insights into human pathology in general and female pathology in particular." Mossberg, working from an examination of the Plath "precosia" at the Lilly Library, proposes that Plath's mother functioned as an elicitor of two different voices in Plath, "the nuzzling little 'Sivvy' who wants to be loved, and the angry woman sulking upstairs, finding her mother's world intolerable."

My biographical essay on Anne Sexton returns to problems like those posed by Gilbert, regarding the apprentice poet's difficulties in achieving recognition for her originality. I describe Sexton's conflict with her first teacher over the subject matter of her early poems, arguing that Sexton protected her strengths as an artist by opposing his advice.

Just as the recognition of women writers as women makes visible the significance of gender in literature, so the emergence of writers who are women of color exposes the imprint of racial dominance in the literary tradition. Responding to the civil rights movement, which among other social changes brought significant numbers of black and Hispanic writers into print, literary criticism in the 1970s began integrating them according to genre, period, influence, theme, and other more rarefied categories specific to prevailing schools of criticism. This was, of course, a criticism produced by and for the dominant group. A countercriticism developed to challenge the validity of the bipolar classification white/nonwhite—for example, by illuminating the specificity of language in black writing and by contemplating material influences, including African origins, which thinned the relevance of traditional (white) literary categories. Two of the essays in *Coming to Light* indicate ways in which racial consciousness may be introduced into traditional notions of the literary canon.

Andrea Benton Rushing makes use of the individual case, exploring the separatist aesthetics and politics of black consciousness which enrich the subjectivity of Lucille Clifton's lyrics. Rushing observes that the work of the writer displays temporary forms of reconciliation among contending loyalties and threats which resist institutional solutions. Self-revealing and "confiding," Clifton's poetry "diverges from the creations of her contemporaries," both male and female, in the qualities of introspection and humor that mark her style. Yet inseparable from what might otherwise be called her "individuality" is her (and the reader's) consciousness that "the soul-changing crusade" of the Black Arts movement of the 1960s and 1970s was "the crucible which most searingly shaped her art."

Paula Gunn Allen's "Genocide and Continuance in American Indian Women's Poetry" is a personal essay reflecting on the cultural legacies that fall due in the life of a well-educated woman identified with her tribe. "It has long appeared that the survival of any tribal people required the acceptance of tribal extinction," she observes. "Transformation—metamorphosis—is the oldest of tribal themes, of metaphysical manipulations, of sacred transactions, and it comes again into focus in the poetry of extinction and regeneration . . . , the only poetry a contemporary Indian woman can write."

Allen's essay also illuminates the ambiguity of the category "race," for her references range across tribal boundaries which are ethnic and linguistic as well.

Susan Stanford Friedman's contribution brings the collection of essays on individual poets full circle, back to themes raised in Ostriker's "Thieves of Language," examining the relationship of the modernist poet H.D. to the feminist poet Adrienne Rich. Friedman outlines an intellectual biography in Rich's poetry and prose, pursuing Rich's in-

creasing engagement with the work of H.D. as an example of the way
Rich absorbed other women writers in the process of developing her
own theory and poetics. Friedman argues that *Helen in Egypt,*
"Trilogy," and other works of H.D. are complex influences on the
thought and the poetics of Adrienne Rich since 1973. Demonstrating
the presence of H.D. woven into all of Rich's feminist writing, Fried-
man also considers Rich's "increasing disillusionment with radical hu-
manism" to be an implicit critique of H.D.'s vision.

Coming to Light closes with an epilogue by Patricia Klindienst
Joplin. In "Philomela's Loom," Joplin comments on the significance of
the female reader, the female audience to the practice of feminist crit-
icism, a subject unexamined in preceding essays. Conceiving of essays
such as those collected here as, in part, a form of redress, Joplin also
raises the (open) question of the motives behind compiling such a book.
"Any claim to a privileged possession of the truth, any appropriation of
sole power to speak carries with it the potential to violate an-
other. . . .Can women now weave texts and interpret them without
reproducing another sacrificial crisis?" Among women as well as be-
tween women and men, feminist criticism has been used both to con-
solidate a sense of community and to patrol the boundaries that separate
ideological camps. But Joplin's hopeful reply to her own question
evokes the spirit of the epigraph from Adrienne Rich with which we
opened, in which the weaponry of hunting is appropriated as a meta-
phor for insight:

> light
> lacing, lancing the water
> the blue knife of a radiant consciousness
> bent by waves of vision as it pierces
> to the deepest grotto.

NOTES

1. *On Lies, Secrets and Silence: Selected Prose 1966–1978* (New York:
W. W. Norton & Co., 1979), pp. 33–50.

2. In his address on receiving the National Book Award in 1960, Lowell
compared two "competing" kinds of poetry: "The cooked, marvelously expert
and remote, seems constructed as a sort of mechanical or catnip mouse for
graduate seminars; the raw, jerry-built and forensically deadly, seems often like
an unscored libretto by some bearded but vegetarian Castro." Quoted in Ian
Hamilton, *Robert Lowell: A Biography* (New York: Random House, 1982), p.
277.

The Thieves of Language: Women Poets and Revisionist Mythmaking

Alicia Ostriker

I

What would become of logocentrism, of the great philosophical systems, of world order in general if the rock upon which they founded their church were to crumble?

If it were to come out in a new day that the logocentric project had always been, undeniably, to found (fund) phallocentrism, to insure for masculine order a rationale equal to history itself?

Then all the stories would have to be told differently, the future would be incalculable, the historical forces would, will, change hands, bodies, another thinking as yet not thinkable, will transform the functioning of all society.

—Hélène Cixous[1]

> Nudgers and shovers
> In spite of ourselves,
> Our kind multiplies:
> We shall by morning
> Inherit the earth.
> Our foot's in the door.

—Sylvia Plath[2]

A major theme in feminist theory on both sides of the Atlantic for the past decade has been the demand that women writers be, in Claudine Herrmann's phrase, *voleuses de langue,* thieves of language, female Prometheuses.[3] Though the language we speak and write has been an encoding of male privilege, what Adrienne Rich calls an "oppressor's language"[4] inadequate to describe or express women's experience, a "Law of the Father"[5] which transforms the daughter to "the invisible women in the asylum corridor"[6] or "the silent woman" without access to authoritative expression,[7] we must also have it in our power to "seize speech" and make it say what we mean.

Women writers have always tried to steal the language. What several recent studies demonstrate poignantly is that throughout most of her history, the woman writer has had to state her self-definitions in code form, disguising passion as piety, rebellion as obedience.[8] Dickinson's "Tell all the Truth but tell it slant" speaks for writers who in every century have been inhibited both by economic dependence and by the knowledge that true *writer* signifies assertion while true *woman* signifies submission. Among poets, even more than novelists, the thefts have been filchings from the servant's quarters. When Elaine Marks surveys the *écriture féminine* movement in Paris, she observes that in their manifestos of desire "to destroy the male hegemony" over language, "the rage is all the more intense because the writers see themselves as prisoners of the discourse they despise. But is it possible," she asks, "to break out?"[9]

Does there exist, as a subterranean current below the surface structure of male-oriented language, a specifically female language, a "mother tongue"? This is a debated issue. A variety of theorists argue in favor, others argue against, while a number of empirical studies in America seem to confirm that insofar as speech is "feminine," its strength is limited to evoking subjective sensation and interpersonal responsiveness; it is not in other respects powerful.[10]

The question of whether a female language, separate but equal to male language, either actually eixsts or can (or should) be created, awaits further research into the past and further gynocentric writing in the present. My argument in this paper concerns the already very large body of poetry by American women, composed in the last twenty years, in which the project of defining a female self has been a major endeavor.[11] What distinguishes these poets, I propose, is not the shared, exclusive *langage des femmes* desired by some but a vigorous and various invasion of the sanctuaries of existing language, the treasuries where our meanings for "male" and "female" are themselves preserved. I have elsewhere examined the ways in which contemporary women poets employ traditional images for the female body—flower, water, earth—retaining the gender identification of these images but transforming their attributes so that flower means force instead of frailty, water means safety instead of death, and earth means creative imagination instead of passive generativeness.[12] Here I want to look at larger poetic structures and suggest the idea that revisionist mythmaking in women's poetry may offer us one significant means of redefining ourselves and consequently our culture.

At first thought, mythology seems an inhospitable terrain for a woman writer. There we find the conquering gods and heroes, the deities of pure thought and spirituality so superior to Mother Nature; there we find the sexually wicked Venus, Circe, Pandora, Helen, Medea, Eve, and the virtuously passive Iphigenia, Alcestis, Mary, Cinderella. It is thanks to myth we believe that woman must be either "angel" or "monster."[13]

Yet the need for myth of some sort may be ineradicable. Poets, at least, appear to think so. When Muriel Rukeyser in "The Poem as Mask" exclaimed "No more masks! No more mythologies,"[14] she was rejecting the traditional division of myth from a woman's subjectivity, rejecting her own earlier poem that portrays Orpheus and the bacchic women who slew him as separate from herself. "It was myself," she says, "split open, unable to speak, in exile from myself." To recognize this, however, is evidently to heal both the torn self and the torn god; the poem's final lines describe a resurrected Orpheus whose "fragments join in me with their own music." When Adrienne Rich in "Diving into the Wreck" carries with her a "book of myths . . . in which / our names do not appear" and declares that she seeks "the wreck and not the story of the wreck / the thing itself and not the myth," while enacting a watery descent that inverts the ascents and conquests of male heroism, she implies the necessity, for a woman, of distinguishing between myth and reality. Yet when Rich identifies with a "mermaid" and "merman" and says that "We are, I am, you are . . . the one who find our way / back to this scene," the androgynous being and the fluid pronouns imply that "the thing itself" is itself mythic.[15]

When Circe in Margaret Atwood's "Circe/Mud Poems" snarls at her lover, "It's the story that counts. No use telling me this isn't a story, or not the same story. . . . Don't evade, don't pretend you won't leave after all: you leave in the story and the story is ruthless," she too describes the depersonalizing effects of myths on persons, the way they replay themselves over and over and "the events run themselves through / almost without us." But at the point of stating this, the poet declares that there are "two islands" that "do not exclude each other" and that the second "has never happened," "is not finished," "is not frozen yet."[16] In all these cases the poet simultaneously deconstructs a prior "myth" or "story" and constructs a new one which includes, instead of excluding, herself.

Let me at this point therefore define the term "revisionist myth-making" and sketch the background behind the work I will discuss. Whenever a poet employs a figure or story previously accepted and defined by a culture, the oet is using myth, and the potential is always present that the use will   revisionist: that is, the figure or tale will be appropriated for altered ends, the old vessel filled with new wine, initially satisfying the thirst of the individual poet but ultimately making cultural change possible. Historic and quasi-historic figures like Napoleon and Sappho are in this sense mythic, as are folktales, legends, and Scripture. Like the gods and goddesses of classical mythology, all such material has a double power. It exists or appears to exist objectively, in the public sphere, and consequently confers on the writer the sort of authority unavailable to someone who writes "merely" of the private self. Myth belongs to "high" culture and is handed "down" through the ages by religious, literary, and educational authority. At the same time, myth is quintessentially intimate material, the stuff of dream life, forbidden desire, inexplicable motivation—everything in the psyche that to rational consciousness is unreal, crazed, or abominable.

In the wave of poetic mythmaking that broke over England in the Romantic period, we hear two strains. One is public antirationalism, an insistence that there were more things in heaven and earth than were dreamt of by Newton and Locke. The other is an assurance that the poets had personally experienced forces within the self so overwhelming that they must be described as gods and goddesses, titans, demiurges, and demons. But Romantic revisionists do not simply take seriously what the Augustans took ornamentally. When Shelley invents for his defiant Prometheus an anima not present in any classical source, or when "knowledge enormous" of divine and human suffering makes a god and a poet of Keats's Apollo, who then dies into immortal life with a scream: that is mythic revisionism. (The same scream, by the way, tears through the young throat of Edna St. Vincent Millay, in a poem many women loved as girls and later learned to despise; "Renascence," too, is a poem about the genesis of a poet.)

Like the Romantics, the early Moderns—Yeats, Pound, Eliot—turned to myth as a means of defying their culture's rationalism and materialism. But while the women poets I will speak of share a distrust for rationalism, they do not share the Modernist nostalgia for a golden age of past culture, and their mythmaking grows at least as much from a subterranean tradition of female self-projection and self-exploration as from the system building of the Romantics and Moderns.[17]

Since 1960 one can count over a dozen major works (poem sequences, long poems, or whole books) of revisionist myth published by American women, and one cannot begin to count the individual poems in which familiar figures from male tradition emerge altered. These poems generically assume the high literary status that myth confers and that women writers have often been denied because they write "personally" or "confessionally." But in them the old stories are changed, changed utterly, by female knowledge of female experience, so that they can no longer stand as foundations of collective male fantasy. Instead, as I hope by a few brief examples to show, they are corrections; they are representations of what women find divine and demonic in themselves; they are retrieved images of what women have collectively and historically suffered; in some cases they are instructions for survival.

II

> Women have had the power of *naming* stolen from us. . . . To exist humanly is to name the self, the world and God. . . . Words which, materially speaking, are identical with the old become new in a semantic context that arises from qualitatively new experience.
> —Mary Daly[18]

Since the core of revisionist mythmaking for women poets lies in the challenge to and correction of gender stereotypes embodied in myth, revisionism in its simplest form consists of hit-and-run attacks on familiar images and the social and literary conventions supporting them. Thus in the stroke of a phrase, Sylvia Plath's Lady Lazarus dismisses "Herr God, Herr Lucifer" as the two faces of a single authoritarian and domineering being for whom a woman's body is "your jewel . . . your valuable." Anne Sexton in "Snow White" disposes of centuries of reverence for the virgin "rolling her china-blue doll eyes. . . . Open to say / Good Day Mama / and shut for the thrust / of the unicorn." Jean Tepperman's "Witch" begins with the lines "They told me / I smile prettier with my mouth closed" and ends calling for a black dress, wild hair, and her broomstick. Of the passive Euridice who exists only as the tragic object of Orpheus's love, the poet Alta writes a motto for any woman poet:

> all the male poets write of orpheus
> as if they look back & expect
> to find me walking patiently
> behind them. they claim i fell into hell.
> damn them, i say.
> i stand in my own pain
> & sing my own song.

Another solution to the male creator–female muse convention is Erica Jong's "Arse Poetica," a role-reversing prose-poem that contrives at once to deflate centuries of male aesthetic pretentiousness and to assert the identity of female sexuality and female creativity:

> Once the penis has been introduced into the poem, the poet lets herself down until she is sitting on the muse with her legs outside him. He need not make any motions at all.[19]

With poems like these, one imagines the poets stepping out of the ring dusting their hands off. But revisionist poems do not necessarily confine themselves to defiance and reversal strategies.

A more central set of preoccupations concerns female-female relationships and the relation of the female to suppressed dimensions of her own identity. Kate Ellis's "Matrilineal Descent" uses the Demeter-Kore story as an aid in discovering how we may reconstitute lost families, becoming spiritual mothers and daughters for each other in time of need. Mothers, daughters, sisters must be recovered as parts "of the original woman we are"; after dreaming that a rivalrous younger sister is a daughter, and killing her in the dream, the poet movingly realizes that like Demeter she can "go down and get her / it is not too late." Sharon Barba's "A Cycle of Women" depicts women's history before and during patriarchy as "that dream world . . . that dark watery place" presided over by a goddess, which each individual woman must try to remember, although the knowledge is locked from her. "Each one is queen, mother, huntress" and must reconstruct the past "until she knows who she is":

> Until she rises as though from the sea
> not on the half-shell this time

> nothing to laugh at
> and not as delicate as he [Botticelli] imagined her:
> a woman big-hipped, beautiful, and fierce.[20]

Interlocked images of fertility and artistic creativity govern the poem-sequence "Eurydice" by Rachel DuPlessis. Here the heroine not only resents (like Alta's Euridice) the loss of herself to a husband whose powerful sex and art define her "like a great linked chain" but is herself the snake "whose deepest desire was to pierce herself." Withdrawing from her husband, far back into the moist, stony "fissure" and "cave" of herself, she becomes a self-generating plant and finally, amid an efflorescence of organic images, her own mother, giving birth to the girlchild who is herself—or, since the sequence can be read as an allegory of female creativity, her poem. The idea of giving birth, unaided, to the self, is also the conclusion of Adrienne Rich's "The Mirror in Which Two Are Seen as One," and governs the "dry bulb" metaphor of "Necessities of Life."[21]

All such poems are, I believe, aspects of an attempt by women to retrieve, from the myth of the abstract father god who creates the universe *ab nihilo,* the figure on which he was originally based, the female creatrix.[22] And this is a figure *not* divided (as she is in C. J. Jung's and Erich Neumann's versions of her) into Sky Goddess (asexual) and Earth Mother (sexual but brainless).[23] Female attributes of flesh and spirit that traditional culture sets asunder, female writers commonly reunite. "The Goddess" for Denise Levertov is a furious woman who seizes the poet where she lies asleep in "Lie Castle" and hurls her against the walls. Prostrate outside the castle "where her hand had thrown me," the poet tastes the mud of a forest, bites the seed in her mouth, and senses the passing of "her" without whom nothing "flowers, fruits, sleeps in season, / without whom nothing / speaks in its own tongue, but returns / lie for lie!" To identify an active, aggressive woman with Truth is to defy a very long tradition that identifies strong females with deception[24] and virtuous females, including muses, with gentle inactivity. In "Song for Ishtar," one of Levertov's most playful and most compact poems, a Babylonian goddess of both Love and War evokes images for what is divine and mundane, spiritual and animal, delicate and violent in female sexuality and female art:

> The moon is a sow
> and grunts in my throat

Her great shining shines through me
so the mud of my hollow gleams
and breaks in silver bubbles

She is a sow
And I a pig and a poet

When she opens her white
lips to devour me I bite back
and laughter rocks the moon

In the black of desire
we rock and grunt, grunt and
shine[25]

A muse imagined in one's own likeness, with whom one can fornicate with violence and laughter, implies the extraordinary possibility of a poetry of wholeness and joy, as against the poetry of the "age of anxiety" in which Levertov was writing. That a sacred joy can be found within the self; that it requires an embracing of one's sexuality; that access to it must be described as movement downward or inward, in gender-charged metaphors of water, earth, cave, seed, moon: such is the burden of these and many other poems by women. To Stevens's post-Nietzschean formula "God and the imagination are one,"[26] they would add a crucial third element: God and the imagination and *my body* are one.

At the opposite pole from the creatrix is the destroyer, a figure women's poetry has been inhibited from exploring in the past by the need to identify femininity with morality. When they traffic in the demonic, women poets have produced some of the most highly charged images in recent American poetry. One thinks immediately of Plath's "disquieting muses," the three ladies "with stitched bald heads" who assemble around the poet, precipitated by the girl-scout cheeriness of a mother who attempts to deny reality's darkness; or the clinging "Medusa" who is at once classic monster, jellyfish, and the poet's mother; or her image of herself as avenging Phoenix-fiend at the close of "Lady Lazarus"; or the depiction of demonic possession in "Elm." In Anne Sexton, demonic images associated with madness, guilt, and death proliferate with increasing intensity, from the witches in *To Bedlam and Part Way Back* to the set of "Angels" in *The Book of Folly* whom the poet acquaints with "slime . . . bedbugs . . . paralysis," to the staggering "death baby" who is the poet's alter ego in *The Death Notebooks*.[27]

Plath and Sexton are dramatic portraitists, in contemporary poetry, of what Joseph Conrad called "the horror . . . the horror." Like Conrad, they imply that the hypocrisies of civilized rationality are powerless to destroy what is destructive in the world and in ourselves; indeed that "the horror" may well be the most devastating product of our demands for innocence and virtue. But what distinguishes their demonism from Conrad's, and from the standard personifications of "evil" throughout Western poetry, is the common characteristic of passivity. Wherever in these two poets we find images of compelling dread, there we also find images of muteness, blindness, paralysis, the condition of being manipulated.

Inactivity is also a motif in several poems written by women about classic female monsters. Of Medusa, a perennial figure in male poetry and iconography, Ann Stanford's sequence "Women of Perseus" and Rachel DuPlessis's "Medusa" both remind us of the key event in this female's life, though it goes unmentioned in either Bulfinch's or Edith Hamilton's *Mythology:* her rape by Poseidon. In Stanford's poem the trauma "imprisons" Medusa in a self-dividing anger and a will to revenge that she can never escape, though she yearns to. In DuPlessis's sequence the three Graeae—whose one eye Perseus steals—are conflated into one mother-figure for Medusa; her rapist and killer are conflated into one male; and she herself becomes a static boundary "stone" and regresses to an infantile ur-language.[28]

The Homeric earth-goddess and sorceress Circe, who turns Odysseus's fellow sailors to beasts and who throughout Western literature represents the evil magic of female sexuality, is transformed in Margaret Atwood's "Circe/Mud Poems" into an angry but also a quite powerless woman. Men turn themselves to animals; she has nothing to do with it. "Will you hurt me?" she asks Odysseus at his first armor-plated appearance. "If you do I will fear you, / If you don't I will despise you." Circe is "a desert island" or "a woman of mud" made for sexual exploitation, and her encounters with Odysseus are war games of rape, indifference, betrayal, which she can analyze caustically, mounting a shrewd critique of the heroic ethos:

> Aren't you tired of killing
> those whose deaths have been predicted
> and who are therefore dead already?
> Aren't you tired of wanting to live forever?
> Aren't you tired of saying Onward?

But this is passive, not active, resistance and cannot alter Odysseus's intentions. In Atwood's "Siren Song" the figure whose name still means "fatal seductress" sings a libretto of confinement turned vicious, "a stupid song / but it works every time." What Atwood implies, as do other women who examine the blackness that has represented femaleness so often in our culture, is that the female power to do evil is a direct function of her powerlessness to do anything else.[29]

III

> The short, passionate lyric has conventionally been thought appropriate for women poets if they insist on writing, while the longer, more philosophical epic belongs to the real (male) poet.
> —Susan Friedman[30]

If male poets write large, thoughtful poems while women poets write petite, emotional poems, the existence of book-length mythological poems by women on a literary landscape itself signifies trespass. Three such works are H.D.'s postwar masterpiece *Helen in Egypt,* Susan Griffin's extended prose-poem *Woman and Nature: The Roaring Inside Her,* and Anne Sexton's *Transformations.* They revise, respectively, ancient Greek and Egyptian mythology, the myth of objective discourse derived from the Western concept of a God superior to Nature, and a set of fairy tales. All of them challenge not only our culture's concepts of gender but also its concepts of reality.[31]

The *donnée* of H.D.'s three-part *Helen in Egypt* is that Helen of Troy—our culture's archetypal woman-as-erotic-object—was actually a male-generated illusion, a "phantom," and that "the Greeks and Trojans alike fought for an illusion."[32] H.D.'s sources are a fifty-line fragment by Stesichorus of Sicily (ca. 640–555 B.C.) and Euripides' drama *Helen.* According to these texts (themselves revisionist ones), "the real Helen" was transported by the gods from Greece to Egypt, where she spent the duration of the Trojan War waiting chastely for her husband Menelaus. In H.D.'s version Menelaus is a trivial figure, and the poet makes clear that sexual chastity—or any conventional morality—is no more to be expected of an epic heroine than of an epic hero. The poet radically transforms these sources as well as the vast body of Greek and Egyptian mythology of which she was mistress, and which she believed composed "all myth, the one reality" in the same way that she believed all history was a "palimpsest," a reiterated layering of changeless patterns. A more significant issue than the heroine's virtue is her relation to "the iron band of war"—meaning not only the Trojan War but the two world wars H.D. had lived through. Still more significant is the fact that the revised heroine is not woman-as-object at all, is not seen from the outside, but is instead a quintessential woman-as-subject, engaged in what is not a single but a threefold quest.[33]

H.D.'s "real Helen" is a "Psyche / with half-dried wings" (sec. 166), a soul emerging from a chrysalis of ignorance and passivity. Spiritually her quest is to decipher symbols, beginning with the hieroglyphs on the temple of the Egyptian god Thoth-Amen, where we find her alone at the poem's opening. This Helen is an "adept," an initiate seeking knowledge of the gods. Psychologically, she is engaged in the recovery of her splintered selves, elements of her own character and past which, we gradually discover, because they are "hated of all Greece" (sec. 2), have been "forgotten" by herself. These two tasks are one task, because "she herself is the writing" (sec. 22). The goddess who manifests herself as Isis-Aphrodite-Thetis is at first a mother-goddess to Helen but ultimately an aspect of her own identity.

As avatar of Aphrodite, the heroine must reconcile herself with the "Helen of Troy" she has forgotten she ever was. That is, the spiritual seeker must accept the erotic woman within herself. These discoveries coalesce, again, with a third aspect of her quest: the reconstitution of a primal family, which among other things means that Helen must determine the meaning to herself of her Trojan and Greek lovers, the seductive Paris and the militant Achilles, and must choose (not be chosen by) a "final lover."

Achilles, the great protagonist of the *Iliad*, is H.D.'s paradigmatic patriarchal male as Helen is the paradigmatic female. Heroic, male-centered, immortality-seeking, Achilles ruthlessly leads a group of "elect" warriors dedicated to discipline and control, called (punningly) "The Command." To Achilles, woman is either sacrificial victim or sexual spoils. He has forgotten his boyhood love of the mother-goddess Thetis. Precisely for this reason, Thetis—that is, the repressed feminine principle within him—can cause him to fall in love with the figure of Helen pacing the Trojan ramparts, and, in a moment of carelessness over an ankle-greave, to receive the fatal wound from "Love's arrow" in his heel: "it was God's plan / to melt the icy fortress of the soul, / and free the man." Helen's first perception of him in Egypt is of a dim outline growing clearer, "as the new Mortal, / shedding his glory, / limped slowly across the sand" (sec. 9–10).

H.D.'s attitude toward conquest (including the conquest of Time) anticipates Atwood's "Aren't you tired of killing . . . ? Aren't you tired of wanting to live forever?" Her image of masculine defense against feeling as a hard armor that should be dissolved and melted, for the man's own sake, parallels Rich's question in "The Knight": "Who will unhorse this rider / and free him from between / the walls of iron, the emblems / crushing his chest with their weight?"[34] It is cognate as well with the fates meted out to the male protagonists at the conclusions of *Jane Eyre* and *Aurora Leigh*. Brontë's and Browning's heroes are blinded in "fires" of sexual, and punitive, import. H.D.'s "arrow" penetrating a masculine chink is explicitly and evocatively sexual.

But the dissolving of male invulnerability in *Helen in Egypt* is part of a larger pattern. Helen's Trojan lover, Paris, while a less violent, more sensuous and woman-centered figure than Achilles, is ultimately assigned the role of "son" rather than "father" in a mother-father-son romantic triangle. Moreover, late in the poem Helen hears within herself "an heroic voice, the voice of Helen of Sparta," one who glories in "the thunder of battle . . . and the arrows; O the beauty of arrows" and must ask herself, "Do I love War? Is this Helena?" (secs. 176–77). The unveiling of this element in Helen parallels the release of Achilles' capacity to love. Replicating in mortal form the pattern of Isis-Osiris, Aphrodite-Ares (fecundity-knowledge, beauty-war), they link equal and opposite forces, generating a child ("Euphorion," pleasure or joy, equivalent of the Egyptian Horus and the Greek Eros) who will unite the attributes of both.

For the driving intellectual impulse in *Helen in Egypt* is the synthesizing of opposites. Typhon and Osiris, killer and victim of Egyptian myth, were "not two but one . . . to the initiate" (sec. 27); the daughter of Helen's sister Clytemnestra, and her own daughter Hermione, are identified as "one" sacrificial maiden (sec. 69); the Greek Zeus and the Egyptian Amen are "One," though manifested as "a series of multiple gods" (sec. 78). The same is true of some of the poem's key images or hieroglyphs: a beach of white "shells" and one of "skulls," the string of the lyre and the warrior's bowstring, the flaming brazier in the comforter's house and the flame of the burning Troy— these too are cognate, related forms, mutually dependent opposites. Eventually Helen intuits that Love and Death, Eros and Eris (strife), unlike the Eros and Thanatos posited by the aged Freud as eternally dual principles, "will merge in the final illumination" (sec. 271).

At the same time, the poem is primarily psychodrama, and, to a

degree paralleled by very few poems in our literature, nonmimetic of
the external material world beyond the psyche. That world is repre-
sented in it to a great extent by men in ships or at war, and the relation
of such "realities" to Helen's identity is only one of the enigmas she is
solving in the poem. Thus the fascinating, flickering alternation be-
tween prose and verse in *Helen in Egypt* is that of a single mind having
an urgent dialogue with itself, probing, questioning—an extraor-
dinarily large portion of the poem's text takes the form of questions—
and persisting despite confusion ("What does he mean by that? . . .
Helena? who is she?") in the effort of feminine self-definition: "I must
fight for Helena" (sec. 37). "I am not, nor mean to be / The Daemon
they made of me" (sec. 109). "I will encompass the infinite / in time, in
the crystal / in my thought here" (sec. 201). H.D. called the poem her
"Cantos," and it is an implicit challenge to Ezra Pound's culturally
encyclopedic *Cantos,* not only because it assails fascism and hero-wor-
ship, but also for its uncompromising inwardness, its rejection of all
authority. For where Pound fills his poems with chunks of authorized,
authoritative literature and history, history and literature are for *Helen
in Egypt* never authoritative but always to-be-deciphered, tangential to,
incorporated within, the feminine mind.

Helen in Egypt* is first of all personal, one woman's quest epitomiz-
ing the struggle of Everywoman. Its interior life comes to include and
transcend the external historical world represented and inhabited by
males—but it does not reject that world. In Susan Griffin's *Woman·and
Nature: The Roaring Inside Her,* male and female are again represented as
polar opposites, but from a different point of view and with a different
set of conclusions.

"Matter" and "Separation," the long opening books of *Woman and
Nature,* offer a pastiche-parody of the history of occidental patriarchal
intellect. Griffin quotes and paraphrases hundreds of works, ranging
from the clean abstractions of theology, metaphysics, physics, and
mathematics, through the material facts of history, to such practical
subjects as forestry, agriculture, animal husbandry, mining, and office
management. The collective and anonymous "paternal voice" she cre-
ates is emotionless, toneless, authoritative. It pronounces "that matter
is only a potential for form. . . . That the nature of woman is passive,
that she is a vessel" with supposed objectivity.[35]

The attitude of this voice toward Nature ("matter") and toward
Woman is the same. It conceptualizes both as essentially, ideally, and

properly inferior, passive, intended for man's use; yet at the same time potentially dangerous, threatening, wild, and evil, requiring to be tamed by force. Extending in two directions, theoretical and practical, the analogy formulated by the anthropologist Sherry Ortner that "Woman is to Nature as Man is to Culture,"[36] Griffin on the one hand makes clear the connection between the myth (in the sense of metaphor) of active male God and passive female Nature, and the myth (in the sense of falsity) of rational objectivity in the life of the intellect and of civilization. On the other she composes a huge collage of the multiple ways in which male superiority, buttressed by its myths, destroys life.

To justify their exploitation and destruction, woman and nature must be seen both as morally evil and as metaphysically nonexistent. Thus of the "inordinate affections and passions" of Woman and the rich unpredictability of Nature, "it is decided that that which cannot be measured and reduced to number is not real" (p. 11). Scenes depicting depletion of nutrients in soil, courtship as a form of hunting, the extinction of species of beasts, the operation of clitoridectomy, the caging and drugging of a lioness, a woman muted by her husband's violence, the despoiling of forests, peasant women raped by invading soldiers, Karamazov's need to dispose of two female corpses, and the disposal of nuclear wastes become the logical extrapolation of such axioms. Though satiric, Griffin's portrait of the myth of rational objectivity is also playfully inventive with numerous sorts of male discourse, from logic to legalese, from Dantean mysticism to Einsteinian thought-experiment. At times it is also beautiful, as in the section called "Territory"; at times ironic, as in the section called "The Show Horse." Occasionally we hear whispers of the suppressed female/natural voice—confused, suffering, angry.

In the third book, "Passage," and the fourth, "Her Vision," this voice moves toward self-transformation. Through traditional female images of cave, water, earth, and seed, it gradually approaches images of light and flight. Altering from consciousness of "dreams" to knowledge of her body, her history, the body of the world; from passivity to rebellion, violence, dance, song; the "she" and "we" of this voice learn to accept "turbulence": "When the wind calls, will we go? Will this wind come inside us? Take from us? Can we give to the wind what is asked of us? Will we let go? . . . Can we sing back, this we ask, can we sing back, and not only sing, but in clear voices? Will this be, we ask, and will we keep on answering, keep on with our whole bodies? And do we know why we sing? Yes. Will we know why? Yes" (p. 222). Scenes from the first part of *Woman and Nature* reverse in the latter sections. Gynecologists become midwives. The lioness devours her captors. There is also a central asymmetry. Griffin portrays the relationships between mothers and daughters, midwives and birthing mothers; between women as friends, allies, and lovers; and between woman and earth as, in their ideal form, relationships of mirroring or interpenetration. Emotional closeness is derived from acknowledged likeness, not from the patriarchal relationship of dominance and submission, or from the dialectic between polarities envisioned by H.D. Consequently, in the last portion of *Woman and Nature,* the direct quotations are exclusively from women writers, and the male voice disappears from the book. At one point the "we" is a family of mourning elephants whose mother has been killed by a hunter and who vow to teach hatred and fear to their young: "And when we attack in their defense, they will watch and learn this too. From us, they will become fierce. And so a death like this death of our mother will not come easily to them. . . . And only if the young of our young or the young of their young never know this odor in their lifetime, . . . only then, when no trace is left of this memory in us, will we see what we can be without this fear, without this enemy, what we are" (p. 218). This pivotal passage offers a forceful metaphor for feminist separatism—man is simply too dangerous, too much a killer, for woman to do anything but fear, fight, and avoid him. The passage also, by virtue of imagining a time "when no trace is left of this memory in us," releases the author to conclude with a hymn of pleasure at once erotic and intellectual, a lesbian-feminist structural equivalent of the last movement of Beethoven's Ninth Symphony, the close of Blake's *Jerusalem,* Molly Bloom's soliloquy, or the Book of Revelation.[37]

Like *Helen In Egypt, Woman and Nature* is a book about process and psychic struggle. In a recent essay Griffin writes that her initial attempts to organize her "scientific" material logically or chronologically failed. She had to learn to structure "intuitively, putting pieces next to one another where the transition seemed wonderful." She also explains that "all the time I wrote the book, the patriarchal voice was in me, whispering to me . . . that I had no proof for any of my writing, that I was wildly in error."[38] Thus the gradual disclosure of the female voice in the book reproduces the process of its creation.

Unlike both *Helen in Egypt* and *Woman and Nature,* and unlike most

revisionist mythmaking by women, Anne Sexton's *Transformations* is
not structured around the idea of male and female as polar opposites
and is consequently not gynocentric in the fashion of these books.
Rather, it is a brilliant synthesis of public "story" and psychological
revelation, revisionist both in its subversive readings of traditional
plots, characters, and morals and in its portrait of a lady who exists
beyond the plots, the female as creator.

Transformations consists of a prologue and sixteen tales from the
Brothers Grimm, told in a wisecracking Americanese that simul-
taneously modernizes and desentimentalizes them. We have bits like
"the dwarfs, those little hot dogs" ("Snow White"); "a wolf dressed in
frills, / a kind of transvestite" ("Red Riding Hood"); or Sexton's Gretel
who, "seeing her moment in history . . . turned the oven on to
bake."[39] Under cover of entertainment, Sexton demolishes many of the
social conventions, especially those connected with femininity, that
fairy tales ostensibly endorse. She mocks virginity and beauty as values;
the former makes one a fool ("Snow White, that dumb bunny"), the
latter cruel ("pretty enough, but with hearts like blackjacks"). Love, in
Sexton's versions, is a form of self-seeking. The happy ending of mar-
riage is treated ironically as "a kind of coffin, / a kind of blue funk. / Is
it not?"

An important source of Sexton's effectiveness is her striking ability
to decode stories we thought we knew, revealing meanings we should
have guessed. Her "Rapunzel" is a tale of love between an older and a
younger woman, ultimately doomed by heterosexual normality. Her
"Rumpelstiltskin" is about the naiveté and vulnerability of a dwarf ma-
nipulated by a calculating girl—or it is about the ability of the healthy
ego to despise, suppress, and mutilate the libido. In "Hansel and
Gretel," Sexton hints that the witch is a mother-goddess sacrificed by a
female in alliance with the patriarchy.

Though Sexton is obviously indebted to psychoanalytic method in
the retrieval of latent content, she is not limited by its dogmas. For
example, psychoanalytical commentary on the "sleeping virgin" pat-
tern in fairy tales interprets the theme as that of feminine pubescence.[40]
Sexton in "Briar Rose (Sleeping Beauty)" takes this insight almost con-
temptuously for granted and organizes her version like a series of clues
to quite another mystery. There is no mother in Sexton's version, only
a father. The psychoanalytically sophisticated reader may speculate that
the thirteenth fairy, "her fingers as long and thin as straws, / her eyes
burnt by cigarettes, / her uterus an empty teacup" (p. 108) is a dis-

placed mother figure, as evil stepmothers commonly are. The protective father who not only got rid of spinning wheels but "forced every male in the court/to scour his tongue with Bab-o" (p. 109) is apparently a possessive parent hoping to keep his young daughter sexually pure. But after the dénouement, the hundred years' sleep, and the arrival of the Prince, Sexton presents Briar Rose as a lifelong insomniac, terrified of sleeping. For when she sleeps she dreams of a dinner table with "a faltering crone at my place, / her eyes burnt like cigarettes / as she eats betrayal like a slice of meat." Why does the heroine identify with the crone? What betrayal? Only the last lines tell us just why the mother is not "in" Sexton's story. Waking from sleep Briar Rose cries, like a little girl, "Daddy! Daddy!" as she did when the Prince woke her—and what she sees is "not the prince at all" (pp. 111–12),

> but my father,
> drunkenly bent over my bed,
> circling the abyss like a shark,
> my father thick upon me
> like some sleeping jellyfish.

This is, of course, a version of the Family Romance that neither orthodox psychoanalysis nor our legal system is ready to accept,[41] but that countless women will recognize as painfully accurate.

In addition to the revivifying language and the revisionist interpretations of the stories, *Transformations* has another, framing element. The persona of the narrator-poet in the book's prologue is "a middle-aged witch, me" who talks like a den mother. Each of the ensuing tales has its own prologue, offering hints about the meaning of the story to come. The poet's personality alters with each prologue. In "Snow White" she is cynical, in "The White Snake," idealistic. Prior to "Rumpelstiltskin" she announces that the dwarf is the suppressed "law of your members," out of Saint Paul's epistles (p. 17), while in "One-Eye, Two-Eyes and Three-Eyes" she comments disapprovingly on the way parents with defective children "warm to their roles . . . with a positive fervor" where nature would sensibly let its malformed products die (pp. 59–60). In the prologue to "The Frog Prince" she addresses a "Mama Brundig" psychoanalyst, gaily declaiming:

> My guilts are what
> we catalogue.
> I'll take a knife
> and chop up frog.

But the gaiety plummets abruptly to horror: "Frog is my father's genitals. / Frog is a malformed doorknob. / Frog is a soft bag of green" (pp. 93–94).

Sexton as narrator is at times distant from the reader, at times intimate. She is unpredictably sensitive or brutal. What is important to notice here is that while the tales themselves are fixed—and Sexton stresses their ruthless changelessness, never letting us think that her "characters" act with free will or do anything but fill their slots in predetermined plots—the teller is mobile. She emits an air of exhilarating mental and emotional liberty, precisely because she is distanced from the material she so penetratingly understands. Thus the full force of *Transformations* lies not only in its psychosocial reinterpretations of Grimm's tales, however brilliant, nor in the fact that it expressly attacks literary and social conventions regarding women. Philosophically, the axis *Transformations* turns on is Necessity (here seen as fixed and damaging psychosocial patterns) versus Freedom; the "middle-aged witch, me" represents the latter.

IV

What all these poems have in common is, first, that they treat existing texts as fence posts surrounding the terrain of mythic truth but by no means identical to it. In other words, they are enactments of feminist antiauthoritarianism opposed to the patriarchal praxis of reifying texts.

Second, most of these poems involve reevaluations of social, political, and philosophical values, particularly those most enshrined in occidental literature, such as the glorification of conquest and the faith that the cosmos is—must be—hierarchically ordered with earth and body on the bottom and mind and spirit on the top.

Third, the work of these poets is conspicuously different from the Modernist mythmaking of Yeats, Pound, Eliot, and Auden because it contains no trace of nostalgia, no faith that the past is a repository of truth, goodness, or desirable social organization. Prufrock may yearn to be Hamlet, but what woman would want to be Ophelia? While the myth of a Golden Age has exerted incalculable pressure in the shaping of Western literature and its attitude toward history, the revisionist woman poet does not care if the hills of Arcady are dead. Or rather, she does not believe they are dead, Far from representing history as a decline, or bemoaning disjunctions of past and present, her poems insist that past and present are, for better or worse, essentially the same. H.D.'s concept of the "palimpsest" seems to be the norm, along with a treatment of time that effectively flattens it so that the past is not then but now.

Fourth, revisionism correlates with formal experiment. This is important not only because new meanings must generate new forms— when we have a new form in art we can assume we have a new meaning—but because the verbal strategies these poets use draw attention to the discrepancies between traditional concepts and the conscious mental and emotional activity of female re-vision. As it accentuates its argument, in order to make clear that there *is* an argument, that an act of theft *is* occurring, feminist revisionism differs from Romantic revisionism, although in other respects it is similar. [42]

The gaudy and abrasive colloquialism of Alta, Atwood, Plath, and Sexton, for example, simultaneously modernizes what is ancient and reduces the verbal glow that we are trained to associate with mythic material. Even H.D., who takes her divinities entirely seriously, avoids the elevated or quasi-liturgical diction that, in the educated reader, triggers the self-surrendering exaltation relied on by the creators of such poems as *Four Quartets* or *The Cantos.* With women poets we look at, or into, but not up at, sacred things; we unlearn submission.

A variant of colloquial language is childish or infantile language, such as T. S. Eliot used in the nursery rhyme echoes of "The Hollow Men" and at the close of *The Wasteland* to suggest a mix of regression and despair. In DuPlessis's "Medusa," passages of halting and sometimes punning baby talk become a way of revealing the power of sexual pain to infantilize, to thwart growth; the speaker's ultimate articulateness coincides with the growth of her avenging snakes. Regressive language also signals sexual trauma in Sexton. Another variant of the colloquial is the bawdy, a traditionally male linguistic preserve that women like Erica Jong have lately invaded.

The most significant large-scale technique in these poems is the use of multiple intertwined voices within highly composed extensive structures. In the three long works discussed here there is the alternating prose and verse of *Helen in Egypt,* with occasional interludes when one of Helen's lovers speaks, or she imagines him speaking; the male and female voices in *Woman and Nature,* along with the multitudinous direct quotations; and prologue and story in *Transformations.* [43] These balancings are crucially important to the texture and sense of the poems, just as the multiple voices of *The Wasteland, The Cantos,* or *Paterson* are. Insofar as the subject of the poem is always the "I" of the poet, her divided voices evoke divided selves: the rational and the passionate, the active and the suffering, the conscious life and the dream life, animus and anima, analyst and analysand. To read *Helen in Egypt* is uncannily like overhearing a communication between left brain and right brain.

In some ways, too, these poems challenge the validity of the "I," of any "I." Like the speaker of Adrienne Rich's "Diving into the Wreck," whose discovery of her submerged self is a discovery that she is a "we" for whom even the distinction between subject and object dissolves, the heroines we find in women's revisionist mythology are more often fluid than solid. But these are not books—or heroines— about which the authors are saying, as Pound tragically said of *The Cantos,* and his life, "I cannot make it cohere."[44] Although the divided self is probably the single issue women poets since 1960 most consistently struggle with, the most visionary of their works appear to be strengthened by acknowledging division and containing it, as H.D. says, "in my thought here."[45]

APPENDIX

The following are post-1960 myth-poems, listed alphabetically by author. Extended poems and poem-sequences are indicated by an asterisk (*). Readers of contemporary women's poetry will be able to supply other titles.

Alta. "euridice." In *I Am Not a Practicing Angel.* Trumansburg, N.Y.: Crossing, 1975.

Atwood, Margaret. "Eventual Proteus," "Speeches for Dr. Frankenstein," "Siren Song," "Circe/Mud Poems."* In *Selected Poems.* New York: Simon and Schuster, 1976.

Barba, Sharon. "A Cycle of Women." In *Rising Tides: 20th Century Women Poets,* edited by Laura Chester and Sharon Barba. New York: Simon and Schuster, 1973.

Broumas, Olga. "Twelve Aspects of God."* In *Beginning with O.* New Haven: Yale University Press, 1977.

Butcher, Grace. "Assignments." In *Rising Tides: 20th Century Women Poets,* edited by Laura Chester and Sharon Barba. New York: Simon and Schuster, 1973.

Clifton, Lucille, Kali poems.* In *An Ordinary Woman.* New York: Random House, 1974.

H.D. *Helen in Egypt.** New York: New Directions, 1961.

———. *Hermetic Definition.** New York: New Directions, 1972.

Dienstfrey, Patricia. "Blood and the Iliad: The Paintings of Frida Kahlo." In *Newspaper Stories.* Berkeley: Kelsey St., 1979.

DiPrima, Diane. *Loba.** Berkeley: Wingbow, 1978.

DuPlessis, Rachel Blau. "Medusa,"* "Euridice."* In *Wells.* New York: Montemora, 1980.

Ellis, Kate. "Matrilineal Descent." In *US 1: An Anthology,* edited by Rod Tulloss, David Keller, and Alicia Ostriker. Union City, N.J.: Wise, 1980.

Fenton, Elizabeth. "Under the Ladder to Heaven." In *No More Masks: An Anthology of Poems by Women,* edited by Florence Howe and Ellen Bass. Garden City, N.Y.: Doubleday, 1973.

Gilbert, Sandra. "Bas Relief: Bacchante." In *Massachusetts Review* 18, no. 4 (Winter 1976). "Daphne." In *Poetry Northwest* 18, no. 2 (Summer 1977).

Glück, Louise. "Gretel in Darkness," "Jeanne d'Arc." In *The House on Marshland.* New York: Ecco, 1975.

Giovanni, Nikki. "Ego Tripping." In *The Women and the Men.* New York: Willam Morrow, 1975.

Grahn, Judy. "She Who."* In *The Work of a Common Woman.* New York: St. Martin's, 1978.

Griffin, Susan. *Woman and Nature: The Roaring Inside Her.** New York: Harper and Row, 1978.

Hacker, Marilyn. "For Elektra," "The Muses," "Nimue to Merlin." In *Presentation Piece.* New York: Viking, 1974.

Jong, Erica. "Arse Poetica." In *Fruits and Vegetables.* New York: Holt, Rinehart and Winston, 1971.

————— "Back to Africa," "Alcestis on the Poetry Circuit." In *Half-Lives.* New York: Holt, Rinehart and Winston, 1973.

Kizer, Carolyn. "The Dying Goddess." In *Midnight Was My Cry.* Garden City, N.Y.: Doubleday, 1969.

Levertov, Denise. "The Goddess." In *With Eyes at the Back of Our Heads.* New York: New Directions, 1959.

—————. "The Jacob's Ladder," "The Well." In *The Jacob's Ladder.* New York: New Directions, 1961.

—————. "Song for Ishtar." In *O Taste and See.* New York: New Directions, 1964.

—————. "An Embroidery." In *Relearning the Alphabet.* New York: New Directions, 1970.

Morgan, Robin. "The Network of the Imaginary Mother,"* "Voices from Six Tapestries."* In *Lady of the Beasts.* New York: Random House, 1976.

Mueller, Lisel. "The Queen of Sheba Says Farewell," "Eros," " 'O Brave New World. . . .' " In *Dependencies.* Chapel Hill: University of North Carolina Press, 1965.

—————. "Letter from the End of the World." In *The Private Life.* Baton Rouge: Louisiana State University Press, 1976.

Ostriker, Alicia. "Homecoming," "The Impulse of Singing," "Message from the Sleeper at Hell's Mouth."* In *A Woman under the Surface.* Princeton: Princeton University Press, 1982.

Owens, Rochelle. *The Joe 82 Creation Poems.** Los Angeles: Black Sparrow, 1974.

Piercy, Marge. "Icon," "Laying Down the Tower."* In *To Be of Use*. Garden City, N.Y.: Doubleday, 1973.

Plath, Sylvia. "The Colossus," "Lorelei," "The Disquieting Muses," "Magi," "Two Sisters of Persephone," "Witch Burning," "Lady Lazarus," "Medusa," "Mary's Song," "Elm." In *Collected Poems*, edited by Ted Hughes. New York: Harper and Row, 1981.

Rich, Adrienne. "The Knight," "Orion," "Planetarium," "I Dream I'm the Death of Orpheus." In *Poems: Selected and New, 1950–1974*. New York: W. W. Norton, 1974.

Rukeyser, Muriel. "The Poem as Mask," "Myth," "Waiting for Icarus." In *Collected Poems*. New York: McGraw-Hill, 1978.

Sarton, May. "At Lindos," "Orpheus," "The Birth of Venus," "The Muse as Medusa," "The Invocation to Kali." In *Selected Poems*. New York: W. W. Norton, 1978.

Sexton, Anne. *Transformations*.* Boston: Houghton Mifflin, 1971.

———. "Angels of the Love Affair," "The Jesus Papers."* In *The Book of Folly*. Boston: Houghton Mifflin, 1972.

———. "Her Kind," "The Double Image." In *To Bedlam and Part Way Back*. Boston: Houghton Mifflin, 1960.

———. "Gods," "The Death Baby," "Rats Live on No Evil Star," "The Furies," "Mary's Song," "Jesus Walking." In *The Death Notebooks*. Boston: Houghton Mifflin, 1974.

Stanford, Ann. "Women of Perseus."* In *In Mediterranean Air*. New York: Viking Press, 1977.

Tepperman, Jean. "Witch." In *No More Masks: An Anthology of Poems by Women*, edited by Florence Howe and Ellen Bass. Garden City, N.Y.: Doubleday, 1973.

VanDuyn, Mona. "Outlandish Agon," "Advice to a God," "Leda," "Leda Reconsidered." In *To See, To Take*. New York: Atheneum, 1970.

Wakoski, Diane. "The George Washington Poems."* In *Trilogy*. Garden City, N.Y.: Doubleday, 1974.

NOTES

1. Hélène Cixous, "Sorties," in *La jeune née*, translated by Ann Liddle (Paris: Union Générale d'Editions, 10/18, 1975), quoted by Elaine Marks in "Woman and Literature in France," *Signs: Journal of Women in Culture and Society* 3, no. 4 (Summer 1978): 832–42, especially p. 841; appears also in Elaine Marks and Isabelle de Courtivron, eds., *New French Feminisms: An Anthology* (Amherst: University of Massachusetts Press, 1980), pp. 92–93.

2. Sylvia Plath, "Mushrooms," *The Collected Poems*, edited by Ted Hughes (New York: Harper and Row, 1981), p. 139.

3. Claudine Herrmann, *Les Voleuses de langue* (Paris: Des Femmes, 1979).

4. Adrienne Rich, "The Burning of Paper Instead of Children," *Poems: Selected and New, 1950–1974* (New York: W. W. Norton, 1974), pp. 148–51, especially p. 151.

5. Jacques Lacan's term for the symbolic order of language is widely used

by psychoanalytically oriented French feminists (see Jane Gallop, "Psychoanalysis in France," *Women and Literature* 7, no. 1 [Winter 1979]: 57–63).

6. Robin Morgan, "The Invisible Woman," in *Monster* (New York: Random House, 1972), p. 46.

7. Marcia Landy, "The Silent Woman," in *The Authority of Experience,* edited by Arlyn Diamond and Lee Edwards (Amherst: University of Massachusetts Press, 1977), pp. 16–27.

8. See Suzanne Juhasz, *Naked and Fiery Forms: Modern American Poetry by Women* (New York: Harper and Row, 1976); Elaine Showalter, *A Literature of Their Own* (Princeton: Princeton University Press, 1977); Ann Douglas, *The Feminization of American Culture* (New York: Alfred A. Knopf, 1977), which is, however, unsympathetic to the women writers discussed; Sandra M. Gilbert and Susan Gubar, *The Madwoman in the Attic: The Woman Writer and the Nineteenth-Century Imagination* (New Haven: Yale University Press, 1979); Cheryl Walker, *The Nightingale's Burden: Women Poets in America, 1630–1900* (Bloomington: Indiana University Press, 1982). See also Florence Howe and Ellen Bass, eds., "Introduction," in *No More Masks: An Anthology of Poems by Women* (Garden City, N.Y.: Doubleday, 1973); Dolores Rosenblum, "Christina Rossetti: The Inward Pose," and Terence Diggory, "Armored Women, Naked Men: Dickinson, Whitman and Their Successors," in *Shakespeare's Sisters: Feminist Essays on Women Poets,* edited by Sandra M. Gilbert and Susan Gubar (Bloomington: Indiana University Press, 1979), pp. 82–98, 135–50.

9. Marks, "Women and Literature in France," p. 836.

10. Robert Graves argues—without much evidence—in *The White Goddess* (New York: Creative Age Press, 1948) that a "magical" language honoring the Moon-goddess existed in prepatriarchal times, survived in the mystery cults, and was still taught "in the poetic colleges of Ireland and Wales, and in the witch covens of Western Europe" (p. x). Among French feminists, Herrmann claims that women use space and time, metaphor and metonymy differently than men, Cixous that women write with "mother's milk" or "the blood's language." Most interestingly, Luce Irigaray moves from *Speculum d'autre femme* (Paris: Editions de Minuit, 1974), which deconstructs Plato and Freud to demonstrate the history of systematic repression of woman as a concept in Western culture, to *Ce Sexe qui n'est pas un* (Paris: Editions de Minuit, 1977), which attempts to transpose the voices of Freud, Lacan, Derrida, and Lewis Carroll into a feminine language. Among Irigaray's techniques is the rejection of the "proper" name along with "property" and "propriety" in order to recover the self as "elle(s)," a plural being (see Carolyn G. Burke, "Irigaray through the Looking Glass," *Feminist Studies* 7, no. 2 [Summer 1981]: 288–306). This work parallels in many respects Susan Griffin's *Woman and Nature: The Roaring Inside Her* (New York: Harper and Row, 1978), discussed below. Julia Kristeva, on the other hand, argues that woman has no linguistic existence but a negative, preoedipal one. For details of the debate, which in part centers on the question of whether feminists should use male abstractions, see Marks and Carolyn G. Burke, "Report from Paris: Women's Writing and the Women's Movement," *Signs* 4, no. 2 (Summer 1978): 843–55. The most important American theoretical texts prophesying a woman's language are

Mary Daly's *Beyond God the Father* (Boston: Beacon Press, 1973) and *Gyn/Ecology* (Boston: Beacon Press, 1978). *Per contra,* see Robin Lakoff, *Language and Women's Place* (New York: Harper and Row, 1975); Mary Hiatt, *The Way Women Write* (New York: Teacher's College Press, 1977); Barrie Thorne and Nancy Henley, eds., *Language and Sex: Difference and Dominance* (Rowley, Mass.: Newbury House, 1975); and the empirical studies referred to in Cheris Kramer, Barrie Thorne, and Nancy Henley, "Perspective on Language and Communication," *Signs* 3, no. 3 (Spring 1978): 638–51.

11. Here and in other essays on contemporary American women's poetry, I take 1960 as an approximate point of departure. Among the breakthrough works appearing between 1959 and 1965 are Mona Van Duyn, *Valentines to the Wide World* (Boston: Houghton Mifflin, 1959); H. D., *Helen in Egypt* (New York: New Directions, 1961); Anne Sexton, *To Bedlam and Part Way Back* (Boston: Houghton Mifflin, 1960) and *All My Pretty Ones* (Boston: Houghton Mifflin, 1962); Denise Levertov, *The Jacob's Ladder* (New York: New Directions, 1961) and *O Taste and See* (New York: New Directions, 1964); Diane Wakoski, *Coins and Coffins* (Garden City, N.Y.: Doubleday, 1962); Adrienne Rich, *Snapshots of a Daughter-in-Law* (New York: W. W. Norton, 1963); Carolyn Kizer, "Pro Femina," in *Knock upon Silence* (Garden City, N.Y.: Doubleday, 1963); Sylvia Plath, *Ariel* (New York: Harper and Row, 1965). It needs to be stressed, however, that the women's movement in contemporary poetry is not confined to these and other well-known poets but includes hundreds of writers whose work appears in small press and magazine publications.

12. Alicia Ostriker, "Body Language: Imagery of the Body in Women's Poetry," in *The State of the Language,* edited by Leonard Michaels and Christopher Ricks (Berkeley: University of California Press, 1980), pp. 247–63, especially pp. 256–60.

13. The case against myth is exhaustively stated by Simone de Beauvoir in chap. 9, "Dreams, Fears, Idols," of *The Second Sex,* translated by H. M. Parshley (New York: Bantam Books, 1970), pp. 157–223. A discussion of the usefulness of some myths for women writers is Susan Gubar's "Mother, Maiden and the Marriage of Death: Women Writers and an Ancient Myth," *Women's Studies* 6, no. 3 (1979): 301–15. Gubar argues that the figures of the Sphinx and the Mother-Goddess represent "secret wisdom," which women identify with "their point of view," and that they use the myth of Persephone and Demeter "to re-define, to re-affirm and to celebrate female consciousness itself" (p. 302). See also n. 22 below.

14. Muriel Rukeyser, "The Poem as Mask," in *Collected Poems* (New York: McGraw-Hill, 1978), p. 435.

15. Rich, "Diving into the Wreck," in *Poems,* pp. 196–98, especially p. 198.

16. Margaret Atwood, "Circe/Mud Poems," in *You Are Happy* (New York: Harper and Row, 1974), pp. 45–70, especially pp. 68–69.

17. Discussion of the ways in which American women poets have used myth to handle material dangerous for a feminine "I" appears in Emily Stipes Watts, *The Poetry of American Women from 1632 to 1945* (Austin: University of Texas Press, 1977).

18. Daly, *Beyond God the Father*, p. 8.

19. Plath, "Lady Lazarus," in *Collected Poems*; Anne Sexton, "Snow White," in *Transformations* (Boston: Houghton Mifflin, 1971), p. 3; Jean Tepperman, "Witch," in *No More Masks*, pp. 333–34; Alta, "euridice," in *I Am Not a Practicing Angel* (Trumansburg, N.Y.: Crossing, 1975); Erica Jong, "Arse Poetica," in *Fruits and Vegetables* (New York: Holt, Rinehart and Winston, 1971), p. 27.

20. Kate Ellis, "Matrilineal Descent," in *US I: An Anthology,* edited by Rod Tulloss, David Keller, and Alicia Ostriker (Union City, N.J.: Wise, 1980), pp. 31–34; Sharon Barba, "A Cycle of Women," in *Rising Tides: 20th Century American Women Poets,* edited by Laura Chester and Sharon Barba (New York: Simon and Schuster, 1973), pp. 356–57.

21. Rachel Blau DuPlessis, "Eurydice," in *Wells* (New York: Montemora, 1980); Rich, "The Mirror in Which Two Are Seen as One," and "Necessities of Life," in *Poems,* pp. 193–95, especially pp. 195, 60–70.

22. The feminist attempt to construct a redefined "Goddess" or "Great Goddess" is, of course, not confined to poetry or even to literature. See, in *Chrysalis: A Magazine of Women's Culture* 6 (1978), Gloria Z. Greenfield, Judith Antares, and Charlene Spretnak, "The Politics of Women's Spirituality" (pp. 9–15); and Linda Palumbo, Maurine Revnille, Charlene Spretnak, and Terry Wolverton, "Women's Survival Catalog: Spirituality," an excellent annotated listing of classic and recent texts, journals, and (a few) environmental artworks relating to "The Goddess" (pp. 77–99).

23. See Erich Neumann, *The Great Mother: An Analysis of the Archetype,* translated by Ralph Manheim (Princeton: Princeton University Press, 1963).

24. Denise Levertov, "The Goddess," in *With Eyes at the Back of Our Heads* (New York: New Directions, 1959), pp. 43–44. Levertov treats the association of women with falsity in "Hypocrite Women," which redefines feminine deception (and self-deception) as compliance with male demands for mothering and with the male pronouncement that "our cunts are ugly," in *O Taste and See,* p. 70.

25. Levertov, "Song for Ishtar," in *O Taste and See,* p. 3.

26. Wallace Stevens, "Final Soliloquy of the Interior Paramour," in *The Collected Poems of Wallace Stevens* (New York: Alfred A. Knopf, 1954), p. 524.

27. Plath "The Disquieting Muses," "Medusa," "Lady Lazarus," "Elm," in *Collected Poems,* pp. 74–76, 184, 244–46, 192; Sexton, "The Exorcists," in *To Bedlam,* pp. 22–23, and "Angels of the Love Affair," in *The Book of Folly* (Boston: Houghton Mifflin, 1972), pp. 57–62.

28. Ann Stanford, "The Women of Perseus," in *In Mediterranean Air* (New York: Viking Press, 1977), pp. 34–48; DuPlesis, "Medusa," in *Wells.*

29. Atwood, pp. 51, 38–39.

30. Susan Friedman, "Who Buried H. D.? A Poet, Her Critics, and Her Place in 'The Literary Tradition,'" *College English* 37 (March 1975): 807.

31. I have selected these three works for both their excellence and their diversity—including their diverse perspectives on female sexuality, from which much else, ideologically and formally, follows. H.D.'s orientation is (in this

book) heterosexual, Griffin's lesbian, Sexton's (in this book) asexual. I believe that these works illuminate, in a profound way, both the common ground and the differences among these three orientations toward women's sexuality, and I believe it is vital for feminist critics not to "prefer" one perspective to the others; we have only begun to learn what sexuality means to us and how various our options may be.

32. H.D., *Helen in Egypt*, sec. 1. Future references to this poem will be included in the text.

33. I am indebted to Susan Friedman, *Psyche Reborn: The Emergence of H.D.* (Bloomington: Indiana University Press, 1981), for her illuminating analysis of H.D.'s revisionist use of occult and mystical tradition in her quest for what she called "spirituality," and for her revisionist use of psychoanalytic doctrines and methods in her quest for self-affirmation. As Friedman makes clear, the quests and methods are projected onto the Helen of *Helen in Egypt*. I am also indebted to Rachel Blau DuPlessis's "Romantic Thralldom in H.D." (*Contemporary Literature* 20, no. 2 [Spring 1979]: 178–203) for the discussion of H.D.-Helen's need to construct a "sufficient family" as an alternative to "romantic thralldom." Helen's successful quest for (*a*) knowledge of the gods, (*b*) integration of self, (*c*) a family consisting of parent figures, siblings, lover, and progeny, might be related to a revisionist scheme of superego, ego, libido, in terms of what is sought and necessary for human wholeness.

34. Rich, "The Knight," in *Poems,* pp. 43–44.

35. Griffin, *Woman and Nature*. Future references to this work will be incorporated in the text.

36. Sherry Ortner, "Is Female to Male as Nature Is to Culture?" in *Woman, Culture and Society,* edited by Michelle Zimbalist Rosaldo and Louise Lamphere (Stanford: Stanford University Press, 1974). Annette Kolodny's *The Lay of the Land* (Chapel Hill: University of North Carolina Press, 1978) pursues the metaphor of land as "virgin" or "mother" in American history and literature, with findings parallel to Griffin's. Mary Daly's *Gyn/Ecology* might provide a gloss on much of Griffin; Griffin and Daly review each other's books in *Chrysalis* 7 (1979): 109–12.

37. Lest these comparisons appear outrageous, let me point out with respect to the most (apparently) outrageous of them that the ratio of "male" to "female" in the text of *Woman and Nature* is roughly equivalent to that between Old and New Testaments, with the "male" coming first. The "male" books of *Woman and Nature* cover a huge time span, are encyclopedic, multigenre, and polyvocal; they concern Conquest and Law but also contain Prophecy, like the Old Testament. Its "female" books cover a relatively brief time span, approach univocality, concern Salvation and Grace, and contain Fulfillment of Prophecy, like the New Testament. I do not suggest that Griffin intended the parallels; they are nonetheless visible and consonant with her overall purpose of retrieving from patriarchal discourse a woman's language.

38. Susan Griffin, "Thoughts on Writing: A Diary," in *The Writer on Her work,* edited by Janet Sternburg (New York: W. W. Norton, 1980), pp. 112–13.

39. Sexton, *Transformations*, pp. 6, 76, 104–5. Future references to this work will be incorporated in the text.

40. See, e.g., Bruno Bettelheim, *The Uses of Enchantment: The Meaning and Importance of Fairy Tales* (New York: Alfred A. Knopf, 1976), pp. 225 ff. See Juhasz, pp. 118–32, for a discussion of "the psychoanalytic model" and Sexton's outgrowing of it.

41. See Florence Rush, *The Best-Kept Secret: Sexual Abuse of Children* (Englewood Cliffs, N.J.: Prentice-Hall, 1980), especially chap. 7, "The Freudian Cover-Up," which discusses Freud's conviction that incest is a female fantasy and the consequences of Freudian orthodoxy for incest victims today. See also Judith Lewis Herman (with Lisa Hirschman), *Father-Daughter Incest* (Cambridge, Mass.: Harvard University Press, 1981), especially the appendix, "The Incest Statutes," by Leigh Bienen.

42. For a discussion of formal experimentation and its aesthetic and political significance in women's prose, see Julia Penelope Stanley and Susan J. Wolfe [Robbins], "Toward a Feminist Aesthetic," *Chrysalis* 6 (1978): 57–71.

43. Similar techniques appear in Diane Wakoski's "The George Washington Poems," in *Trilogy* (Garden City, N.Y.: Doubleday, 1974), pp. 113–66; and Robin Morgan's "Network of the Imaginary Mother," in *Lady of the Beasts* (New York: Random House, 1976), pp. 61–88. I cannot think of any major modern poem by a man in which the self is presented as split or plural while the total poetic structure remains cohesive rather than fragmented. In the closest approximation, John Berryman's *Dream Songs* (New York: Farrar, Straus and Giroux, 1969), the "blackface" voice plays a distinctly minor role. *The Wasteland, The Cantos,* and *Paterson* are, of course, classics of personal, social, *and* aesthetic fragmentation.

44. Ezra Pound, *The Cantos of Ezra Pound* (New York: New Directions, 1970), p. 796.

45. H.D., *Helen in Egypt,* p. 201.

The New Poetry and the New Woman: Mina Loy

Carolyn Burke

Soon after her arrival in New York for the first time (1916), Mina Loy was contacted by a newspaper reporter who wanted to interview a representative "new woman." The reporter began her article by asking, "Who is . . . this 'modern woman' that people are always talking about," then reflected, "Some people think that women are the cause of modernism, whatever that is." Loy's name had been suggested because of her radically modern poetry: already published in such avant-garde magazines as *Camera Work, Rogue,* and *The Trend,* she was known as the author of the most widely quoted poems in *Others, A Magazine of the New Verse,* the scandalous new rival to Harriet Monroe's *Poetry.* For the average reader, Loy's writing was of a piece with the baffling artistic projects of Alfred Steiglitz, Gertrude Stein, and the Italian Futurists, and her subject matter with the public soul-searching and lawbreaking of the new woman. The reporter remembered her poems as "the kind that people kept around for months and dug out of corners to read to each other." Not only were they written in an original kind of free verse, but they also presented a new female perspective. The reporter came away from the interview with the impression that this new woman believed it out-of-date to write or live according to the rules and thought it necessary "to fling yourself at life" in order to discover new forms of self-expression. Loy's art was modernist (whatever that was) because she threw the rule book out the window and wrote direct from life.[1]

The interview is of interest because it makes explicit the connection between the politics of the new woman and the principles of the new poetry. Although Mina Loy's name is no longer familiar, in 1916 it was synonymous with the most daring poetic experimentation. Until very recently, however, historians of American poetry have tended to ignore the importance of *Others,* unless it is to observe that Marianne

Moore, Wallace Stevens, and William Carlos Williams got their start in its pages. Yet Harriet Monroe thought it wise to stake out her own territory by observing that *Others* stood for "a rather more youthful effervescence than I am quite ready to endorse publicly," and Ezra Pound described the new magazine as "a harum scarum vers libre American product, . . . useful because it keeps 'Arriet from relapsing back into the Nineties." Among anthologists, William S. Braithewaite categorized *Others* poets as disciples of Pound in order to distinguish them from his more sedate former associates, the Imagists, while the influential Louis Untermeyer dismissed them as "crank insurgents," offering Loy's "Love Songs" as Exhibit A in what reads like an attempt to have the whole group indicted for poetic rebellion.[2] Although Loy's radicalism was obviously disconcerting in her own time, contemporary readers are rediscovering her elliptical, fragmented images of a modern woman's psychosexual experience as the revisionary histories of both modernism and feminism are gradually pieced together.

Although many women continued to publish traditional lyric poetry during the 1910s, poets like Loy, H.D., and Marianne Moore were writing poems that spoke from the brain as well as from the heart. Critical response to these intellectual poets depended upon the individual's opinion of the modern woman as well as personal aesthetics. When Untermeyer called Loy and her contemporaries "cerebralists" and complained of their "eroticism gone to seed," Pound praised them for their obvious intelligence.[3] Opting for a Poundian version of modernism (in *Revolution of the Word: A New Gathering of American Avant-Garde Poetry),* Jerome Rothenberg recently resituated Loy at the center of her peers' attempts to articulate what she called "the crisis in consciousness" (1914). Similarly, David Perkins's characterization of Loy's best poetry as "witty, physical, philosophical, anti-sentimental and vigorously phrased" places her once again in the context of the New York avant-garde and the *Others* poets.[4] Rothenberg and Perkins both fail, however, to speculate upon the convergence of Modernism and feminism in her (and her generation's) writing. I intend to reconstruct the climate of opinion in the explosive prewar years, first in relation to feminist issues of the period, and next in the context of the free verse controversy, in order to understand the impact of Loy's poems on those readers who kept them around for months and dug them out of corners to read to each other.

I

Mina Loy's chief source of information about the New York avant-garde prior to her arrival was Mabel Dodge, her close friend from the Anglo-American expatriate community in Florence. While Loy remained in Florence until 1916, Dodge had returned to New York in 1912, having, as she said, "done" the Renaissance and wishing to catch the tempo of modern life. Soon Dodge's name was linked with modernism in the arts and radicalism in social and political thought. By 1913, her elegant salon in Greenwich Village brought together "Socialists, Trade-Unionists, Anarchists, Suffragists, Poets, Relations, Lawyers, Murderers, "Old Friends," Psychoanalysts, I.W.W.'s, Single Taxers, Birth Controlists, Newspapermen, Artists, Modern-Artists, Clubwomen, Woman's-place-is-in-the-home Women, Clergymen, and just plain men." Dodge wanted to see what would happen when "all sorts of people could meet under one roof and talk together freely on all subjects." At this point, Dodge considered herself one of the "pioneers for the renewed expression of life in art,"[5] for whom radicalism in all domains sprang from the same impulse.

Dodge wrote to Loy of her many activities on behalf of the new spirit. She organized publicity for the controversial Armory Show, published a provocative appreciation of Gertrude Stein's prose, and distributed Stein's "Portrait of Mabel Dodge at the Villa Curonia" as if it were a sort of press release. She also worked in support of the new socialist magazine *The Masses* and the reenactment of the Paterson strike, where she began an affair with journalist John Reed. Reed was, however, less certain than Dodge that changes in the means of expression would go hand in hand with changes in forms of social organization. When she waxed enthusiastic over his coverage of the Mexican revolution, he bantered, "Mabel has already decided that the rebels are part of the great world-movement. . . . I think she expects to find General Villa a sort of male Gertrude Stein, or at least a Mexican Steiglitz." But at this point, she was still convinced that the radicals, herself included, were "out in the untried—feeling our way towards the truth of tomorrow."[5]

Still digesting the philosophy of Henri Bergson, which she had read in Florence with Mina Loy, Dodge decided that a sort of cosmic "élan vital" was at work, and that she and her friends were playing their parts in its unfolding. Did not Bergson's visit to New York at the time of the Armory Show confirm her intuitions? She was equally enthusiastic about Loy's quasi-Bergsonian prose poem, "Aphorisms on Futurism," and recommended it to Steiglitz for *Camera Work*. Loy's first published writing, "Aphorisms,"[7] reads like a set of prescriptions for psychic liberation.

TODAY is the crisis in consciousness.

CONSCIOUSNESS cannot spontaneously accept or reject new forms, as offered by creative genius; it is the new form, for however great a period of time it may remain a mere irritant—that moulds consciousness to the necessary amplitude for holding it.

CONSCIOUSNESS has no climax.

LET the Universe flow into your consciousness, there is no limit to its capacity, nothing that it shall not re-create.

Although they would later grow apart, at this point, Dodge included Loy in her world movement for psychic and social emancipation.

Another new woman whom she met in radical circles soon showed Dodge the way to her vocation as a priestess of "It," or a mystical eroticism. Although Margaret Sanger was still involved in the political struggles of the International Workers of the World (IWW) in 1913, she was, in Dodge's view, more important as a prophet of sexual liberation. "It was as if she had been more or less arbitrarily chosen by the powers that be to voice a new gospel of not only sex knowledge in regard to conception, but sex knowledge about copulation and its intrinsic importance." At the same time that she was forming her commitment to birth control, Sanger was also "an ardent propagandist for the joys of the flesh. . . . It was her belief that the attitude towards sex in the past of the race was infantile, archaic, and ignorant." Dodge learned that the body was full of wondrous possibilities for "sex expression," a sacred yet scientific mode of communion. She received Sanger's teaching as if it were the new gospel and Sanger herself a female precursor of D. H. Lawrence.[8]

Although Mabel Dodge showed little interest in birth control, Mina Loy was curious about Sanger's activities. She asked Dodge for the details of Sanger's legal battles and may have been familiar with Sanger's magazine, *The Woman Rebel*. When Sanger began to publish information on contraception and sexual hygiene, another friend in New York commented on the scandal to Loy, "There are those of us over here who won't believe that 'That's' all Love is."[9] Loy in turn observed to Dodge that their friend was having "virginal hysterics. . . . Of course '*Thats*' all nothing and yet '*Thats*' all it is— the *more* is spiritual effervescence." Loy was sympathetic to efforts for greater sexual honesty, which she saw as a prerequisite for psychic and social liberation. Even though Sanger's activities might put "That" in proper perspective, however, activism was not Loy's way: "what I feel now are feminine politics—but in a cosmic way that may not fit in anywhere."[10]

In an effort to define her version of "feminine politics," Loy wrote her own "Feminist Manifesto" and sent a copy to Mabel Dodge. She added, "Do tell me what you are making of Feminism. . . . Have you any idea in what direction the sex must be shoved—psychological I mean."[11] Apparently uninterested in what she called the "bread and butter" issues, the vote and other political solutions to the woman question on the basis of equality, Loy emphasized instead the differences between the sexes. Her manifesto calls for women to "leave off looking to men to find out what you are *not*—seek within yourselves to find out what you are." Convinced that "no scratching on the surface of the rubbish heap of tradition will bring about Reform," she concluded, "the only method is Absolute Demolition." Loy agreed with Sanger, however, that women's ignorance of sexual realities stood in the way of their self-fulfillment: "Nature has endowed the complete woman," Loy wrote, "with a faculty for expressing herself through all her functions—there are no restrictions." Furthermore, like Sanger, she believed that "every woman has a right to maternity," whether married or not.[12] Children should no longer be defined according to the marital status of their parents, who, in turn, should remain free to follow their own paths of personal development. Such freedom would restore the "spontaneous creative quality" long repressed by "the Anglo-Saxon covered up-ness," she wrote to another friend, adding, "all this modern movement—is keeping entirely on the surface—and gets no further psychologically."[13] Loy's manifesto prescribed psychic liberation as the necessary prelude to both artistic and social regeneration. Her conclusion would have been appropriate in the pages of *The Woman Rebel*: "There is nothing impure in sex—except in the mental attitude to it."[14]

Such views were not shared by the American postal authorities, however. Sanger was soon indicted for publishing "a pamphlet of obscene, lewd and lascivious character, containing articles of such vile, obscene, filthy and indecent nature that a description of them would defile the records of the United States District Court."[15] Sanger gathered numerous supporters in New York and abroad, while the newspapers gave her case increasingly abundant publicity. By the time of her trial early in 1916 (when the indictment was dropped), birth control had become the central social issue of the period, dividing pro-family progressives from radicals, who saw the issue in the larger context of the class struggle.

Although Sanger later disavowed her friendship with Emma Goldman, she first learned of birth control methods in Goldman's anarchist circles. The first issue of *The Woman Rebel* carried an article in which Goldman declared that the modern woman "desires fewer and better children, begotten and reared in love and through free choice, not by compulsion, as marriage imposes." Like Mina Loy, Goldman believed that most exponents of women's rights held too narrow a conception of female emancipation. In her view, "independence from external tyrannies" was not enough, for the "internal tyrants . . . —ethical and social conventions" still ruled the hearts and heads of most feminists.[16] Since women's access to information about their sexuality was a prerequisite for dealing with these tyrants, Goldman took up the cause of birth control again soon after Sanger's indictment and served a brief sentence in a New York jail in the winter of 1916. Throughout this period, Greenwich Village feminists (including Henrietta Rodman, Ida Rauh, Floyd Dell, Crystal and Max Eastman, and John Reed) lectured, wrote editorials, and organized protest meetings in support of the cause. This publicity was so effective that by the summer of 1916, large groups of people were voicing their opposition to the classification of birth control literature as obscene, and the police no longer arrested those who distributed it. By the time of Mina Loy's arrival in the autumn of 1916, many were ready to agree that "a woman's body belongs to herself alone."[17]

In this context, it is not surprising that Loy's poems on sexual love and its consequences were read as if they were the statements of the woman rebel. She had dared to write of the "lascivious revelation" of childbirth in "Parturition" (1914) and of free love in her infamous "Love Songs" (1915). Like Dodge, Loy called for freedom of "sex expression"; like Sanger, she wrote of female sexuality as the woman's own prerogative; and like Goldman, she questioned the sway of the inner tyrants that caused even emancipated women to accept the conventions of romantic love and patriarchal marriage. Her writing confirmed the popular view that free verse probably led to free love. Before turning to a reading of her poetry in this context, I would like to illustrate the important literary issue of 1915–16—the vers libre controversy—by discussing critical responses to *Others* in relation to the question of the new woman.

II

Depending upon one's point of view during the prewar years, new developments in the arts were seen either as "conditions of vital growth" or as immoral and decadent.[18] Progressives and conservatives agreed that "much of the expression of those explosive days was the same, whether in art, literature, labor expansion, or sexual experience."[19] The *New York Times*'s art critic considered the modernists "cousins to the anarchists in politics," and as if in confirmation of his view, Emma Goldman called *The Little Review* "a note of rebellion in creative endeavor."[20] At Mabel Dodge's salon, friends discussed the connections among what their hostess called "the possibles: the possible revolution, the possible New Art, the possible new relation between men and women."[21] The general sense that political, artistic, and sexual experimentation spring from the same impulse lay behind the vers libre controversy. Free verse was denounced by the press and taken up by the public as yet another symptom of the impulse of the day.

William Carlos Williams remembered that the summer of 1915 saw "a strange quickening of artistic life" with the publication of Alfred Kreymborg's *Others*. Kreymborg and Walter Conrad Arensberg, his financial backer, intended to publish more experimental verse than could be found in *Poetry,* which, they felt, "admitted too many compromises."[22] The first issue featured Orrick Johns's "Olives" and Mina Loy's "Love Songs," both of which caused something of an uproar in the press. One could be amused by Johns's "Now I know/ I have been eating apple-pie for breakfast/ In the New England/ Of your sexuality," but few readers knew what to make of Loy's peculiar love songs:

> Spawn   of   Fantasies
> Silting the appraisable

Pig Cupid   his rosy snout
Rooting erotic garbage
"Once upon a time"
Pulls a weed   white and star-topped
Among wild oats   sewn in mucous-membrane

I would   an   eye in a bengal light
Eternity in a sky-rocket
Constellations in an ocean
Whose rivers run no fresher
Than a trickle of saliva

Although Kreymborg noted approvingly at the time, "Women are finding their most intimate expression through free verse," he recalled later that many readers "shuddered at Mina Loy's subject matter and derided her elimination of punctuation marks and the audacious spacing of her lines."[23] Perhaps these readers sensed that Loy's antisentimental stance and formal experimentation subverted both literary decorum and received cultural norms.

For supporters of *Others,* however, "it seemed that the weight of centuries was about to be lifted. . . . America had at last found a democratic means of expression." Not the least of their excitement was caused by the realization that the magazine had created "wild enthusiasm among free-verse writers, slightly less enthusiasm among Sunday Magazine Section reporters, and really quite a stir in the country at large."[24] Detractors soon objected that the unrestrained expression of individualistic emotions produced only crank insurgency, "a perfumed and purposeless revolt." A letter in the *New York Sun* denounced poetry like Loy's as "erotic and erratic."[25] Soon the newspapers, eager to promote a controversy, were ridiculing the new poetry: it was skinny, impoverished, preoccupied with sex and empty of thought, save the thought of its own emancipation. Parodies of the poems in the first issues of *Others* appeared throughout the autumn and winter of 1915.

Don Marquis devoted a number of columns in the *New York Evening Sun* to gentle mockery of the new fashion. "A Key to the New Verse" declares:

Not only do we understand the New Verse, but we are the only person who does understand all of it. When Alfred Kreymborg writes one of his mushroom poems, no one but Mina Loy knows exactly what it means, and she never tells anyone but Sadakichi

Hartmann. Sadakichi Hartmann is sometimes comprehended by Ezra Pound, but never by himself.

After linking free verse to the activities of Gertrude Stein and Alfred Steiglitz, Don Marquis shared his key with the reader: such poems need only to be rearranged into traditional meters to be understood, for "in every *vers libre* poem of the wilder sort, a poem of the academic, old-fashioned conventional type . . . is hidden."[26] Those who were bewildered by the new poetry could, at last, breathe a sigh of relief.

But it would have been impossible to find reassuringly old-fashioned poems hidden in Loy's "Love Songs." Readers accustomed to the conventions of romantic poetry were totally unprepared for her frank exploration of sexual love from a woman's perspective. Even the ostensibly modern Amy Lowell was so shocked by Loy's poems that she threatened to withdraw her support from *Others*. In the meantime, readers alarmed by the image of Eros as "Pig Cupid" denounced Loy's verse as "swill poetry" or, more succinctly, "Hoggerel."[27] What Kreymborg described as her "utter nonchalance in revealing the secrets of sex," others saw as lewd and lascivious writing, in the same class as the pamphlets of Margaret Sanger or the lectures of Emma Goldman. Worse still, Loy did not imitate their straightforward prose but wrote "in a madly elliptical style scornful of the regulation grammar, syntax and punctuation." Kreymborg concluded, "To reduce eroticism to the sty was an outrage, and to do so without verbs, sentence structure, punctuation, even more offensive. . . . Had a man written these poems, the town might have viewed them with comparative comfort."[28] His point is well taken: Loy's frankness and experimentalism were all the more unacceptable because she was a woman.

When Loy decided to write about the predicament of the modern woman as avant-garde artist, she chose as her model an acquaintance from the expatriate colony in Florence, Isadora Duncan. Possibly she recalled her fellow radicals' high esteem for the dancer's art: when Duncan appeared in New York in 1915, she seemed to represent "woman's emancipation, sexual liberation, artistic freedom and political protest" all in one."[29] Floyd Dell asserted in *The Masses*, "It is not enough to throw God from his pedestal, to dream of superman and the cooperative commonwealth: one must have seen Isadora Duncan to die happily." Mabel Dodge thought Duncan "the most truly living being I had ever seen," the embodiment of the élan vital.[30] Her unfettered move-

ments, which seemed to the modernists to express creativity in its pure
state, soon suggested a metaphor for the "free feet" of free verse. The
image of bare feet, emancipated from the stiff shoes and outworn cho-
reographies of classical ballet, recurred whenever reporters began to
write of the revolution in poetry.

When, for example, the *New York Tribune* sent a reporter to the
artists' colony in New Jersey where Kreymborg printed *Others,* the sto-
ry appeared under the provocative headline, "Free Footed Verse is
Danced in Ridgefield, N.J." Although the reporter concentrated on the
more bohemian aspects of life in Ridgefield, she discussed free verse as
a new cultural phenomenon. After comparing the poems in *Others* to
the paintings in the Armory Show, she explained that *vers libre*
demands an intellectual effort of the reader: "in the new poetry there is
a riddle, something to be solved. It is like . . . a Gertrude Stein rhap-
sody or a Shoenberg [*sic*] symphony." To illustrate the point she
quoted not Loy's infamous lines about Pig Cupid, but the puzzling
conclusion of her first love song:

> I must live in my lantern
> Trimming subliminal flicker
> Virginal   to the bellows
> Of experience
>   Coloured glass

After a glance at Loy's significant blank spaces, the rest of the article
details the poets' attempts to live in a style appropriate to their verse.
The reporter did, however, observe that a "notable feature of the
movement is the early prominence taken in it by women."[31] The con-
nection was implicit: like Isadora Duncan, the emancipated female poet
would naturally express herself in "free-footed verse."

Of course there were those who doubted the wisdom of allowing
either poets or women to dance as they desired, and parodists con-
tinued to mock the Isadora-like abandon affected by free verse writers.
The author of "Lines to the Free Feet of Free Verse" (the *New York
Tribune*) noted that once poetry was emancipated, it lost its grace and
hobbled clumsily. He concluded with an argument familiar from other
controversies: the feet that once pattered prettily were being deprived
of their natural rhythm by the new freedom; everyone knew that they
were happiest when dancing to the familiar choreographies.[32] Soon

Don Marquis was explaining that modernism in verse was merely a return to a language freed of Victorian excrescences. Under the guidance of Harriet Monroe, "a rather conservatively inclined chaperone of the radical brood," vers librists would return to their senses.[33] Although a few *Others* poets did return to meter and to romantic love poetry, Loy had irrevocably abandoned the chaperonage of the late Victorian sensibility. Her unsentimental depiction of sexuality—"No love or the other thing / Only the impact of lighted bodies / Knocking sparks off each other / In chaos"—suggested a modernist disillusionment with both the myth and metrics of romance.[34] Her poetry appeared, furthermore, to corroborate a contemporary's observation: "When the world began to change, the restlessness of women was the main cause."[35]

III

As an English woman familiar with contemporary artistic movements on the Continent, Mina Loy brought an original perspective to the American scene. Although she too was in revolt against Victorian social and aesthetic standards, unlike the American modernists she did not have to do combat with a genteel poetic tradition. In fact, Loy had the peculiar advantage of knowing very little of literary convention. She began to write poetry around 1912 in a kind of historical vacuum, as if there were no models of poetic speech for or by women. In the 1910s, Emily Dickinson was known by very few readers, and she was, in any case, too idiosyncratic to serve as a model. Although Elizabeth Barrett Browning wrote suggestively of "woman's claim," she was at once too learned and too much of her own generation (that of Loy's grandparents). Similarly, although Loy read Christina Rossetti's poetry with great interest, its eroticized piety and self-deprivation provided her with a negative model only. Loy was, however, reading Gertrude Stein's experimental rhythmic prose as early as 1911, when they met in Florence. In contrast to nineteenth-century poetry, Stein's writing revealed a strikingly contemporary concern with psychological analysis and the effects of consciousness upon perception. For Loy, Stein's battle with grammatical, rhetorical, and narrative convention actually "stretches the muscles of the intellect." Loy's writing was undoubtedly stimulated by Stein's innovations, which may have pointed the way toward her own development of a highly visual form of free verse. In any case, she praised Stein as a type of female genius:

> Curie
> of the laboratory
> of vocabulary
>   she crushed
> the tonnage of consciousness
> congealed to phrases
>   to extract
> a radium of the word[36]

In a similar spirit, the new poetry might also liberate language from the weight of tradition.

Both Stein and Loy could approach writing in this typically modernist spirit, in part because of their familiarity with contemporary art movements, especially cubism. Loy actually studied painting in London, Munich, and Paris during the 1890s and 1900s and achieved recognition for her work at the Salon d'Automne before moving to Florence in 1907. Like her contemporary Guillaume Apollinaire, whose *Soirées de Paris* column on modern art she probably read, Loy was a "poète fondé en peinture."[37] But even if she knew Apollinaire's *Alcools* and *Zone,* she was already composing her own visually oriented, "simultanist" poetry when Apollinaire began to publish his spatially ordered *calligrammes.* (Indeed, Loy's 1913 "Costa San Giorgio" may have been one of the first English poems to employ simultaneity and juxtaposition as formal principles.) Furthermore, by 1913, Loy was involved with the Italian Futurists. Marinetti and his followers claimed in their provocative manifestos that they intended to break down the barriers between art and life, as well as the barriers separating one art from another. To Loy, their reorientation of artistic attention to the urban flow and bustle seemed to throw open the windows of both poetry and art to modern life. In spite of her later criticisms of Futurist misogyny, Loy wrote that Marinetti nevertheless deserved credit for waking her up: his theories of dynamism suggested a way out of the passivity of *fin de siècle* aestheticism. Although her own poetry was never as extreme in its syntactic and grammatical emancipation as Marinetti's *parole in libertà,* like Stein he acted as a catalyst in her own personal and artistic awakening.

It is not surprising that American modernists welcomed a poet with this impressive background in European avant-gardisms. They saw Loy as a sophisticated expatriate at home with the latest developments of modern art, as well as an ally in their battle with the genteel tradition. What they did not see was that Loy, like themselves, had her own "subconscious archives,"[38] the layers of interwoven images and memories that had to be exhumed and analyzed while she was finding her voice as a modern woman. As an art student in London during the nineties, Loy attempted to distance herself from her middle-class family and the waning ideals of Victorian womanhood by adopting the aestheticism and antibourgeois stance of the Decadents. Later, when she began to write poetry from a woman's perspective, the imagery of the nineties rose to the surface of her consciousness: women were either sensitive Ophelias or dangerous Salomés, or these two extremes might seem to be combined in such complex female presences as the imaginary Mona Lisa or the real Sarah Bernhardt. Although few women spent their lives in languorous poses outside the art studio, such images retained their hold on her imagination. Several groups of poems from the early 1910s constitute a kind of aesthetic and personal self-analysis, in which images of gender and sexuality are dredged up from the subconscious, carefully examined, and, finally, demystified.

In "Three Moments in Paris," a sequence of three related poems, Loy paints portraits of women whose dependence upon a traditional view of the sexes shapes their self-awareness. This *fin de siècle* Paris is, of course, as much a state of mind or an artistic vision (suggesting Toulouse-Lautrec or the early Picasso) as it is an actual city, and Loy's perceptive female speakers all acknowledge the limitations of its aesthetic ambience. In the first poem, "One O'Clock at Night," the speaker is bemused by her response to a male companion's virile posturings. While this man tries to argue his interlocutor into accepting his theories of "Plastic Velocity," the woman falls asleep at his side:

> Indifferent to cerebral gymnastics
> Or regarding them as the self-indulgent play of children
> Or the thunder of alien gods

When she wakes to catch the thread of the argument, however, and assumes "a personal mental attitude," she ceases to be "a mere woman / The animal woman / Understanding nothing of man." Asleep, she had been "indifferent," or unaware of the structure of sexual difference, but now she awakens to an understanding of its effects. She could criticize their "pugilis(m) of the intellect" if she chose to abandon the security of living "indifferent." The ironic conclusion—"Let us go home she is tired and   wants to go to bed."—appears to give the last word to the men while permitting their arguments to be undercut by the physical presence of the "mere woman."

The second poem evokes an imaginary "Café du Néant," whose airless atmosphere and melancholy poses suggest a Symbolist painting. In this world of artifice, seeing is not necessarily believing, when "eyes that are full of love" become "eyes that are full of kohl." Pairs of lovers are grouped in a composition that focuses on the central figure, again a woman defined by her male companion's power over her. Acquiescing in her role as dependent, however, the women "As usual / Is smiling as bravely / As it is given to her to be brave." Although her languid acceptance of self-abasement marks her as a Symbolist ideal, the speaker's heavy irony makes it clear that there are, nevertheless, alternatives to this morbid romantic script. The final line—"Yet   there are cabs outside the door."—implies that this woman (and women in general) must distance herself from the aestheticism of the Café du Néant before she can see what it has made of her. Perception and consciousness are intimately related. One whose eyes are blurred with love may lack the ability to perceive her own complicity in the process of being reduced to an image.

In "Magasins du Louvre," the final poem of the sequence, another watchful speaker studies the images of femininity available for purchase at the Paris department store. Boxes of dolls are on display: their vacant glass eyes see nothing, like the "virgin eyes" they represent, "Beckoning / Smiling / In a profound silence." The speaker also studies the other women in the shop, who, like the dolls, are available objects of the female sex. Both the salesgirl harassed by the shop-walker and the two *cocottes* in provocative costumes are defined by their subordination to masculine powers. When the *cocottes* catch sight of the dolls, their knowing eyes are held by the vacant gazes of these icons of innocence: "their eyes relax / And now averted / Seek each other's   surreptitiously." The speaker, meanwhile, watches this double exchange of glances, then lowers her own eyes in shame, "Having surprised a gesture that is ultimately intimate." She regrets the loss of innocence that her lucidity entails. The complex relationship between the "eye" and the "I," between perception and (self) consciousness, sets her apart from these women even in her attempt to understand their situation. The sequence of poems as a whole rethinks masculinity and femininity as perceptual and conceptual categories, or as habits of the eye and the mind.

Loy's "Love Songs," published in the same year as "Three Moments in Paris" but more innovative both thematically and formally, constitute a passionately clinical analysis of a failed love affair from a woman's perspective. The first person speaker's focus has moved in them from the exterior world to an inner space or psychological reality. There, the conventions of romantic love may be reenacted rhythmically and imagistically to evoke both their power and their status as illusory fictions. The entire sequence of thirty-four poems deserves attention in the context of modernist experimentation by her contemporaries T. S. Eliot, Williams, Pound, and Marianne Moore. A kind of verse collage, Loy's fragmented form itself participates in the thematic examination of the gaps between art and life, but her shards of "colored glass" (the final image of the first poem) constitute a kaleidoscope of psychic and sensual impressions rather than a stable mosaic. The experience they embody is the disintegration of an ideal, or, more positively, the process of "deconstruction" that Gertrude Stein described to Loy as the aim and technique of modernist art.[39] In the deeply ironic last line of the sequence, "Love— — — the preeminent litterateur," romantic love is "deconstructed" and dismissed as a self-enclosed system of creative illusions.

What shocked her contemporaries, however, was Loy's treatment of gender and sexuality in these so-called love songs. She alluded to the "suspect places" of sexual intercourse with such frankness that no one could miss her meaning. As if references to female sexuality in a series of water images (e.g., "an ocean / Whose rivers run no fresher / Than a trickle of saliva") were not sufficiently scandalous, poem II evokes both the male sexual principle and the apparently insurmountable differences between the sexes.

> The skin-sack
> In which a wanton duality
> Packed
> All the completions of my infructuous impulses
> Something the shape of a man
> To the casual vulgarity of the merely observant
> More of a clock-work mechanism
> Running down against time
> To which I am not paced
> My finger-tips are numb from fretting your hair
> A God's door-mat
> On the threshold of your mind

Her sexual timing is incompatible with the lover's "clock-work mecha-
nism," yet their intercourse could fulfill both her physical desires and
her spiritual aspirations, were they similarly "paced." Given the biolog-
ical and emotional scripts for heterosexual romance, communion be-
tween the sexes seems doomed to frustration.

Loy's "Love Songs" may be compared with similarly antiromantic
poetry by her better-known contemporaries. Despite Harriet Monroe's
misgivings, *Poetry* pubished T. S. Eliot's "The Love Song of J. Alfred
Prufrock" in 1915, and his "Portrait of a Lady" appeared in *Others* soon
after the publication of Loy's "Love Songs." Although both poets share
an ironic approach to the demise of romantic love and traditional love
poetry, Eliot's tepid tales are emotionally evasive and self-protective,
while Loy's verses spring from passionate self-revelation. Where Eliot
writes of what did not happen, of "carefully caught regrets," Loy
plunges the reader into the suspect places of sexuality and generates
surrealistic images of spiritual transgression. Unlike Eliot, the generally
shy William Carlos Williams nevertheless "frankly and fearlessly un-
dressed himself down to the ground" in his poetry during this period,[40]
when he was close to Mina Loy. Her daring subject matter and tech-
nique probably stimulated him to attempt more contemporary subjects
and greater stylistic innovation. His "Romance Moderne" (published in
Others in 1919) evokes "the unseen power of words" in the shaping of
desire and juxtaposes romantic declarations of love with violently anti-
sentimental references to its physical apparatus: "God how I love
you!—or, as I say, / a plunge into the ditch. The end. I sit / examining
my red handful. . . ." Loy's love poems exhibit a lingering fondness
for "something the shape of a man," compared with Williams's delib-
erately crude demystification of the phallic principle. Although hardly a
feminist, Williams was intensely interested in the woman's perspective,
especially when he wanted to appropriate it for his own uses. Like Loy,
he learned to make sexual difference a poetic subject, and he undoubt-
edly agreed with her that women's experience differed radically from
men's.

If sexual intercourse simultaneously heightened and frustrated the
female subject's sense of herself, the experience of childbirth provided
another, perhaps even more extreme occasion for the definition of
female difference. Fifty years before such a subject became acceptable,
Loy traced what she called the "spatial contours" of childbirth in "Par-
turition" (1914). Her originality and daring should not be underesti-

mated. Few women discussed childbirth in public, except in the pages of *The Woman Rebel,* and none wrote poems about it. Whitman's ecstatic celebration of physical being may have provided Loy with a distant precedent, but she had to revise his song of the (male) self to suit a female subject. While his Biblically cadenced free verse sang the body electric by casting aside poetic conventions as if they were tight-fitting garments, Loy, by contrast, worked out a compact, compressed free verse line that could simulate the rhythmic contractions and expansions of labor. At the same time, she approached the blank page as if it were a canvas: a visual medium in which to recreate the inner spaces of the female body.

> I am the centre
> Of a circle of pain
> Exceeding its boundaries in every direction
>
> The business of the bland sun
> Has no affair with me
> In my congested cosmos of agony
> From which there is no escape
> On infinitely prolonged nerve-vibrations
> Or in contraction
> To the pin-point nucleus of being
>
> Locate an irritation   without
> It is   within
>   within
> It is without

The white space around the words joins in the play of speech and silence. Gradually the spaces between words and phrases become the inner space from which the birth/poem is issuing, and the area around the poem becomes a version of the larger cosmos in which the birth is taking place. By abandoning punctuation, Loy creates a kinesthetic sensation of opening from within: childbirth becomes the process of "knowing / All about / Unfolding," an "elusion of the circumscribed." The female subject is released from dependence upon the male into an unbounded knowledge of female libido, a "lascivious revelation." In giving birth to the child, she also gives birth to the poem and to herself in an almost mystical acknowledgment of female creative potential. "Parturition" answered the prescription for psychic liberation in Loy's "Feminist Manifesto": "leave off looking to men to find out what you are *not*—seek within yourselves to find out what you are."[41]

IV

But even in the radical literary and political circles of pre–World War I Greenwich Village, few readers were prepared for poetry like Loy's. Probably it demanded too much of them, intellectually, aesthetically, and emotionally, because, as Kreymborg pointed out, it was spoken in a woman's voice. Even sympathetic literary men generally saw women poets first "as humans," then "as lovers," and finally "as artists," as in the appropriate chapter title from Kreymborg's *Our Singing Strength,* a history of American Poetry.[42] (In it, Kreymborg observes that women are better craftsmen because they set themselves "a narrower range.") John Reed, for example, lent his support to feminist causes but responded with ambivalence to the new woman's writing. His mixed feelings are apparent in the mock drama that he composed for Mabel Dodge, which included a part for Mina Loy: the play is of interest because it concerns God's efforts to create the ideal woman from a pattern book containing all the familiar stereotypes. Only the formula for a femme fatale has been slightly modernized: "Figure that will stand a Greenwich Village uniform; thorough comprehension of Matisse; more than a touch of languor; a dash of economic independence; dark hair, dark eyes, dark past."[43] Reed might have been describing Mina Loy or someone like her, except that this femme fatale would have painted her own canvases or written her own poems. Even the most committed radicals were often intimidated by the modern woman's conjunction of independence, intellect, and what Loy called her "personal mental attitude."

Always on the alert for what was "new," however, Ezra Pound was not so much intimidated as surprised by the presence of intellect in poetry by women. After championing H.D. as the exemplary "imagiste," he asserted in 1918 that Mina Loy and Marianne Moore both wrote "logopoeia," a kind of poetry which he described as "a dance of the intelligence among words and ideas." While welcoming them to the club of intellectual poets (including Pope, Laforgue, and T. S. Eliot), he warned that their poetry would disconcert readers unaccustomed to using their wits. Moreover, he found in their poetry "the utterance of clever people in despair." Although Pound went out of his way to avoid speaking of Moore and Loy as women, his criticism of their poetry is typically astigmatic, however, because it ignores both the striking differences between them and the fact that being a woman mattered to each of them as much as being intelligent. Pound concluded that both poets were "interesting and readable," but that their poems "would drive numerous not wholly unintelligent readers into a fury of rage-out-of-puzzlement."[44]

Although Moore's relation to feminism is ambiguous, her poetry is well known today, while Loy's still puzzles numerous not unintelligent readers. In a gloss on Pound's comments, Kenneth Rexroth offered a provocative explanation for Loy's neglect that made a clear connection between the politics of the new woman and the poetics of the new poetry:

> Erotic poetry is usually lyric. Hers is elegiac and satirical. . . . If it is bitter and dissatisfied, it is at least passionate. She commonly transforms the characteristic envy of little girls into the super-ciliousness of an unhappy suffragette. People don't like poetry like that.

Arguing for Loy's importance in the history of American modernism, he observed, "her material is self evidently more important than Miss Moore's. . . . She writes of . . . the presence or absence of sexual satis-faction; and of the results: recreation, marriage, procreation; sterility, disorder, disaster, death."[45] It was no wonder that adventurous readers kept Loy's poems around for months and more conservative readers were shocked. Perhaps as the reporter suspected in their 1917 inter-view, women like Mina Loy were indeed a "cause of modernism, whatever that is."

NOTES

I am indebted to Jane Bostwick, whose patient and thorough research in the New York periodicals of the period 1915–17 allowed me to develop and docu-ment the argument of this article.

1. "Do You Strive to Capture the Symbols of Your Reactions? If Not You Are Quite Old Fashioned," *New York Evening Sun*, February 13, 1917, p. 10.

2. Monroe cited in Ellen Williams, *Harriet Monroe and the Poetry Renais-sance: The First Ten Years of Poetry* (Urbana: University of Illinois Press, 1977), p. 150; *The Letters of Ezra Pound: 1907–1941*, edited by D. D. Paige (New York: Harcourt Brace and World, 1950), p. 82; William S. Braithewaite, ed., *Anthology of Magazine Verse for 1916* (New York: Laurence J. Gomme, 1916), p. xv; Louis Untermeyer, *American Poetry Since 1900* (New York: Henry Holt, 1923), pp. 183–85.

3. Untermeyer, *American Poetry Since 1900,* pp. 192, 346–50; Pound, "'Others,'" in *Little Review* 4, no. 11 (March 1918): 57.

4. Jerome Rothenberg, *Revolution of the Word* (New York: Seabury Press, 1974), pp. xix, xxi; David Perkins, *A History of Modern Poetry, From the 1890's to the High Modernist Mode* (Cambridge, Mass.: Harvard University Press, 1976), p. 532.

5. Mabel Dodge Luhan, *Intimate Memories,* vol. 3, *Movers and Shakers* (New York: Harcourt, Brace and Co., 1936), pp. 83, 93, 94.

6. Reed cited in Robert Rosenstone, *Romantic Revolutionary: A Biography of John Reed* (New York: Vintage Books, 1981), p. 151; Luhan, *Movers and Shakers,* p. 94.

7. In *Camera Work* 45 (January 1914): 13–15; reprinted in Loy, *The Last Lunar Baedeker,* edited by Roger L. Conover (Highlands, N.C.: Jargon, 1982), henceforth abbreviated as *TLLB*. This edition of Loy's writing includes all works discussed here, unless otherwise noted.

8. Luhan, *Movers and Shakers,* pp. 69–70. On Sanger, see Linda Gordon, *Woman's Body, Woman's Right: A Social History of Birth Control in America* (London: Penguin, 1977), pp. 206–45.

9. Loy to Luhan, c. 1915, in Collection of American Literature, Beinecke Library, Yale University (henceforth abbreviated as YCAL).

10. Loy to Carl Van Vechten, c. 1915, YCAL.

11. Loy to Luhan, c. 1915, YCAL.

12. Loy, "Feminist Manifesto," November 15, 1914, in Dodge papers, YCAL; reprinted in *TLLB*.

13. Loy to Van Vechten, c. 1915, YCAL.

14. Loy, "Feminist Manifesto."

15. *The Woman Rebel* 1, no. 7 (September–October 1914): 49. The offensive material included information on family planning, contraception, and abortion.

16. *The Woman Rebel* 1, no. 1 (March 1914): 3; Emma Goldman, *Anarchism and Other Essays* (New York: Mother Earth Publishing Association, 1910), pp. 243, 220, 227.

17. *The Woman Rebel* 1, no. 4 (June 1914): 25.

18. Hutchins Hapgood, cited in Barbara Rose, *American Art Since 1900: A Critical History* (London: Thames and Hudson, 1967), p. 76. Hapgood continued, "this beneficent agitation is as noticeable in art and the woman's movement as it is in politics and industry."

19. Hapgood, *A Victorian in the Modern World* (New York: Harcourt, Brace and Co., 1939), p. 341.

20. Cited in Rose, *American Art Since 1900,* p. 76; Goldman, *Living my Life,* cited in Blanche Wiesen Cook, "Female Support Networks and Political Activism," in *A Heritage of Her Own,* edited by Nancy F. Cott and Elizabeth H. Pleck (New York: Simon and Schuster, 1979), p. 434.

21. Luhan, *Movers and Shakers,* p. 242.

22. Williams, "The Great Opportunity," *The Egoist* 3, no. 9 (September 1916): 137; Alfred Kreymborg, *The Troubadour, An Autobiography* (New York: Boni and Liveright, 1925), p. 221.

23. Kreymborg, *The Troubadour,* p. 235.

24. Williams, "The Great Opportunity," p. 137.

25. Untermeyer, *The New Era In American Poetry* (New York: Henry Holt and Co., 1919), p. 326; Lincoln Phifer, letter to the editor, *New York Sun,* August 21, 1915.

26. Don Marquis, *New York Evening Sun,* July 24, 1915, p. 6.

27. T.N.P., "Or Hoggerel, As You Might Say," *New York Tribune,* July 3, 1915, p. 7.

28. Alfred Kreymborg, *Our Singing Strength, An Outline of American Poetry (1620–1930)* (New York: Coward-McCann, 1929), pp. 488–89.

29. Arthur Frank Wertheim, *The New York Little Renaissance, Iconoclasm, Modernism, and Nationalism in American Culture, 1908–1917* (New York: New York University Press, 1976), p. 89. Wertheim's chapter on feminism (pp. 79–96) has more to say about male feminists than about female ones.

30. Dell, "Who Said that Beauty Passes Like a Dream," *The Masses* 8 (October 1916): 27; Luhan, *Movers and Shakers,* p. 333.

31. Margaret Johns, *New York Tribune,* July 25, 1915, sec. 3 p. 2.

32. L.W.D., *New York Tribune,* June 29, 1915, p. 7.

33. Don Marquis, "The Business of Poetry," *New York Sun,* September 12, 1915, p. 8.

34. Loy, "Love Songs," poem XIV.

35. Hapgood, cited in Gordon, *Woman's Body, Woman's Right,* p. 198.

36. Loy, "Gertrude Stein," *Transatlantic Review* 2 (October 1924): 305, and *TLLB.* On Stein and Loy as female modernists, see Carolyn Burke, "Without Commas: Gertrude Stein and Mina Loy," in *Poetics Journal* 4 (1984): 43–52.

37. Roger Shattuck, *The Banquet Years: The Origins of the Avant-Garde in France, 1885 to World War I* (New York: Vintage Books, 1968), p. 319.

38. Loy's phrase, in her poem "O Hell," *Contact* 1 (December 1920): 7, and *TLLB.* On Loy's social and familial background, as well as her involvement in Futurism, see Carolyn Burke, "Becoming Mina Loy," in *Women's Studies* 7 (Summer 1980): 136–50.

39. Loy, "Phenomenon in American Art," YCAL. Stein may have coined the term *deconstruction,* by which she meant dismantling both the structural principles of the object and the traditional habits of perception.

40. Kreymborg, *The Troubadour,* p. 242.

41. See note 12.

42. Kreymborg, *Our Singing Strength,* p. 438.

43. Luhan, *Movers and Shakers,* p. 224. On male feminists' personal dilemmas, see Ellen Kay Trimberger, "Feminism, Men and Modern Love: Greenwich Village, 1900–1925," in *Powers of Desire, The Politics of Sexuality,* edited by Ann Snitow, Christine Stansell, and Sharon Thompson (New York: Monthly Review Press, 1983), pp. 131–52.

44. Pound, " 'Others.' "

45. "Les Lauriers Sont Coupés," *Circle* 1, no. 4 (1944): 69–70.

To Have the Winning Language:
Texts and Contexts of Gertrude Stein

Ulla E. Dydo

I

In February of 1903, Gertrude Stein, aged twenty-nine, returned to New York from London, hoping to work out a love affair that had tortured her for two years. Within a few months, she realized that she had lost her friend's affection to a rival. In a state of acute depression, she joined her brother Leo at 27 rue de Fleurus, his new apartment in Paris. Late that year, she told the story of the aborted lesbian love affair in conventional narrative manner in the novel *Q. E. D.* The manuscript was put away and not published until after her death.

In the spring of 1905, Stein began the first of three stories—echoing Flaubert, she at first called them histories—that she completed by February of 1906 and published in 1909 under the title *Three Lives*. The three pieces were written in a manner entirely different from that of familiar narratives of the period and of Stein's own *Q. E. D.* The new stories exhilarated some of Stein's friends, who read them in manuscript, and baffled others. But they conveyed a sense of purpose and control so clear and urgent that they marked Stein as a serious professional writer in a new mode. The last of the three tales, "Melanctha," was not only written in the new style of phrases repeated and modulated in such a way that they created descriptions, but it also used the subject matter of *Q. E. D.* in an entirely new, heterosexual form. Between 1903 and 1906, then, Stein had come to look at her experience as material for writing—as writing—rather than as events for confessional telling.

That Stein had become a writer was clear to herself and to friends and family, whom she informed that she had found her life's work. Her first step was the creation of the new aesthetic of *Three Lives,* which led directly to *The Making of Americans* (1902–11)[1] and the early portraits.

Her second step was to find a publisher. The introductory pages of this essay consider not only Stein's progress as a young writer but also some of the problems of publication which affected her work.

When Stein moved to Paris, she left behind not only a wrecked love affair but also an enormous and powerful family, which in her own generation included more than forty living first cousins (not counting cousins by marriage), in addition to her four siblings. Most of the family lived in Baltimore though a sizable and important group was in New York. Stein knew both groups well.

The Steins were a cohesive Jewish family whose members' sense of identity derived primarily from the family rather than from individuality, locality, or nationality. The power and importance of the family may be heard in one phrase from her long poem "Patriarchal Poetry" (1927)[2] and especially in its insistent, triple reiteration: "Their origin and their history patriarchal poetry their origin and their history patriarchal poetry their origin and their history." (The phrase surely also echoes *The Making of Americans: Being A History Of A Family's Progress*.) In the same poem the sentence, "Patriarchal poetry makes no mistake" suggests, ironically, in part, the powerful family constraints and in part Gertrude Stein's capacity to convey in her poetry without mistake the nature of family power. The grammar of family living limited individual freedom and set firm rules for family members.

When Stein's father died in Oakland in 1891, his will was filed in Baltimore. His affairs were taken care of not only by his eldest son, Michael, in Oakland, but also by the eldest son of his senior brother in Baltimore, as tradition required. After his death, Gertrude and her older sister Bertha naturally moved to Baltimore to live with family. Bertha married in Baltimore, but Gertrude went on to college in Cambridge, where she found greater physical and intellectual freedom than continued life in Baltimore offered.

When Stein moved to Paris, she moved out of necessity, freeing herself to live and work. One of her entries in an early notebook states her need in emphatic rhythms: "I am wanting freedom for myself always in living" (*NB-M-6*, YCAL). Though she moved far away from Baltimore, the family remained a powerful presence in her life, even in Paris. The kind of freedom she needed had to be sought far from the grammar of her Baltimore family.

Years later, when Stein wrote her own will in 1928, she considered deaths, wills, and family in a six-act "Baltimore Opera" entitled *A Bouquet. Their Wills*.[3] The opera includes a Chorus of Baltimoreans that becomes a powerful family voice, characterized by ironic descriptive phrases like "Chorus of Amiability" or "Chorus of Baltimoreans distinguished by their management." The context of wills affects the extent to which people become friendly or lovable, as the word *amiability* with its unmistakable French overtone (*aimable*) suggests; the *distinguished management* in the second phrase refers to the management of money—the Steins were bankers.

What allowed Stein to initiate an entirely new approach to composition in 1905–6 was not only her growing mastery of her own experience and her capacity to use her freedom but also her discovery of Flaubert ("Flaubert has no emotion about his material but complete emotion about his expression" *NB-13-12*, YCAL). and above all her encounter with the work of Cézanne, "the master of realization of the object itself" (*NB-A-14*, YCAL).

Stein came to understand how Cézanne distributed interest equally throughout the painting so that the work would not be organized around a central focus of interest and would not subordinate minor to major elements. In her writing, she also came to include not only the things perceived but the act of perceiving them. Once the process of perception and indeed the act of writing was a part of what she was writing, traditional narration vanished and the composition became a description. At that point, genre distinctions lost their meaning and the designation of written pieces as poems, novels, histories, and so on became unimportant. Stein poked fun at genres by using titles that made classification impossible and subtitles that made nonsense of genres: "Scenery and George Washington. A Novel or a Play" (1931) is a good example.[4] She thought of her own pieces as compositions or constructions.

In a radically disjunctive world Stein affirmed the need for raw experience, unfiltered by systems of interpretation and rules for composition. With passionate dedication she began to explore and to compose in words the elements of that world. When she said, "Aesthetic has become the whole of me" (*NB-14-7*, YCAL), she was speaking of the unpremeditated perception of what she saw and what she set out to name.

Stein's discovery of the new aesthetic was also a discovery of her own gift—her genius. She had known for a long time that she was gifted. Leo and Gertrude were both keenly aware of their endowments and never thought of concealing them. The Steins' fascination with the idea of genius, which reflected an interest of their time, is also evident in their reading. They knew William James's comments on genius in *Psychology*, the textbook for his course at Harvard, and in other works. They were familiar with Lombroso's study of the criminal as genius and with the work of Havelock Ellis, and Gertrude had a lifelong fascination with Napoleon as a genius. When in the winter of 1907–8 Leo and Gertrude discovered Otto Weininger's *Sex and Character*,[5] they were absorbed by his discussion of genius and by their sense that Weininger himself was a genius.

The meaning of genius became clear to Stein in the course of her study of personality types and of her developing friendship with Picasso, whom she considered the prototype of the genius. Stein watched Picasso with the greatest care, hoping that he would not betray his gift by allowing weaknesses of character to interfere with his art. She felt a profound personal affinity with Picasso, and she was fascinated by the psychology of artistic perception and expression.[6]

Stein's encounter with Picasso led her to understand and to define—not in theory but in the practice of actual composition—who she was as an artist. It also led her to differentiate herself from her brother. She came to reject the abstract, systematic thinking and theorizing to which Leo was given as lacking in the "power of construction" (*NB-A-3*, YCAL) and to assert that only a person who maintained at all times a firm sense of the objects of the world was a true artist. Increasingly, she distrusted those who "run themselves by their minds" (*NB-A-3*, YCAL), like her brother. Stein distinguished between those whose eyes turn in and those whose eyes turn out: "it is only sentimentalists and unexperiencing thinkers whose eyes turn in. Those having wealth of experience turn out or are quiet in meditation or repose" (*NB-N-1*, YCAL). This distinction is exemplified on the one hand by "unexperiencing thinkers" like her brother Leo and on the other by artists like Picasso and herself. Once Stein had formulated the difference between these two ways of apprehending life, she was ready to reject her brother and to devote herself passionately to the creation in words of her perception of the world.

Reinforcing her sense of her own gift was Stein's sense of professionalism and vocation, familiar from student days. In the 1890s, students at the Harvard Annex (which was to become Radcliffe College in

1894, Gertrude's second year) were aware of the need for independent purpose and for a vocation. The women at Radcliffe, at Smith, at Bryn Mawr—all colleges where Stein had friends—were systematically taught to think about vocations. When, in 1897, Stein entered the Johns Hopkins Medical School, the first to admit women students on the same terms as men, she was committed to the study of medicine as her life's vocation, and although medicine turned out to be the wrong choice, professional seriousness remained a permanent characteristic of Stein's view of her work. Once she chose writing as a profession, her commitment was total and unsentimental. She never saw herself as an amateur lady writer. She spoke of her *métier*—her trade—as an uncompromising professional.

Stein knew that writing involved struggle. Often her words, in the voice of a military leader considering strategy, speak of the need to "concentrate," to "manoeuver," to "confederate." "Arthur A Grammar" (1928)[7] is filled with military language and with allusions to Hannibal, Grant, Wellington: "A grammar makes an attack" (p. 74). "Grammar in resistance" (p. 86). Writing is the product of the grammatical interplay of attack and resistance, a dynamic process in constant movement rather than in static opposition: "There is no grammar in opposition but there is if there is omnipresent successful intermediation. Best and most in interplay" (p. 64). The interest of the work of art is in its dynamic construction.

Stein's experience of painting had taught her that new forms in art appeared ugly until they became accepted as beautiful. But that knowledge offered little solace when it came to publication. Though friends understood and praised her work from *Three Lives* on, publishers rejected her submissions, saying that they did not make sense.[8] Privately many readers called them mad—another word for ugly. Stein's work constituted an attack not only upon inherited forms of perception and expression used without thought (she called them "associational habits") but on the very instrument of perception—language itself. Her work was the result of her consistent refusal to rely on language habits and of her insistence that each piece was a new problem of perception which required its own form of construction in words. Her readers' battles with her words are in part battles against ingrained reading habits.

If Stein's work was to be known, she needed readers. The wish to be known, however, led imperceptibly to the wish for fame. A part of

Stein's personality craved fame even in her earliest years. Again and again there are references to the wish to be "lionized." She recognized the temptation of writing to please an audience rather than to create literature. When, upon the publication of *The Autobiography of Alice B. Toklas* in 1933, she became a best-selling author and a public personality, she feared that she had abandoned God for Mammon. *The Geographical History of America* (1935), written at the height of her fame, discusses the problem of audience writing at length.[9]

Gertrude Stein's ambition also included the wish to be published by the literary establishment in its classiest form—the very establishment whose values her writing challenged. No wonder Ellery Sedgwick of the *Atlantic Monthly* returned three poems which she had submitted, saying that they "would be a picture puzzle to our readers. All who have not the key must find them baffling—and—alack! the key is known to very very few." Undaunted, Stein replied:

> I may say without xageration [*sic*] that my stuff has genuine literary quality . . . let us say the only important literature that has come out of America since Henry James. After all Henry James was a picture puzzle, but the Atlantic did not hesitate. To be sure he was connected with the heart of Boston but then I did graduate from Radcliffe and I was a favorite pupil of William James and that combination ought to encourage the Atlantic to take a chance. (25 October 1919)[10]

And she concluded, "I am sending you a few earlier things that may be easier. Do your best for them it really is important." It is easy to condemn these words as gross immodesty and to forget that Stein lacked experience in dealing with the literary establishment. Naively, she valued candor in self-appraisal more highly than modesty. Yet she never wavered from her conviction that she knew what she was about: "Nobody knows what I am trying to do but I do and I know when I succeed" ("More Grammar for a Sentence," 1930).[11] Not until 1933, when *The Autobiography of Alice B. Toklas*—serialized in the *Atlantic Monthly*—made a celebrity of its author, did the literary establishment pay attention to her. But by that time, Stein had already written most of the serious literary compositions for which she remains important. While after 1933 it became easier to get published, it never became a matter of course, especially not for the pieces that most mattered to her.

Those were the pieces that even Alfred Harcourt, who had made a handsome profit from the publication of the *Autobiography,* remained reluctant to publish, asking instead for more of the "open and public" books—autobiographical works and critical pieces like the lectures she delivered in America. In responding to Harcourt, Stein avoided the antonym "closed" to describe her books. "The open and public books are really illustrations for the other books, and . . . illustrations should be accompanied by what they illustrate," she said, making it clear that the popular books were not the important ones. Harcourt, she felt, "ought to be willing to risk some of my real kind of books" if he wished to go on with her open and public ones.

But her early works were never public books and were difficult to publish. Three years after completing *Three Lives* she solved the problem of the first book by paying for its publication. Later she financed the publication of other works, often collections of pieces written at various times. *The Making of Americans* (1902–11), the work that Stein considered her most important, was published in book form in Robert McAlmon's Contact Editions after financial and personal problems throughout the year 1925. The struggle for book publication culminated in the late twenties, when she most seriously examined the nature of writing and of language, That was also when she decided to assume control of the book publication of Gertrude Stein.

She sold one of her Picassos, and with Alice Toklas in 1929 started the Plain Edition, "an edition of the first editions of all the work not yet printed of Gertrude Stein." Five volumes appeared in the Plain Edition between 1930 and 1933: *Lucy Church Amiably,* written in 1927; *Before the Flowers of Friendship Faded Friendship Faded,* written in 1930; *How to Write,* a collection of pieces written between 1928 and 1931; *Operas and Plays,* a collection of some of the plays written between 1913 and 1931; and *Matisse Picasso and Gertrude Stein,* three early works written between 1909 and 1912.

To refer to these books and to many other volumes of Stein by publication date is almost meaningless since the time gap between composition and publication is usually enormous. The dates of composition, however, are of the greatest importance since Stein's work evolves gradually, step by step, from one piece to the next. That is why the dates given in this essay are the dates of composition.

In 1928, Stein for the first time asked for the help of an agent. William Aspenwall Bradley, a critic, poet, and translator in his own right, was also the best-known American agent in Paris. According to Bradley, Stein engaged him because she wanted him to help her make money; money, of course, was an aspect of fame. As Stein put it in "More Grammar for a Sentence" (1930),

> They have to be without doubt well known. He likes to have him be hired for that in that with their care named Bradley which made whenever they do more than that deliberately making a mine of use of their acknowledge meant for them a reason assistance made curious and by and nearly which is that. Make without call. It is very beautiful to have the winning language.[12]

(Grammar is for sentences; other units of writing, such as paragraphs, do not rely on grammar. The opening, declarative sentence tells of the simple need for fame. The next sentence renders in oblique fashion, with echoes of business and contractual language as well as various bits of polite verbiage, the complexities of realizing the simple desire to be known. For such a sentence more grammar was indeed needed. The statement in "More Grammar" is a far cry from the language of her letter to Ellery Sedgwick.) Bradley, who considered himself far more than a mere salesman of writing, tried to "erect a publishing structure" for Gertrude Stein's work, and little by little negotiated numerous publications.

By the mid-thirties, Stein had a large audience—larger for her public books than for her real kind of books—and a sense of her importance. In 1936–37, Thornton Wilder brought that sense home to her by encouraging her to deposit her manuscripts and papers at the Yale University Library. Wilder well understood that the gift of a writer's papers to a major library spelled a kind of immortality. To Stein, who had always looked to universities for her best readers, the prospect of the Stein Collection gave great satisfaction.

The papers in the Stein Collection form a context for Stein's work. Although Stein firmly maintained that a knowledge of her life was irrelevant for the reading of her work, and though she took pains to keep her private life strictly private, all her writing comes from her own experience. Yet her pieces are not representations of what she experienced. She creates in her word constructions a reality that can be recognized though it is not a mimetic reality. The Stein papers show a part of the context—the source of the vocabulary—out of which she created her texts. Without an understanding of this context, which is never invented, the ways in which Stein abstracted or discontextuated when she wrote are difficult to understand. A few of the ways in which the context sheds light on the text will become apparent in the following pages.

II

Gertrude Stein's sources are all the small things in daily life, including her own writing, her reading, overheard comments, distractions, interruptions, walks, eating, sitting down, talking to the dog, clouds, vegetables—anything can become an occasion for a composition and a perception that takes verbal form. Sometimes Stein works with a big plan and a large shape: her novels, plays, and long poems are always based on designs for the whole that create coherence and continuity (though these designs are also capable of absorbing the small and immediate detail that daily life offers in unending variety). Rather than examine the large designs, I shall look at how Stein made writing out of what she called "everything." She said she relied on the immediate—the here and now—and the commonplace to give shape to word constructions. How did she draw on her sources and how did she use them to write?

Stein arranged her whole life around the fact that she was a writer. Of course she did a great many things beside writing, but when these things entered her writing, they entered as words and were no longer the actions or objects or feelings of Miss Stein, the person with a visiting card that announced her name and her identity. Here is a tiny playlet with a few statements and forms of direct address alternating with asides that contain bits of narrative:

> Dear dog
> He likes to see
> Dear dog
> But did he know it was he
> Leave dear dog where he is
> Otherwise it is
> Not satisfied
>
>   ("Hotel François Ier," 1931)[13]

In these lines Stein is talking about nothing extraordinary at all. The lines may concern leaving her poodle, who has seen his reflection. They

certainly speak about whether the dog knows who he is. All these mat-
ters, however, are of interest only as a series of "composed" verbal
reflections—the phrase "Dear dog," which becomes pathetic in repeti-
tion; the rhyme *see / he;* the mirrored *is / is.* The dog, who likes to see
images but does not know how to look at them, fails to recognize his
own reflection. This incapacity reduces him to an *it.* The reader familiar
with Stein may recall that this is the dog who occasioned the sentence,
"I am I if my little dog knows me," which Stein had originally read in
Josiah Royce's work and which she used for her own purposes in her
discussions of identity.[14] In her lines the dog's "seeing" has become an
occasion for an insight in words.

   All of Stein's writing insists on the pleasure of *now*—being now,
doing now, seeing now, and of course writing now. She wrote, as she
often said, what she knew, and that was her immediate daily life rather
than remote memories and theories. Her work is what Leon Katz calls
"a hymn of pleasure in the actual." The actual includes herself: "I am
trying to say something but I have not said it. / Why. / Because I add
my I," she wrote in "Stanzas in Meditation" (V, xli, 1932).[15] She tries
to say what cannot be said in itself—cannot *say itself*—because the per-
ceiver of it is mixed up in the seeing and the saying of it. "Study
nature," Stein advises herself in a 1915 piece that also uses the phrase as
its title.[16] The advice provokes a deadpan response: "I do." It is then
repeated in modified form ("Study from nature") with overtones of
painting or drawing. (The work *study* may be a verb or a noun.) A
further response follows in a shapely, symmetrical form:

Study from nature.

I
Am
Pleased
Thoroughly
I
Am
Thoroughly
Pleased.
By.
It.

The response includes the "unscientific" pleasure in an *it* with no sin-
gle, clear antecedent. It may be the study of nature, or nature itself, or a
drawing from nature, or the words Stein has just written that end with

it. Plainly, however, the study of nature gives pleasure, for it is the beginning of art.

What is nature? "Study Nature" makes clear that it is not merely fields and flowers though these are among the little things that Stein trained herself to perceive in words. Nature includes the many people whom Stein studied and of whom she wrote word portraits. Daily life is a form of nature. It includes composed talk—conversation, commentary, chitchat, asides:

> I have lost the thread of my discourse.
> This is it it makes no difference if we find it
> If we found it
>
> ("Stanzas in Meditation," V, xvi)

There are echoes from primers: "Come here Ben / Come here Hilda." Dressmakers and clothes appear: "Garments were a separate desire pleasure, / She made hours a desired separated measure" ("Hotel François Ier").[17] The Stein meditation puts into words the actualities that Stein perceives, including the act of perceiving them. The act of meditation is the composition of actualities.

Though Stein's subject is not nature and she does not write "nature poetry," nature in this large sense is the source of words and the occasion for insights. In the twenties, however, nature as the countryside became increasingly important. Stein's stay in St. Rémy for several months in 1922–23 began a powerful experience of landscape. And from 1924 on, Stein and Toklas spent their summers in Belley, in the Rhone Valley, settling in 1929 for six months out of every year in nearby Bilignin, in a house that they rented for many years. These summers gave Gertrude Stein access to an enriched vocabulary of experience and a new source of sights, sounds, and insights. A few examples from "Stanzas in Meditation" illustrate their importance: "They shell peas and of the pea shell they make a soup to eat and drink" (IV, i).

> Often as evening is as light
> As once for all
> Think of how many often
> And they like it here
>
> (I, ii)

> They call peas beans and raspberries strawberries or two
> They forget well and change it as a last

That they could like all that they ever get
As many fancies for which they have asked no one.

(I, vi)

Stein often speaks of the here and now as the source of her com-
positions. This is the world of the commonplace things of daily life
which are always the same and always different. What do people do in
this world? They "get up sit down and walk around." One of the
many variations on this recurrent sentence describes her people in Bal-
timore: "Suppose in walking up and down they sat around" ("Business
in Baltimore," 1923).[18] To use everything means to waste nothing that
can be composed in writing. Gertrude Stein's world is full of writing
ideas.

The long poem "Winning His Way" (1931)[19] shows another
source of composition: the relation of poetry, friendship, and fame—
three cardinal concerns in Stein's life. The subtitle of the poem in the
manuscript notebook is "A narrative poem of poetry and friendships."
In the printed version, based on the corrected typescript, the subtitle is
more tightly focused: "A Narrative Poem of Poetry." However slight,
the change is quite in Stein's style: a single revision pinpoints the central
word: poetry. Friendship and fame are mere adjuncts to poetry.

What. In what. Way. Do they differ.
And. In what. Way. Are they. The same.
Those of them that have. Fame. From those of them.
That do not. Have. Fame. In what way.
Are they. The same. Those. Of them. That do not. Have fame.
What is. Fame. That they. Have.
And what. Is different. In them. That gives to them. This. Fame.
From those of them. That do not have.
Given to them. Fame. Or is it. Not the same.
Not. To have fame. As to. Have fame.
And are they. Who have fame. The same.
As those. Who do not have. Fame.
This is why. It is. The same.

This series of modulations on fame, with its periods and halts, sounds
like an enormously deliberate effort at defining a great difference that
turns out to be meaningless. The sentences are broken into slow and
heavy phrases by the periods, and the varied phrases create a movement
and a tone that characterize the voice of the poem, which is a particu-

larly good example of Stein's interest in the weight of words and in slow and fast speed in writing.

Elsewhere in "Winning His Way" Stein wonders why she keeps writing.

> The problem resolves itself. Into this.
> Does a poem. Continue. Because of. A kiss.
> Or because. Of future greatness.
> Or because. There is no cause. Why.

A kiss means Alice Toklas, the central presence in Stein's life and behind her work, who sometimes also entered her work.

> Lifting Belly praises
> And she gives
> Health.
> And fragrance.
> And words.
>
> ("Lifting Belly," 1915–17)[20]

"When it is not with her he can make no verses and this is why because she is hallowed even" ("Narrative," 1930).[21] Alice Toklas's love allowed Gertrude Stein to use her gift of words. It was not a matter of writing *for* Alice or of writing *about* love although Stein did write a great deal about Alice, especially in the language of everyday detail discussed earlier. Alice Toklas validated Stein's wish to write and gave her access to her life's work. She became the bridge from life to art and from art to life, even when they quarreled.

At the beginning of the first manuscript notebook of "Natural Phenomena" (1925–26),[22] a long, complex meditation, appears a personal note, not a part of the piece she eventually composed, that tells something about how Stein got off the ground when she began to write: "What shall I write about not about a volcano not about war but about love, my dear dear love. . . ." Alice Toklas, who typed Stein's pieces, would of course receive this love letter as soon as she began to type. Why not write about volcanoes and war? The notebook in which this piece begins—one of the French school notebooks with educational covers that give information about various topics in words and pictures—is from a series entitled "Les Phénomènes de la Nature." The name of the series, in English translation, becomes the title and probably the starting point for Stein's piece. This particular notebook concerns volcanoes as natural phenomena and includes, through Vulcan, references to war. Gertrude Stein did not always have a subject or a word idea ready when she began to write. Sometimes she looked for a way to get started. The thought of Alice offered one way of starting; the other, which became the eventual subject of the piece, came from the world around her—in this case, the text and illustrations of her notebook.[23]

Alice Toklas was not Stein's subject when she wrote; her subject was always writing. But Alice often gave her access to the world which held the ideas for writing. As Stein's primary audience, she had immense power, and she provided Stein with far more than sexual satisfaction, a functioning household, and typescripts. She delineated the world in which Stein lived and wrote. When necessary, Toklas disciplined Stein to do the writing that in laziness she shunned. Toklas protected her from interference. She kept Stein's world large enough for writing and small enough for intimate living. All this allowed the slightest event to become an occasion for composition in words.

Words as signs refer to the world in which Stein lived. But in a composition, words refer to other words. They no longer point outward to the world, denotatively and centrifugally, but inward, centripetally, to one another. Stein's work consists of successive attempts to make words move within the composition rather than in the world.

If Stein did not invent anything but used everything from the world around her, what is the invention of her art? The invention is in the construction. Stein uses words with all their referential meanings—her pieces never sever the connection with the objects she perceives. But in her construction, she frees words from traditional rules for behavior. She refuses to allow habits to dictate phrasing. She liberates the little words and the subordinate elements, which had been bound by rules of grammar, to move freely and meaningfully in the choreography of her composition. She liberates the parts of speech.

In "More Grammar for a Sentence," at the end of the paragraph quoted earlier about her agent Bradley, about the problems of publication and other worldly matters which required words, Stein returned to what mattered most: "It is very beautiful to have the winning language." As long as people love the English language, they will know what she meant.

NOTES

Research for this essay, a part of a study of the work of Gertrude Stein from 1925 to 1932, was supported by a Fellowship for College Teachers from the National Endowment for the Humanities and by grant number 13220 from the PSC-CUNY Award Program of the City University of New York.

1. Thinking of a family history, Stein wrote her earliest notes for *The Making of Americans* in the winter of 1902–3 in London and New York. By 1906, she returned to the family history. Both the details of the aborted love affair and the genesis of *The Making of Americans* are told by Leon Katz in his introduction to Gertrude Stein's *Fernhurst, Q.E.D. and Other Early Writings* (New York: Liveright, 1971).

Quotations from printed sources are identified in the text by title and date of composition; volumes that print the pieces are cited in notes. Quotations from manuscripts and other papers in the Stein Collection are identified as belonging to the Yale Collection of American Literature (YCAL), Beinecke Rare Book and Manuscript Library, Yale University. Quotations from Stein's unpublished Early Notebooks at Yale are identified by the abbreviation *NB*.

2. *Bee Time Vine* (New Haven: Yale University Press, 1953), pp. 249–94.

3. *Operas and Plays* (Paris: Plain Edition, 1932), pp. 195–218. The 1928 will does not survive because it was replaced by a new will or wills later. It is fascinating that in the last will of 1946 (and perhaps even in the 1928 will), Stein returned to family form. The will was deposited in Baltimore. While naming Alice Toklas as beneficiary for her lifetime, Stein appointed as the heir her nephew Allan Stein, the son of her eldest brother, who had taken charge of family affairs after her father's death. It appears likely that even the 1928 will may have named Allan Stein as heir. A long paragraph of "Patriarchal Poetry" moves from the question of the patriarchy to "no farther" (father) to the question of supporting Allan: ". . . is it best Allan will to support patriarchal poetry . . . Allan will patriarchal poetry Allan will" (p. 290).

4. The piece was incorporated in the George Washington section of *Four in America* (1933), published by the Yale University Press in 1947.

5. First German edition published 1903; English translation, 1906.

6. Stein's relationship with Picasso and her interest in Cézanne are discussed in detail by Leon Katz in "Matisse, Picasso and Gertrude Stein," *Four Americans in Paris* (New York: Museum of Modern Art, 1970), pp. 51–63.

7. *How To Write* (Paris: Plain Edition, 1931), pp. 37–101.

8. Both some comments by friends and some letters from editors are printed in *The Flowers of Friendship: Letters Written to Gertrude Stein,* edited by Donald Gallup (New York: Alfred A. Knopf, 1953).

9. *The Geographical History of America* (New York: Random House, 1935). The book was published with an introduction by Thornton Wilder, with whom Stein had discussed the problem of audience at length.

10. Donald Gallup, "Gertrude Stein and the *Atlantic*," *Yale University Library Gazette* 28 (January 1954): 109–28.

11. *As Fine As Melanctha* (New Haven: Yale University Press, 1954), p. 365.

12. Ibid., p. 361.

13. *Mrs. Reynolds and Five Earlier Novelettes* (New Haven: Yale University Press, 1952), pp. 301–20.

14. Richard Bridgman, *Gertrude Stein in Pieces* (New York: Oxford University Press, 1970), p. 242n.

15. *Stanzas in Meditation and Other Poems (1929–1933)* (New Haven: Yale University Press, 1956).

16. *Bee Time Vine*, p. 181. As a student at Johns Hopkins, Stein had with difficulty learned to abandon broad generalizations and to observe detail as scientific research required. Her passionate commitment to detail may have originated here, but it was surely reinforced by her study of Cézanne, whose insistence upon detail she knew: "Le Bon Dieu existe dans le détail."

17. *Mrs. Reynolds and Five Earlier Novelettes*, p. 305.

18. *Useful Knowledge* (New York: Payson and Clarke, 1928), pp. 64–77.

19. *Stanzas in Meditation and Other Poems (1929–1933)*, pp. 153–209.

20. *Bee Time Vine*, pp. 61–115.

21. *Stanzas in Meditation and Other Poems (1929–1933)*, pp. 250–56.

22. *Painted Lace* (New Haven: Yale University Press, 1955), pp. 167–233.

23. Both Richard Bridgman in *Gertrude Stein in Pieces* and Wendy Steiner in *Exact Resemblance to Exact Resemblance* (New Haven: Yale University Press, 1978) comment on Stein's use of the French *cahiers*. However, these notebooks require further study.

H.D.: Hilda in Egypt

Albert Gelpi

H.D. always wrote her own personal and psychological dilemma against and within the political turmoil of the twentieth century, the toils of love enmeshed in the convulsions of war. Her marriage to and separation from Richard Aldington turn on World War I, and that concatenation of private and public trauma stand behind the Imagist poems of her first phase, summed up in the *Collected Poems* of 1925. The sequences of *Trilogy,* written through the London blitzes of World War II, usher in the longer, multivalent, and more associative poems of her later years. But her last years were to bring a third great burst of creativity. The travail of aging and illness did not issue in the stoic silence which made Pound leave incomplete his life's work in the *Cantos,* but instead, as with William Carlos Williams, made for a final and climactic efflorescence of poetic expression. The results of this third phase were *Helen in Egypt,*[1] published in 1961 almost concurrently with her death, and *Hermetic Definition,* published posthumously in 1972.

Even the reviewers who shied away from dealing with *Helen in Egypt* as a poem by detaching particular lyrics for dutiful praise (as though they were still Imagist pieces) recognized dimly that *Helen* was the culmination of a life in poetry. But it is an event even more culturally signal than that: it is the most ambitious and successful long poem ever written by a woman poet, certainly in English. It is so often observed as to take on a kind of fatality that no woman has ever written an epic, that women poets seem constrained to the minor note and the confabulations of the heart. H.D. confounds that complacent dictum by assuming and redefining the grounds of the epic. Early on (p. 32) the poem asks:

> Is Fate inexorable?
> does Zeus decree that, forever,
> Love should be born of War?

The *Iliad* showed War born of Love, but H.D. repossessed the Trojan materials that have inspired the Western epic from Homer to Pound and converted them into an anti-epic centered less on heroes like Achilles and Hector than on a heroine, none other than the fabulous woman who, male poets have told us, roused men to Love, and so to War.

Many of the masterworks of American writing—*Walden* and *Moby-Dick* and *Absalom, Absalom!*, *Leaves of Grass* and *The Cantos, Four Quartets* and *Paterson*—are *sui generis*. They make their idiosyncratic statement in their own unique form. So *Helen in Egypt* draws Greek and Egyptian myths, epic and psychoanalysis and occult gnosticism into an "odyssey" of consciousness played out as a series of lyrics written in irregular free verse tercets of varying length, linked by prose commentaries sometimes longer than the lyrics. The poem is divided into books, eight lyrics to a book, seven books to Part I, "Pallinode," and to Part II, "Leuké," and six to the concluding part, "Eidolon." "Pallinode" was written at Lugano in the summer of 1952; "Leuké," the next year at the Küsnacht Klinik near Zurich, H.D.'s base of residence after 1953; and "Eidolon" again at Lugano during the summer of 1954. H.D. came to think of the poem as a trilogy, and the narrative too is laid out in a number of interrelated triangles. The speakers in "Pallinode," which takes place in an Egyptian temple near the coast after the war, are Helen, who was rumored to have spent the war there rather than at Troy, and Achilles, the Trojan nemesis lost at sea and shipwrecked in Egypt; the speakers in Part II are Helen and her old lover Paris on Leuké, *l'isle blanche,* and then Helen and Theseus, her old benefactor and counselor in Athens; the triad of voices in "Eidolon" are Helen and Paris and Achilles. Through the other male voices Helen's is, of course, not only the point of view but the subsuming consciousness. And Helen is, of course, H.D.'s persona.

A notebook entry in 1955 observed: "I had found myself, I had found my alter-ego or my double—and that my mother's name was Helen has no doubt something to do with it." And the configuration of male characters around Helen recreates fantasized versions of her governing relationships with men as she strove, now on an epic scale, to lift "the tragic events and sordid realities of *my* life" into myth.[2]

Theseus is the easiest to designate. Most readers have recognized in him an image of Sigmund Freud. He served H.D. during the thirties and after as wise old man, surrounded in his study by ancient Greek figurines, as he applied reason to help her sort out the confusion of her life and feelings. Like Freud for H.D., Theseus is for Helen the wise, paternal authority who offers his couch to her for rest and an analytic rehearsal of her amatory embroilments.

The associations with Paris and with Achilles are more important and elusive because less fixed and more inclusive; they span all H.D.'s adult life up to the time of her writing of the poem. As for Paris, her involvement with Dr. Eric Heydt, her doctor and analyst at Küsnacht Klinik, had almost immediately passed from the professional into the personal and romantic despite the fact that she was decades older than he, and in a notebook she confessed that the complications of the relationship extended the poem into its second part and specifically led to the introduction of Paris. But behind Heydt stood Pound: in *HERmione* she saw the young Pound as "Paris with the apple," saw his luxuriant red hair as "the Phrygian Cap of Paris." He called her his "Dryad," and so she signed her letters to him to the end of her life. He wrote his famous invocation "A Tree" to her in the "Hilda Book" during their courtship, and *HERmione* echoes her acceptance. "I am a tree. TREE is my new name out of the Revelations."[3] And now years later Paris calls Helen "Dendritis, . . . Helena of the trees" (p. 141).

In the "Compassionate Friendship" notebook (which also dates from the mid-1950s), H.D. rehearsed "the sequence of my initiators" throughout her life: Pound; Aldington; from the London days of World War I John Cournos and D. H. Lawrence and Cecil Grey (the father of her daughter Perdita); Bryher's second husband Kenneth MacPherson (who had been H.D.'s lover); Walther Schmideberg, her analyst and close friend during the time of the final divorce decree from Aldington in 1938; and now Eric Heydt as the "inheritor" of the long male line of initiators.[4] In much the same way the figure of Paris summed up all the men in her life, from Pound to Heydt, including Aldington.

Moreover, she particularly associated Heydt with Pound. When Heydt gave her an injection at perhaps their initial encounter at the Klinik, he transfixed her with the question "You know Ezra Pound, don't you?" "This was a shock coming from a stranger," she told her journal. "Perhaps he injected me or re-injected me with Ezra." The sexual image is appropriate enough; Heydt persisted in pressing her about her relationship with her first lover, and once even asked her—to her distaste—whether the relationship had been sexual. The Pound memoir *End to Torment* H.D. wrote in 1958 only after repeated urging from Heydt that she recover her memories of the young man who had loved her and confirmed her a poet. Testimony that Pound was a living presence in her mind extends beyond *End to Torment* to the separate Helen sequence "Winter Love," written in 1959 and published in *Hermetic Definition,* in which Helen/Hilda relives her early love for "Odysseus." So she incorporated into the Paris of her *Helen,* she said, an imaginative presence or medium who stood behind Heydt and was associated with "the history of poor Ezra and my connection with him."[5]

The figure of Achilles is composite in much the same way as Paris. Notebook entries specifically connect him with Lord Hugh Dowding, the Air Marshal of the Battle of Britain with whom H.D. shared spiritualist experiences and for whom she served briefly as medium. Though she saw Dowding only at two lectures about his communications with lost RAF pilots and at seven meetings, she felt a spiritual affinity for him that was like an "engagement." She was shattered when he broke off their acquaintance, and "in 1952, after I knew of the Air Marshall's [sic] marriage (Sept. 1951), I wrote the first section of the *Helen* sequence." The rupture released creative energy to cope with the situation, as had the separation from Aldington earlier.[6]

> We had come together through and for the messages. There was a feeling of exaltation in my later discovery, it was not I, personally, who was repudiated. An "engagement" was broken, but broken on a new level. . . . My life was enriched, my creative energy was almost abnormal. I wrote the *Avon,* I wrote three "works" (unpublished) on my unparalleled experiences. I wrote the long *Helen* sequence. . . .

But Achilles was associated with other figures as well. Dowding reminded her of her father in some ways: "I know *ad astra,* my father's profession, the iridescent moons he shows us. I know *ad astra,* the Air Marshall's profession. I know the wide-faring, hypnotic, rather mad grey eyes of both of them." In another notebook she recounts a dream in which her older brother Gilbert (for whom she felt such love and such competition for her mother's love) is strangling her, and associates the dream with the episode in which Achilles tries to strangle Helen.[7] But more importantly, just as Pound stands behind Heydt in Paris, so Aldington stands behind Dowding in Achilles. Paris's and Achilles'

initials are as significant as Helen's. And where Paris represents the line
of initiators in H.D.'s life who in one way and another carried her
away, Achilles represents specifically the rough and devastating threat
of the masculine, not unrelated to the romantic Paris-aspect, but specif-
ically that aspect of the masculine which cast her off and cast her down.
The poem enacts Helen's apotheosis as she transcends Paris's power
over her and transforms Achilles' rejection into a divine marriage, a
conjuctio oppositorum ordained by the gods.

"Is Fate inexorable? / does Zeus decree that, forever, / Love should
be born of War?" (p. 32). The poem finally answers *yes:* divine decree
requires that we submit ourselves to life, for all the war wounds and
mortal blows, so that, providentially, in comprehending the train of
temporal events, we can accept and transcend them; participation in the
design decreed for time at last earns identity. *Helen in Egypt* is, then,
H.D.'s death song which is at once a capitulation to and a reconstitu-
tion of life.

Helen's union with Achilles is posited from the start. She tells his
lost companions (p. 5):

> . . . God for his own purpose
> wills it so, that I
>
> stricken, forsaken draw to me,
> through magic greater than the trial of arms,
> your own invincible, unchallenged Sire. . . .

Paris and Theseus will play their parts; but everything contributes,
however unwittingly, to the foreordained syzygy of Helen and
Achilles. And God's emissary and instigator is the mother-goddess of
the sea Thetis. Thetis it was who had unintentionally precipitated the
war by failing to invite Eris (Strife) along with the other gods to the
banquet for her marriage to Peleus. Excluded from the celebration of
Eros, Eris sowed the discord which ended in the Trojan conflict, and
the death of Achilles, son of Thetis and Peleus. Eris was devious in her
revenge; she tossed a golden apple marked "for the fairest" into the
banquet hall and when Hera, Athene, and Aphrodite began to wrangle
for it, Zeus ordered that the quarrel be settled by the judgment of Paris,
the youthful shepherd-son of the Trojan king. Aphrodite won the apple
by promising Paris the most beautiful woman in the world, who
turned out to be Helen, Menelaus's queen. Thetis had counterschemes

to thwart Eris's vengeance and save her son: she sought immortality for her son by dipping him into the river Styx, she charged Chiron with tutoring him in peaceful pursuits, she settled him into a safe, remote marriage with the daughter of the king of Scyros. All in vain: Achilles left that haven with Patroclus to fight before the walls of Troy and to take various women as his sexual prize, only to meet his death; with Greek victory at hand under Achilles' leadership, the vengeful Paris slew Achilles with an arrow shot into the heel Thetis had held when the Stygian waters rendered Achilles otherwise invulnerable.

All this background is sketched in through flashbacks and memories, but the poem begins with the dramatic encounter between Helen and Achilles. Dead and past the "fire of battle" and the "fire of desire" (p. 285), he is ferried to Egypt, an alien shore where he does not recognize as the dread Helen the women brooding on the hieroglyphs in the temple of Amen. From the time when Helen's glance from the Trojan ramparts had locked with his below on the plains, his fate was set. They had moved, all unknowing, to this meeting, and Thetis is the link and catalyst: "How did we know each other? / was it the sea-enchantment in his eyes of Thetis his sea-mother?" (p. 7). When Achilles grieves with a boy's petulant outrage at suffering the mortal fate of a mere man, Helen prays to comfort him like a mother (p. 14):

> let me love him, as Thetis, his mother,
> for I knew him, I saw in his eyes
> the sea-enchantment, but he
>
> knew not yet Helen of Sparta,
> knew not Helen of Troy,
> knew not Helen, hated of Greece.

When he does recognize her, he "clutched my throat / with his fingers' remorseless steel," but Helen's plea to Thetis relaxed his grip (p. 17). The last book of "Pallinode" presents Thetis speaking now "in complete harmony with Helen" (p. 93). For Thetis becomes Helen's mother too—her surrogate mother, adopted by the mutually consenting love of "mother" and "daughter"; Thetis is the biographical Helen, and the fictional Helen is Hilda.

From her mother Helen, Hilda felt that she drew her poetic and religious capabilities, her affinity with the power of the word and the Word. But that Helen gave Hilda no maternal confirmation or blessing, she seemed to prefer her brother Gilbert. Even before she brought the problem to Freud in the thirties, H.D. stated her disappointment in _HERmione_. There the daughter resents her mother, a failed artist conforming to patriarchal norms, because she has "no midwife power," "can't lift me out of" her thwarted inarticulateness; and yet "one should sing hymns of worship to her, powerful, powerless, all-powerful. . ." (pp. 80–81). _Trilogy_ and, even more strongly, _Helen_ are the hymns she could not sing in _HERmione_. For in the _Helen_ poem Hilda assumes her mother's name at last, and the word she is given by Thetis to speak to her murderous son is Thetis's own name, the mother-name. With that word aggressor becomes brother, hetaira becomes sister, mother embraces daughter with son; with that name Helen and Achilles are reconciled as lovers and siblings.

So complete is the mother's harmony with the filial Helen at the climax of "Pallinode" that she acts as psychopomp revealing Helen's selfhood, to be achieved under her aegis. Thetis's lyric rune inaugurates Helen's initiation into arcane female mysteries, drawn from the deeps of nature and of the psyche (pp 93–94):

> A woman's wiles are a net;
> they would take the stars
> or a grasshopper in its mesh;
>
> they would sweep the sea
> for a bubble's iridescence
> or a flying-fish;
>
> they would plunge beneath the surface,
> without fear of the treacherous deep
> or a monstrous octopus;
>
> what unexpected treasure,
> what talisman or magic ring
> may the net find?
>
> frailer than spider spins,
> or a worm for its bier,
> deep as a lion or a fox
>
> or a panther's lair,
> leaf upon leaf, hair upon hair
> as a bird's nest,
>
> Phoenix
> has vanquished
> that ancient enemy, Sphinx.

Thetis's unriddling of the temple hieroglyphs reveals Helen's name rising from the rubble of war (p. 95):

> The Lords have passed a decree,
> the Lords of the Hierarchy,
> that Helen be worshipped,
>
> be offered incense
> upon the altars of Greece,
> with her brothers, the Dioscuri;
>
> from Argos, from distant Scythia,
> from Delos, from Arcady,
> the harp-strings will answer
>
> the chant, the rhythm, the metre,
> the syllables H-E-L-E-N-A;
> Helena, reads the decree,
>
> shall be shrined forever;
> in Melos, in Thessaly,
> they shall honour the name of Love,
>
> begot of the Ships and of War;
> one indestructible name,
> to inspire the Scribe and refute
>
> the doubts of the dissolute;
> this is the Law,
> this, the Mandate:
>
> let no man strive against Fate,
> Helena has withstood
> the rancour of time and of hate.

Thetis goes on to distinguish Helen's fate from that of her twin sister Clytemnestra, for Clytemnestra's relation to the masculine has been destructive and self-destructive. As Helen's "shadow" (pp. 2, 68) Clytemnestra has obscured her sister's quest for identity, but now Thetis directs Helen to self-discovery through a creative connection with the masculine. Helen shall be immortalized with her twin brothers the Dioscuri. The decree (p. 104) of Amen-Thoth, "Nameless-of-many-Names," is

> that *Helena* shall remain
> one name, inseparable
> from the names of the Dioscuri,

who are not two but many,
as you read the writing, the script,
the thousand-petalled lily.

And the union with the brothers is concurrent with, or consequent to, the divine decree that "Helena / be joind to Achilles" (p. 102). The hieroglyphs have sealed Helen's destiny, but the periplum to Achilles is a circumnavigation, first to Paris on the white isle of Leuké and then to Theseus in Athens to find the future by sorting out the past.

Why Leuké, *l'isle blanche?* "Because," the prose commentary says, "here, Achilles is said to have married Helen who bore him a son, Euphorion" (p. 109). The import of this remark will become clear later, but at the present it seems misleading since the first three books of "Leuké" narrate the reencounter between Paris and his "*Dendritis, . . . Helena of the trees*" (p. 141). Paris calls them "Adonis and Cytheraea" (p. 140), associating Helen with his goddess Aphrodite, and seeks to rouse her from Egyptian secrets and Greek intellection to rekindled sexual passion: "O Helena, tangled in thought, / be Rhodes' Helena, *Dendritis*, / why remember Achilles?" (p. 142); "I say he never loved you" (p. 144). Paris harkens back to a life of passion on the old terms, now to Helen past feeling and past recall.[8]

Helen flees Paris's importuning to seek the sage counsel of the aged Theseus, who wraps her in the security of warm blankets on his couch, like a swaddled baby or cocooned butterfly. At first Theseus counters her recoil from "Paris as Eros-Adonis" (p. 160) with Athenian reasonableness, urging happiness with Paris and denouncing Achilles as a choice of death over life: "even a Spirit loves laughter, / did you laugh with Achilles? No" (p, 161); "you found life here with Paris . . ." (p. 173). Why should she choose to "flame out, incandescent" in death (p. 187) with Achilles, who has exploited women all his life? Nevertheless, though Theseus may not want to admit it, Helen is no longer Dendritis, and Achilles may not be his old self either. In any case, Paris seems too fevered and puerile to be the one she seeks.

Theseus comes to see that she longs for a new and perfect lover "beyond Trojan and Greek" (p. 165); she is the Phoenix ready to rise from the ashes, the butterfly cracking the chrysalis and "wavering / like a Psyche / with half-dried wings" (p. 166). Though Theseus sees Helen's development and stops pleading for Paris, he tries importuning for himself. He had been captivated by Helen since she was a girl, and H.D. may have had in mind Freud's angry complaint during a therapeutic session that his pupil found him too old to love when she had Theseus offer to serve Helen as someone "half-way" to her ideal Lover. The suggestion is tender and touching—but out of the question. As with Freud and H.D., Theseus becomes Helen's "god-father" by bringing her to a wisdom which essentially differs from his own. His response requires her to clarify her own and prepares her to leave him behind as well as Paris in order to seek out Achilles once and for all. As for old transgressions, Achilles and she are "past caring" (p. 177); the future need not be blocked by the past, life can lead only to afterlife.

Paris's adolescent eroticism makes him seem her own child, per-haps even Achilles' son—in fact, "incarnate / Helen-Achilles," so that, in an inversion of chronological time, "he, my first lover, was created by my last . . ." (p. 185). On one level this line may recall again the special connection between Pound and Heydt in the sequence of male initiators, and the reappearance of Pound as a potent psychological presence during these late years in part through the agency of Heydt. But a more relevant reading of the line would see Helen as setting aside as outdated and outgrown all the lovers and initiators of her previous life for a new kind of love to be found with Achilles. When the prose commentary at the beginning of Part II said that on Leuké "Achilles is said to have married Helen who bore him a son" (p. 109), the statement seemed erroneous or misleading, for Helen met not Achilles but Paris. But, as it turns out, her refusal to turn back the life cycle makes Paris seem, regressively, a child to her. Through Theseus she reconstitutes herself, reclaiming her past with a new maturity. And so by a kind of backward illogic the recognition of Paris as child confirms Achilles as husband-father in her heightened consciousness.

For in this poem Achilles and Paris matter only in relation to and in definition of Helen. The central insight which opens the resolution of the poem is the realization that she is the Phoenix, the Psyche self-born (p. 187):

> beyond all other, the Child,
> the child in the father,
> the child in the mother,
>
> the child-mother, yourself. . . .

Helen enwombs the entire process; the "child-mother" bears herself. When Helen asks in the next lyric how the masculine dualities—her twin brothers Castor and Pollux, Achilles and Theseus—can be reconciled, the wise old Theseus answers that the polarities meet in herself. His words carry him past Greek common sense into ecstatic vision, the sound-echoes and rhythms of the words rocking the lines to a hallucinated resolution beyond words. His incantation, at once limpid and opaque, veiling the revelation in the act of revealing the veiled secret, brings "Leuké" to a climax (p. 190):

> Thus, thus, thus,
> as day, night,
> as wrong, right,
>
> as dark, light,
> as water, fire,
> as earth, air,
>
> as storm, calm,
> as fruit, flower,
> as life, death,
>
> as death, life;
> the rose deflowered,
> the rose re-born;
>
> Helen in Egypt,
> Helen at home,
> Helen in Hellas forever.

The prose commentary informs us that "Helen understands, though we do not know exactly what it is that she understands" (p. 191), but the interplay of opposites in a transcendent pattern (which Emerson called the cosmic law of Compensation) is now to her "very simple" (p. 192). Reconciled "to Hellas forever," she sets out to return to Achilles in Egypt for the long-appointed union; Theseus has no choice but to bless her voyage to "Dis, Hades, Achilles" (p. 199). Her fate is not her dead life with Paris, but renewal with the dead Achilles; her myth is not Venus and Adonis, as Paris urged, but Persephone and Hades. And the hierogamy will be personal and psychological: "I will encompass the infinite / in time, in the crystal, / in my thought here" (p. 201).

Early in Part III, "Eidolon," Paris abandons his recriminations against Pluto-Achilles ("his is a death-cult," p. 216), and accepts him as father with Helen replacing Hecuba as mother. Now the poem circles back with deeper comprehension to the meeting with which it began, when Achilles, raging against his mortality, attacks Helen, until his

mother's—Helen's god-mother's—intervention relaxes his death-grip
into an embrace. Achilles had forsaken his mother when he went to
war; only after ten years on the Trojan plains did he promise to return
to her if she helped him seize victory. But with triumph in his grasp, he
suffered his human destiny. Paris's arrow found Achilles' heel, and he
returned to his mother in a strange land, finding her in the eyes and
person of Helen. With Paris reclaimed as son, Helen reaches her apoth-
eosis as mother. Now we understand more clearly than in Book I why
the single word "Thetis," gasped in Achilles' strangle-grasp, meta-
morphoses Helen in his eyes into a sea-goddess. For that mother-name
(p. 278)

> would weld him to her
> who spoke it, who thought it,
>
> who stared through the fire,
> who stood as if to withstand
> the onslaught of fury and battle,
>
> who stood unwavering but made
> as if to dive down, unbroken,
> undefeated in the tempest roar
>
> and thunder, inviting mountains
> of snow-clad foam-tipped
> green walls of sea-water
>
> to rise like ramparts about her,
> walls to protect yet walls to dive under,
> dive through and dive over. . . .

The two "will always" for that "eternal moment" comprise a syz-
ygy of L'Amour, La Mort (pp. 271, 277): "this is Love, this is Death, /
this is my last Lover" (p. 268). Paris, discarded as lover, is reborn as
their child, and the offspring of their syzygy is not just Paris, but them-
selves restored: Achilles "the child in Chiron's care," Helen the maiden
at Theseus's knee (pp. 289–90). The mythic psychological status which
Helen attains in the poem encompasses mother and wife and restored
daughter: Demeter-Persephone-Kore in one. In writing her own Helen-
text, H.D. arrived at a reading of identity which resumed and surpassed
the past. That moment—between time and eternity and participating in
both—is the "final illumination" of the poem (p. 271), and it is the
moment of death. Through the mother-goddess she has conceived and
come full term, dying and rising to herself. That metamorphosis,

spelled out in the poem, has sealed her life cycle in the eternal pattern. "Sealed" in several senses: it brings her life to fulfillment and conclusion, it impresses on that life its distinctive signet or hieroglyph, and it affirms that life with irrevocable authority. Helen had said: "to me, the wheel is a seal . . . / the wheel is still" (p. 203). Under the name of Helen, H.D. spelled out her hermetic definition. Though *Helen in Egypt* is a death-hymn, H.D. told her notebook: "I am alive in the *Helen* sequence" because "there I had found myself"; those poems "give me everything."9

Early in the poem Helen asks: "is it only the true immortals / who partake of mortality?" (p. 28). The poem's response inverts the proposition: true partakers of mortality achieve immortality. The moment of death is the moment of gnosis, in which life and consciousness conclude and transcend themselves; Helen becomes, with Achilles, a "New Mortal" (pp. 10, 263, 300)—L'Amour/La Mort in a higher configuration. This is what the last lyric of Book III postulates in lines whose declarative simplicity does not designate the mystery they bespeak.

> Paris before Egypt, Paris after,
> is Eros, even as Thetis,
> the sea-mother, is Paphos;
>
> so the dart of Love
> is the dart of Death,
> and the secret is no secret;
>
> the simple path
> refutes at last
> the threat of the Labyrinth,
>
> the Sphinx is seen,
> the Beast is slain
> and the Phoenix-nest
>
> reveals the innermost
> key or the clue to the rest
> of the mystery;
>
> there is no before and no after,
> there is one finite moment
> that no infinite joy can disperse
>
> or thought of past happiness
> tempt from or dissipate;
> now I know the best and the worst;

the seasons revolve around
a pause in the infinite rhythm
of the heart and of heaven.

To some readers the "final illumination" to which *Helen in Egypt* builds will seem gnomic, perhaps nonsensical. But the vision of the eternal moment, with time concentered individually and cosmically in eternity, is H.D.'s occult version of Eliot's Christian "still point of the turning world." In fact, the conclusion of *Helen in Egypt* deserves to be set beside such exalted moments in poems of old age[10] as Eliot's in the *Quartets,* when "the fire and the rose are one." Or Frost's arrival in "Directive" back at the spring-source which is his watering place ("Drink and be whole again"). Or Williams's declaration through his dead "Sparrow": "This was I, / a sparrow. I did my best; / farewell." Or Pound's conclusion to *The Cantos:* "Do not move. / Let the wind speak. / That is Paradise"; or his version of Herakles' expiring words:

                                what
    SPLENDOUR,
                    IT ALL COHERES.

Different in tone and perspective as these moments are, the reader either is or is not already there with the poet. By this point, in the particular poem and in the evolution of the poet's life's work, evocation has become invocation; image and symbol, bare statement. Further demonstration is out of the question.

Where Frost's final sense of things remained skeptical and Williams's naturalistic, H.D.'s was like Eliot's religious, and like Pound's heterodoxly so. No resume or excerpting of passages can indicate how subtly the images and leitmotifs of *Helen in Egypt* are woven into the design. Some reviewers found the prose passages distracting intrusions among the lyrics, but H.D. wanted, like the other poets I have cited, a counterpoint of lyric expression and reflective commentary. In identification with the mother-goddess, assimilating Greek and Egyptian, Christian and gnostic wisdom, H.D. came to read the scribble of her life as hieroglyph. Nothing need be forgotten; nothing could be denied; everything was caught up in the resolution.

The summons of Thetis the sea-mother which closes Part I, "Helen—come home" (p. 108), initiates a refrain that echoes throughout the poem and receives a gloss in a notebook entry: "We say (old-fashioned people used to say) when someone dies, he or she has *gone home*. I was looking for home, I think. But a sort of heaven-is-my-home. . . ."[11] The recovery of the human mother as goddess, the discovery of the mother in herself and herself in the mother constituted "heaven-is-my-home," and allowed, in the concluding lyric, a return of the lover-twin of Helen-Achilles to the mother-sea.

> *But what could Paris know of the sea,*
> *its beat and long reverberation,*
> *its booming and delicate echo,*
>
> *its ripple that spells a charm*
> *on the sand, the rock-lichen,*
> *the sea-moss, the sand,*
>
> *and again and again, the sand;*
> *what does Paris know of the hill and hollow*
> *of billows, the sea-road?*
>
> *what could he know of the ships*
> *from his Idaean home,*
> *the crash and spray of the foam,*
>
> *the wind, the shoal, the broken shale,*
> *the infinite loneliness*
> *when one is never alone?*
>
> *only Achilles could break his heart*
> *and the world for a token,*
> *a memory forgotten.*

As the poem indicates, Helen's recovery of the mother coincides with a shift in her relation to the masculine, away from the dominating Paris, who used to have power over her, to a new Achilles as filial-fraternal partner, and the shift signals a reimagining of the central theme of H.D.'s fiction and verse.

The biographical source of the sexual anxiety is clear: the broken engagement to Pound, the broken marriage to Aldington in the years during and immediately after the war. But she continued to seek the reconciliation that would heal the psychic wounds. Her correspondence with John Cournos, a member of their London circle, shows her intense concern about Aldington before, during, even after the separation. As late as February, 1929, she wanted to scotch any rumor

Cournos had heard of a "final quarrel" with Aldington, and in July she
sent Cournos this excited word:

> without any intervention R. wrote me and I have been in close
> touch with him ever since. . . . We saw one another much in Paris
> and write constantly. We are very, very close to one another intel-
> lectually and spiritually. There may be some definite separation
> later, but if there is, it will be because of FRIENDLINESS and
> nothing else. There is no question of R. and self ever becoming in
> any way "intimate" again and that is why this other relationship is
> so exquisite and sustaining.[12]

In fact, as she might well have known, she was never to reach "this
other relationship"—intellectual and spiritual without the compulsions
and vulnerabilities of the physical—with Aldington, but even their di-
vorce in 1938 did not break off communication between them. They
went their separate, and often stormy, ways; but during the years at
Küsnacht Klinik they were still corresponding, and Dr. Heydt was as
curious about Aldington as he was about Pound.

It is clear that after she fell from the innocence of that first love
with Pound into the betrayals and counterbetrayals of sexual rela-
tionships, she often asked herself "Why had I ever come down out of
that tree?" By the time Achilles succeeds Paris at the end of *Helen,*
those male characters have archetypal functions within the design of
female consciousness which the poem formulates. H.D. saw the whole
succession of initiators, including Dr. Heydt, in Pound, and she also
saw in Achilles, as she told her notebook, the "héros fatale" who had
failed her repeatedly—from Pound and Aldington down to the "Lord
Howell" (Dowding) of the unpublished World War II novels and now
Heydt at the Klinik. Yet since the "héros fatale" held the key to her
self-fulfillment, she must imagine the terms on which Helen would
marry Achilles. An Achilles who had undergone a sea-change: the Al-
dington she lost early in her marriage, possessed once and for all in the
consanguinity of the mother. The mother gave her the word and the
word was her own name: Hilda's Helen poem. There, in the imagined
possibilities of the word, she attained at last after great cost the "ex-
quisite and sustaining" relationship she could never establish in life.

More especially so, since the union resolved the parental as well as sexual crisis. In a notebook passage, quoted above, which notes the association of her astronomer father with the airman Dowding in the figure of Achilles, H.D. notes again the association of Helen with her mother. The passage then continues: "in the sequence, Helen is ideally or poetically or epically 'married' to Achilles. . . . I know the father, the mother, and the third of the trio or trilogy, the poem, the creation, the thing they begot or conceived between them. It is all perfect." The creation of the poem has brought Helen to perfection as mother-daughter-wife: the completed feminine archetype. In the ideal-poetic-epic marriage of Helen to Achilles H.D. attains "the final and complete solution of the life-long search for the answer—the companion in-time and out-of-time together."[13] In the poem Achilles is Helen's "Achilles" now, father-husband-son, and together they consign themselves to the sea.

The perfect union of Helen and Achilles is therefore a death marriage, as in the "marriage" poems of Emily Dickinson, realized in the imaginative creation. If Dickinson's "love" poetry remains more indirect and inhibited than *Helen in Egypt,* the cause may lie in part in Dickinson's attachment to her stern father: a bonding so strong that it kept her from the experience of the wife and the mother; she knew the masculine as the virgin-daughter, at the furthest extreme as virgin-bride: Kore rather than Persephone or Demeter. H.D.'s Helen would not be daughter to Theseus or hetaira to Paris; through Thetis she made Achilles her own, husband and father and son as she was wife and mother and daughter. Helen Doolittle was the source of Hilda's visionary power over the word, and in her Helen-poem Hilda formulated her hermetic definition.

The scope of that vision also made for another notable difference between *Helen in Egypt* and Dickinson's love poems. Wrenching and exhilarating as they are, Dickinson's love poems remain a collection of individual pieces at cross-purposes, recording ambivalences that kept her the father's virgin daughter. In the long, tortuous, fragmented history of women writing about their womanhood, the supreme distinction of *Helen in Egypt,* with all its idiosyncrasies, is that it transforms the male war epic into the woman's love lyric sustained at a peak of intensity for an epic's length, and the woman's myth it evolves posits the supremacy of the mother: Helen self-born in Thetis, Hilda self-born in Helen.

NOTES

1. *Helen in Egypt* (New York: Grove Press, 1961; New York: New Directions, 1974). Since the New Directions edition is in print and available where the Grove Press edition is not, page references henceforth given in the text come from the New Directions edition.

2. The first quotation comes from the typescript of an unpublished journal, dated February 18, 1955 through September 21, 1955, and entitled *Compassionate Friendship* in the H.D. Archive at the Beinecke Library, Yale University, p. 17. The second quotation comes from the *Hirslanden Notebooks* 3: 28, also at the Beinecke.

3. *HERmione* (New York: New Directions, 1981), pp. 82, 173, 131.

4. *Compassionate Friendship,* pp. 79, 35.

5. *End to Torment: A Memoir of Ezra Pound, with the Poems from "Hilda's Book" by Ezra Pound* (New York: New Directions, 1979), p. 11; *Compassionate Friendship,* p. 111.

6. *Hirslanden Notebooks* 3: 7, 26, 24.

7. Ibid. 3: 27, 1: 4.

8. *End to Torment* recounts an ecstatic moment of passion shared by Pound and his "Dryad" in a tree in the Doolittles' back yard; in 1958 H.D. still feels, but with poignance, that emotion: "Why had I ever come down out of that tree?", out of that paradisal garden-love into a world torn by love and war, Eros and Thanatos. The love poems of "Hilda's Book," inscribed and bound for her by Pound and only recently reprinted with *End to Torment,* celebrate her as Hilda of the trees: "My Lady is tall and fair to see / She swayeth as a poplar tree . . ."; "Thou that art sweeter than all orchard's breath"; "She hath some tree-born spirit of the wood / About her . . ."; and, most glowingly, "The Tree," which survived the juvenilia of "Hilda's Book" into *A Lume Spento* and *Personae:* "I stood still and was a tree amid the wood / Knowing the truth of things unseen before / Of Daphne and the laurel brow . . ." (*End to Torment,* pp. 73, 71, 84.) From his prison camp at Pisa, Pound had called out to his "Dryad" in Canto 83, and again in the famous lynx-song of Canto 79. Now after years of separation they were again in touch. After his return to Italy he invited her to Venice (Venus's city), but her identification with Helen-Thetis kept her from going back to old loves and old lovers.

9. *Compassionate Friendship,* pp. 64, 17.

10. *Collected Poems 1909–1962* (New York: Harcourt, Brace and World, 1963), pp. 177, 209; *The Poetry of Robert Frost,* edited by Edward Connery Latham (New York: Holt, Rinehart and Winston, 1969), p. 379; *Pictures from Breughel and Other Poems* (New York: New Directions, 1962), p. 132.; *The Cantos* (New York: New Directions, 1957), pp. 49–50.

11. *Compassionate Friendship,* pp. 12–13.

12. Letter to John Cournos, Feb. 5, 1929, in the collection of H.D. correspondence with John Cournos, in the Houghton Library, Harvard University.

13. *Hirslanden Notebooks* 3: 27.

"My Scourge, My Sister":
Louise Bogan's Muse

Mary DeShazer

"What makes a writer?" Louise Bogan asks in a lecture given at New York University during the 1960s. Rejecting the "purist" notion of a passionate love for the act of writing in itself, she explores such contributing factors as intellectual power, talent, and, in particular, "gift."

> It is as a gift that I prefer to think of it. The ancients personified the giver of the gift as the Muse—or the Muses: the Daughters of Memory. The French use the word *souffle* figuratively for what passes between the Muse and the artist or writer—*le souffle du génie*—the breath of inspiration; and any writer worth his salt has felt this breath. It comes and goes; it cannot be forced and it can very rarely be summoned up by the conscious will.[1]

This passage reflects the importance for Bogan of the muse as a metaphor for poetic creativity, a concern she shares with many other modern women poets. Furthermore, the language of the quotation suggests that peculiar brand of creative ambivalence, the problem of reconciling one's poetic identity with one's gender, which often permeates the woman poet's struggle for autonomous expression. Traditionally the writer, especially the poet, has been assumed to be male: a prophet, a priest, an Orphic bard who sings eloquently and forcefully to and for those less gifted. The muse, on the other hand, has typically been personified as female, an inspiring "other" imaged as the male poet's beneficent maternal helpmate, his seductive, elusive beloved, or a combination of the two. For Bogan as for other women poets, this paradigm does not hold, yet she finds that tradition offers no alternative. Unable or unwilling here to speak directly from her frame of reference as a woman poet—to say, that is, "any writer worth *her* salt"—she is equally hesitant to attribute a specific sex to the muse. The poetic gift is "the breath of inspiration," "it," and the issue of who or what may be the source of this gift is not directly addressed.

Yet Bogan is aware of the problematic nature of the relationship between woman poet and muse. Despite the improved status of women effected by the modern feminist movement, she asserts,

> the problem of the woman artist remains unchanged. Henry James in *The Tragic Muse* speaks of "that oddest of animals, the writer who happens to be a woman." Robert Graves has more recently said that women poets have a distinctly difficult problem, since they must be their own Muse.[2]

Bogan does not discuss the implications of these remarks, choosing instead to analyze the various powers and terrors attributed through the ages to woman in her roles as goddess, mother, wife, and lover; thus the questions she raises here remain unanswered. Who or what does Bogan perceive as her inspirational source? And is Graves's assertion that the woman poet must be her own muse applicable to Louise Bogan?

Like women poets from Sappho to Emily Dickinson to Adrienne Rich, Bogan invokes a muse very different from that of her male counterparts. For Bogan, the muse emerges as a female figure whom she "re-visions" and remythologizes as an active rather than a passive inspirational force, a powerful alternate "self" rather than an externalized, objectified "other." Often Bogan images the muse as a demonic goddess with whom she must wrestle and yet through whom her own powers of creativity are given rise, to take shape in a perverse but potent language and voice. This fascination with a demonic muse, along with a tendency to redefine the "monster" within as a source of creative nurture and sustenance, reflects a paradox inherent in Bogan's poetry and poetics: an intense conflict over her own artistic powers, and yet a keen desire for poetic subjectivity and strength.

For Bogan, then, this issue of the poet-muse relationship is an extremely complex matter closely connected to her ambivalence toward both her womanhood and her art—or her "craft," as Bogan, with her emphasis on technique and poetic process, might prefer. "Craft" suggests this poet's preoccupation with the formal and linguistic elements of poetry, as well as her "crafty" aesthetic strategy of employing female personae as distancing or masking devices. Through a process of dissociation she creates guises and images which let her conceal her central poetic concerns at the same time she reveals them, thereby producing what she describes in one poem as "terrible, dissembling music."[3] In a letter to Morton Zabel, Bogan claims that the poet must opt for "reticence" but not "guardedness," but the difference to which she alludes is often difficult to distinguish in her own work.[4] Like many women poets, Bogan experiences the conflict of the "double bind": how to function successfully as both woman and poet in a culture which considers the two a contradiction in terms.[5] Her poems are filled with images of fragmentation, division, things "riven," to use a favorite Bogan adjective; her strategies for coping with this conflict are suggested in an imagery of rage, solitude, and, finally, silence: an isolation fraught with despair and anger, which culminates in her prevalent metaphor of the silent voice. Yet from this silent voice emerges a paradoxically powerful speech, one informed by an inspirational source born of the poet's own female experience and creative energies. Ultimately it is from a female perspective that Bogan creates her "aesthetic of silence," and it is as a female force both demonic and benevolent that she perceives and personifies the giver of her gift, the muse: "my scourge, my sister."[6]

Bogan's female muse often emerges from a rubric of silence, which she employs as a metaphor for the female artistic struggle. Many poems about the creative process contain at least one central image of silence or thwarted speech.

- People without palates trying to utter, and the trap seems to close.
- Must I tell again / In the words I know. . . ?
- This mouth will yet know song / And words move on this tongue.
- A smothered sound . . . long lost within lost deeps.
- Still it is good to strive . . . to echo the shout and the stammer.
- Hearing at one time . . . / that checked breath bound to the mouth and caught / Back to the mouth, closing its mocking speech. . . .
- And it is my virtue . . . that it is silence which comes from us.

Similar lines appear in other Bogan poems, and an imagery of silence or aborted speech informs the various renderings of the poet's female muse. Why does Bogan insist upon this perverse imagery which asserts even as it denies her poetic power?

Silence is hardly a new poetic image; indeed, textual silence—the absence of dialogue, the presence of elliptical, cacophonous speech—serves as a key metaphor in modern literature. In his discussion of silence as a central mode of expression, if not a *raison d'être,* in modern and postmodern works, Ihab Hassan asserts that it is a "sense of outrage" which induces literary silence, "a metaphysical revolt and at the same time metaphysical surrender, which is the desire for nothingness." Hassan views this tendency toward negation as a paradoxically healthy sign, "a new attitude that literature has chosen to adopt toward itself" as a means of challenging traditional assumptions, and he offers an interesting argument that the metaphor of poetic silence parallels and extends the myth of Orpheus in a context applicable to the modern poet. Faced with existential despair and the possibility of annihilation, Hassan asserts, the modern poet *must* speak from a severed head; only by directly confronting his own fragmentation and the volatile nature of his world can he continue to sing.[7] I use the generic "he" deliberately, for although Hassan's analysis does not specifically exclude women writers, his focus is primarily on male writers, his assumptions about the artist's sex and nature those of traditional patriarchal literature and scholarship.

Tillie Olsen offers a different perspective on the significance of silence for the woman writer, for whom it has traditionally been an obstacle to overcome, "the unnatural thwarting of what struggles to come into being, but cannot."[8] Olsen is especially interested in Louise Bogan, and although she does not analyze Bogan's use of an imagery of silence, she does speculate about why this "consummate poet" wrote so little. Olsen views Bogan's passion for perfection as a compensatory mania which, she believes, often consumes women writers, who feel stigmatized by their gender and thus make excessive demands of themselves. Citing a letter in which Bogan describes her own critical bent as "the knife of the perfectionist attitude in art and life," Olsen concludes that this poet represents "one of our most grievous 'hidden silences'" (p. 145).

Both Hassan's and Olsen's analyses are relevant to the issue of silence as a prominent metaphor in Bogan's poetry, but neither accounts completely for the use of silence as a strategy in women's art. Like many other writers, Bogan uses silence as a means of transforming the liabilities of isolation and fragmentation into assets. But, as Olsen suggests, Bogan's search for voice is not merely that of the typical modern poet confronting the existential void, but rather that of the modern *woman* poet experiencing the predicament of gender alienation as well. Remote from the enterprise of poetry due to her sex and her time, she frequently responds to this isolation by setting inordinately high artistic standards and writing little, thus isolating herself still further by her self-imposed demands for perfection. Furthermore, she cannot deny her womanhood; thus her fear that her voice will be viewed by others as less "universal" than that of her male counterparts causes her to become her own harshest critic. She not only "consents to [her own] dismemberment," she actively participates in it.[9] This is not to suggest a masochism at work, however, for the woman writer typically dismembers in order to reconstruct. Once the old stance is broken down, she starts to "re-member" on her own terms, and by her own means. For Louise Bogan, one such means of "re-membering" is a perverse and stony silence which, ironically, provides a strong voice from which to speak. This silence is neither Hassan's "desire for nothingness" nor Olsen's "atrophy," but rather a singular response to the woman poet's quest for autonomous expression, a means by which she can both reveal and conceal her powerful poetic voice.

Bogan is not alone among women poets in adopting this strategy of the silent voice. In "The Art of Silence and the Forms of Women's Poetry," Jeanne Kammer discusses the tendency among a number of women poets—notably Emily Dickinson, H.D., and Marianne Moore—to use silence as a means of both expressing and denying their gender-related frustrations. Chief among the characteristics of "expression-suppression" is what Kammer, borrowing the term from Philip Wheelwright, calls "diaphoric" metaphor: a type of linguistic and imagistic compression characterized by paradox, ellipsis, syntactic inversion, complex sentence embeddings, and ironic juxtaposition of two or more concrete images.[10] Although Kammer goes on to note that diaphor is a trait of much modern poetry, she argues that the source of this aesthetic choice is unique for the woman poet. Her feelings of cultural powerlessness, her realization that the bardic "epiphoric" voice is not hers, leads her to diaphor.

Silence for Bogan is an aesthetic strategy functioning within the framework of the diaphoric mode. As a method of confrontation with world, art, and self, silence becomes a potent and dynamic strategy of subversion for Bogan and ultimately a central tenet of her art. Silence is necessary for self-apotheosis for Bogan, and the metaphor of the still voice reflects her creative ambivalence and her demonic and benevolent sides. This use of silence is particularly well illustrated in poems about the female muse, those which celebrate the goddess as a source of poetic energy. The line "it is silence which comes from us," then, reveals Bogan's view of the source of her inspiration, the "us" within, and suggests a key image by which she depicts that inspirational force. For Bogan, "the loud sound and pure silence fall as one."[11]

As her "aesthetic of silence" indicates, Bogan both fears and thrives on her creative strength. Female figures serve as muses in her poems, alternate selves at once sources and manifestations of the poet's struggle *with* herself *for* herself. These female figures provide artistic nourishment and sustenance which help Bogan come to terms with "that crafty demon and that loud beast," the demonic side of herself.[12] Bogan's muses are often mythological women, goddesses of vengeance and power who reflect her efforts to depict her creative struggle through the framework of a female-centered mythology. That Bogan recognizes the strong symbolic link between the woman poet and the goddesses of antiquity is indicated in "What the Women Said," an essay in which she explores the beneficent and demonic nature of ancient female figures such as Cybele, "mother of all the gods," Isis, Kali, Plato's Diotima, and Athene.[13] Despite this celebration of mythological women as both "vocal and visible," however, Bogan often portrays her gift from these inspirational forces not as a bardic song but as a Sphinxlike silence, a voice befitting the quiet, solitary, yet paradoxically powerful female whom she envisions. As I have suggested, Bogan's silent voice is a strategy by which she attains poetic power and yet acknowledges the problems inherent in doing so. In this regard she anticipates those contemporary French theorists who regard silence as one of the woman writer's most revolutionary means of self-expression, a key tool in her rebellion against a male-dominated language and literature. One such critic, Hélène Cixous, argues that to symbolize her search for a female language, the woman writer should use an indelible and invisible white ink, thereby creating a hermetic inscription out of "mother's milk." This new "script" would symbolize her alienation from the patriarchy and her community with other female forgers of new truths.[14] Although Bogan would perhaps not have advocated the use of white ink to symbolize female creativity, she uses a similar image in the "Meadow Milk" of "The Crossed Apple"; furthermore, in poems which focus on mythological women as sources of power, she uses silence as a tool similar to Cixous's "white ink." The absence of speech that is present, like the invisibility of an ink which flows, represents women's paradoxical "repressed expression"—her gift of silent speech, born of a female muse. Alongside silence as a dominant image is solitude, which Bogan depicts as a companion-source of creative nourishment, a way by which the female quester can attain the freedom of one whose "body hears no echo save its own."[15] Silence and solitude, then, are the central images of her three most revealing muse-poems.

A solitary silence is implicit in the fate and voice of Cassandra, the female prophet of Greek mythology punished by Zeus for insubordination by being awarded a gift of prophecy to which no one would listen. In "Cassandra" Bogan treats the plight of this female figure as a metaphor for that of woman poet (p. 33):

> To me, one silly task is like another.
> I bare the shambling tricks of lust and pride.
> This flesh will never give a child its mother,—
> Song, like a wing, tears through my breast, my side,
> And madness chooses out my voice again,
> Again. I am the chosen no hand saves:
> The shrieking heaven lifted over men,
> Not the dumb earth, wherein they set their graves.

Cassandra's stance as a female prophet dissociated from other women and from other prophets parallels Bogan's view of herself as a woman poet, alienated from other women and their "silly tasks" as well as from male poets. Like Cassandra, doomed by her own plaintive cry, the poet is isolated by her poetic gift, at once a debilitating and an empowering force. Neither the poet nor Cassandra chooses her gift of isolation, and both are ambivalent toward this power imposed by forces beyond their control. Cassandra's song literally attacks her, tearing through her breast and side; its source, madness, overwhelms its unwilling victim again and again. Ironically, then, both strength and weakness lie at the root of Cassandra's gift of prophecy. She is chosen for divinity yet not saved from suffering, empowered with song but ignored by all. Yet from this same song she derives her power.

Cassandra's mad, screaming voice provides a significant contrast to the deliberate predictions of other prophets from mythology—the blind

Tiresias, for example, or Isaiah. Instead, her warnings might be likened to those of the oracle of Delphi, whose riddled prophecies often went unheeded because their complexity defied mortal interpretation. Cassandra's plight and its attendant powers recall the conflict which Bogan describes in "The Daemon," as the poet is forced to recount repeatedly "the word . . . the flesh, the blow" to "the lot who little bore." Clearly Bogan perceives herself as a modern version of Cassandra, plagued and yet empowered by an insistent muse to speak not in a bardic voice, but in an oracular one.[16] In "Cassandra," Bogan shrieks her seer's truths through the potent voice of a woman twice disenfranchised: by the madness which "chooses out my voice again, / Again," and by the alienating yet restorative silence which receives her unheeded cries, turning them back upon themselves.

Silence also forms the core of "Medusa," a poem in which Bogan directly confronts her own demonic aspect in the guise of the terrifying Gorgon, who according to classical myth turns onlookers into stone. Rather than being a totally debilitating encounter, however, this confrontation enables the poet to assume some of Medusa's frozen, silent power. The poem begins with a description of the awesome meeting, which occurs in a "house, in a cave of trees," under a "sheer sky." As the poet encounters Medusa, a whirlwind carries the reflection of house, trees, and sky into the poet's range of vision. This image of reflection is especially crucial, since according to legend the Gorgon's hideous face must be viewed only indirectly, lest the observer be petrified with fright and cast into stone. Significantly, however, the poet confronts the "bare eyes" and "hissing hair" directly. This act of boldness recalls the male quester of another Bogan poem, "A Tale," who finds endurance only "where something dreadful and another / Look quietly upon each other"; and it also anticipates later poems such as "March Twilight," in which a watcher gazes into "another face," only to see "time's eye"; or "Little Lobelia's Song," whose childlike speaker sees reflected in her own face the image of a potent other.[17] As these other poems suggest, this eye-to-eye encounter between speaker and "shadow," that other self both frightening and recognizable, is crucial to Bogan's poetic imagery and to her perception of the poet-muse relationship. Only by looking squarely at the "beast within," Bogan believes, can the poet come to terms with her own hidden powers.

The last three stanzas of "Medusa" describe a scene transformed, as both time and motion are suspended in the wake of the Gorgon's

power: "a dead scene forever now," in which "Nothing will ever stir."
Medusa has exercised her powers of transformation by recasting her
surroundings into silence and stasis, a state which parallels the perpetual
suspension of the scene on Keats's Grecian urn. Surprisingly, however,
the poet's resolute voice emerges from this silence. Although Bogan
calls this a "dead scene," life flourishes amidst the stasis ("The grass
will always be growing for hay / Deep on the ground"), and her de-
scription conveys a tentative resolution. As the poet stands "like a
shadow / Under the great balanced day," she becomes a new Medusa,
a potent and demonic goddess capable of controlling herself and her
craft, of "killing" life into art. Medusa's silence provides Bogan a
powerful, if static, stance from which to speak. The poet's usurpation
of the goddess's strength recalls Yeats's enigmatic question at the end of
"Leda and the Swan."

> Did she put on his knowledge with his power
> Before the indifferent beak could let her drop?[18]

Unlike Leda, who was forced by Zeus into female subservience, the
poet confronts her goddess as a same-sex equal, and that makes all the
difference. Bogan assumes both the knowledge and the power of
Medusa, her demonic muse, and through this power she redefines
stony silence as vital creative energy.

The transference of power from goddess to poet is a central theme
also of "The Sleeping Fury," another poem of homage to a female muse.
Medusa, Cassandra, the Amazon of "the Dream," the temptress of "The
Crossed Apple"—virtually all of Bogan's strong, demonic women fuse
here into the single evocative image of the fury, "my scourge, my sis-
ter," once violent and vengeful but now at rest. This demonic alternate
self alludes, of course, to the Maenads of Greek mythology, those
orgiastic "madwomen" who avenged Clytemnestra and dismembered
Orpheus, and who are generally associated with matriarchal rule. For
Bogan, the fury represents an awesome and frightening aspect of her self,
one which she has difficulty accepting but which she must confront and
control if her art is to flourish. An imagery of transformation dominates
the poem, as the fury's destructive vengeance is rejected in favor of a
hard-won harmony, a reconciliation of opposing forces: noise and si-
lence, fear and calm, rage and release, demonism and beneficence, war
and peace. Ultimately at one with her "fury," the poet affirms her own

vital powers born of silence, solitude, and strength gleaned from the goddess-muse.

The poem's first two stanzas describe the "raging beast" now sleeping peacefully (pp. 78–79).

> You are here now,
> Who were so loud and feared, in a symbol before me,
> Alone and asleep, and I at last look long upon you.
>
> Your hair fallen on your cheek, no longer in the semblance of
>   serpents,
> Lifted in the gale; your mouth, that shrieked so, silent.
> You, my scourge, my sister, lie asleep, like a child,
> Who, after rage, for an hour quiet, sleeps out its tears.

Confrontation and transformation are key motifs here, as the poet assesses this symbol which has become a reality—a force to be gazed at, reflected upon, and reckoned with. The fury once was overpowering: a Medusa whose hair writhed with deadly serpents, a Cassandra whose shrieking voice would not be silenced. Aware at last, however, of her close link to this female force, still awesome yet paradoxically childlike, Bogan accepts the fury as both scourge and sister. As she reflects in tranquility, she derives new meaning from what was once a symbol of horror; her "fury" becomes a tool for transforming chaos into creative energy. Bogan goes on to describe the furies' fierce nocturnal pursuits, as they travel *en masse* on a reign of terror, avenging themselves through sacramental offerings and clamoring for sacrificial blood. "Hands full of scourges, wreathed with . . . flames and adders," Bogan's fury, the "you" of the poem, is particularly vindictive: "You alone turn away, not appeased; unaltered, avenger." Significantly, this shouting, insatiable fury is both separate from and part of the poet, bound to the speaker's side like a shadow: "You alone turned away, but did not move from my side."

Although revenge is the furies' chief occupation, Bogan suggests, these goddesses also manifest powers of revelation. Stanzas six and seven recount the confrontations insisted upon by the furies, as they expose at dawn "The ignoble dream and the mask, sly, with slits at the eyes, / Pretence and half-sorrow, beneath which a coward's hope trembled." Unmasking the coward, the false lover, the liar is a process crucial to both fury and poet, Bogan implies, and one that must begin with inward exploration. The autonomous self can emerge, however, only after meeting the awesome fury,

> You who know what we love, but drive us to know it;
> You with your whips and shrieks, bearer of truth and of solitude;
> You who give, unlike men, to expiation your mercy.

As in "Medusa" and a host of other poems, Bogan employs here the image of face-to-face confrontation to symbolize the transference of power from goddess to mortal woman, muse to poet. As the eyes of the scourged meet those of the scourge, as the hunted advances to face the hunter, the fury's whip and knives are laid to rest, her shouts silenced.

At last the poet's affirmative voice assumes control, a voice emerging from the quiet aftermath in a manner reminiscent of the last line of "Poem in Prose": "it is silence which comes from us." Having exorcised the demon with the power of the daemon, Bogan confronts a solitary and powerful female self

> Beautiful now as a child whose hair, wet with rage and tears
> Clings to its face. And now I may look upon you,
> Having once met your eyes. You lie in sleep and forget me.
> Alone and strong in my peace, I look upon you in yours.

This essay began with questions essential to an understanding of Louise Bogan's poetry and poetics: who or what does Bogan perceive as her muse, and what images does she use to mythologize her relationship to this inspirational source? Furthermore, to what extent is Robert Graves correct in asserting that the woman poet must "be her own muse"? As indicated in the poems in which she employs powerful female personae, especially those with goddesses and mythological women, the muse for Bogan is an aspect of the self which she envisions as a shadow-figure at once demonic and sustaining, silent and vocal, solitary and strong. The balance achieved when scourge and sister attain a reconciled peace provides the poet with a primary source of artistic nourishment. In turn, her art, specifically her "aesthetic of silence," is a crucial tool by which she learns to control her furies, in order to keep them from controlling her. Thus in Bogan's case, at least, Graves's assertion is accurate. By invoking strong female figures who serve as both sources and manifestations of her creativity, Bogan becomes her own muse. "Like scales, cleanly, lightly played," she admits, "myself rises up from myself."[19] In confronting this shadow-self, Bogan moves closer to a reconciliation of public and private, an affirmation of self and art. In the words of Adrienne Rich, Louise Bogan's work represents "a graph of the struggle to commit a female sensibility, in all its aspects, to language. We who inherit that struggle have much to learn from her."[20]

NOTES

1. "What Makes a Writer?", delivered at New York University, March 18, 1967; cited in Louise Bogan and Ruth Limmer, *Journey Around My Room: The Autobiography of Louise Bogan* (New York: Viking Press, 1980), p. 119.

2. "What the Women Said," delivered at Bennington College, October 11, 1962; cited in *Journey Around My Room*, p. 136.

3. "Men Loved Wholly beyond Wisdom," in *The Blue Estuaries: Poems 1923–1968* (New York: Ecco Press, 1977), p. 16. All further quotations from Bogan's poems are taken from this edition.

For further discussion of Bogan's masking devices and their effects upon her imagery and form, see Gloria Bowles, "Louise Bogan: To Be (Or Not to Be?) Woman Poet," *Women's Studies* 5 (1977): 131–35; and Jaqueline Ridgeway, "The Necessity of Form to the Poetry of Louise Bogan," *Women's Studies* 5 (1977): 137–49.

4. To Morton D. Zabel, August 10, 1936; cited in *What the Woman Lived: Selected Letters of Louise Bogan, 1920–1970*, edited by Ruth Limmer (New York: Harcourt Brace Jovanovich, 1973), p. 135. All further letters will be cited according to recipient, date, and page.

5. For a discussion of the woman poet's "double bind," see Suzanne Juhasz, *Naked and Fiery Forms: Modern American Poetry by Woman, A New Tradition* (New York: Harper and Row, 1976), pp. 1–5.

6. The phrase *aesthetic of silence* is used by Jeanne Kammer, "The Art of Silence and the Forms of Women's Poetry," in *Shakespeare's Sisters: Feminist Essays on Women Poets,* edited by Sandra M. Gilbert and Susan Gubar (Bloomington: Indiana University Press, 1979), pp. 163–64. "My scourge, my sister" is taken from Bogan's "The Sleeping Fury," in *The Blue Estuaries,* pp. 78–79.

7. Introduction to *The Literature of Silence: Henry Miller and Samuel Beckett* (New York: Alfred A. Knopf, 1967), pp. 3–32. The quotations are taken from pp. 5 and 15.

8. *Silences* (New York: Dell, 1979), p. 6.

9. Ihab Hassan, Introduction to *The Dismemberment of Orpheus: Toward Postmodern Literature* (New York: Oxford University Press, 1971), p. 1x.

10. Kammer, "The Art of Silence," p. 157.

11. "Sonnet," in *The Blue Estuaries,* p. 48.

12. To Morton D. Zabel, January 23, 1932; cited in Limmer, *What the Woman Lived,* p. 61.

13. "What the Women Said," in *Journey Around My Room,* pp. 137–38.

14. "Sorties," in *La Jeune Née,* by Catherine Clement and Hélène Cixous (Paris: Union d'Editions, 1975), pp. 114–246.

15. "Sonnet," in *The Blue Estuaries,* p. 36.

16. According to Jeanne Kammer in "The Art of Silence," p. 164, the most appropriate descriptive model for the woman poet's voice is the oracle, not the bard; her chief poetic activity is "seeing, not singing." This model seems quite applicable to Bogan's poetics.

17. "A Tale," p. 3; "March Twilight," p. 127; "Little Lobelia's Song," pp. 132–33. All from *The Blue Estuaries.*

18. *Selected Poems and Two Plays of William Butler Yeats,* edited by M. L. Rosenthal (New York: Macmillan, 1962), p. 114.

19. From "The Situation in American Writing, 1939"; cited in *Journey Around My Room,* p. 57.

20. Adrienne Rich, quotation from the book jacket of *The Blue Estuaries.*

Trial Balances: Elizabeth Bishop and Marianne Moore

David Kalstone

Elizabeth Bishop left unfinished at the time of her death a long memoir of Marianne Moore, a piece she had been eager to do. Of course, she had written to and about Moore all her life: hundreds of letters, tributes in the form of a poem and three critical essays, informal talks about Moore and her work, anecdotes saved and polished over the years, tales told out of school. That critics linked their names both flattered and irritated, amused and puzzled the women—seemed an evasion of what mattered most, the stubborn particular. So, when yet once again a magazine, this time French, spoke of Moore's influence on Bishop, the younger woman wrote to her old friend:

> Everyone has said that—I was going to say, all my life—and I only wish it were truer. My own feeling about it is that I don't show very much; that no one does or can at present; that you are still too new and original and unique to *show* in that way very much but will keep on influencing more and more during the next fifty or a hundred years. In my own case, I know however that when I began to read your poetry at college I think it immediately opened up my eyes to the possibility of the subject-matter I could use and might never have thought of using if it hadn't been for you.—(I might not have written any poems at all, I suppose.) I think my approach is so much vaguer and less defined and certainly more old-fashioned—sometimes I'm amazed at people's comparing me to you when all I'm doing is some kind of blank verse—can't they *see* how different it is? But they can't apparently. [October 24, 1954]

And Moore, with an equally polite and generous irritability, replied:

> As for indebtedness, Elizabeth, I would reverse everything you say. I can't see that I could have "opened your eyes" to subject

matter, ever, or anything else. And a stuffy way of appraising us by uninitiate standards blankets all effort with impenetrable fog! I roam about in carnivorous protest at the very thought of unimaginative analyses. Alexander Pope to the rescue!

Even allowing for Bishop's deferential tone and for Moore's playful archness, the two women show a healthy respect for the distance between them and for the complex of feelings we call "indebtedness." Moore, who had had no tutelary older poet in her own life, must have sensed Bishop's talent and independence from the start. Her role in Bishop's emergence as a poet is more mysterious than any simple comparison of texts could suggest. In a relaxed moment of her memoir, Bishop writes:

> I have a sort of subliminal glimpse of the capital letter M multiplying. I am turning the pages of an illuminated manuscript and seeing that initial letter again and again: Marianne's monogram; mother; manners; morals; and I catch myself murmuring, "manners and morals; manners *as* morals; or is it morals *as* manners?" Like Alice, "*in a dreamy sort of way,*" since I can't answer either question, it doesn't much matter which way I put it; it *seems* to be making sense.

Moore is taken up in an alliterative blur of childhood associations with the remote Nova Scotia village where Bishop grew up: the coiling initial letters that fascinated Bishop in her beloved grandfather's Bible; his old-fashioned village lessons in behavior revisited in at least one of a planned series of poems on "manners"; and beneath it all the unspoken fact of Bishop's childhood, an absent mother. Thinking about Moore must have been in part like recognizing fragments of her Nova Scotia life "through the looking glass." What must it have been like, for example, for a young woman who had not seen her mother since she was five to know an older poet who was by contrast inseparable from hers? And to have met Moore in the very year when Bishop's long-hospitalized insane mother had died? The apartment at 260 Cumberland Street in Brooklyn where Moore lived with *her* mother was "otherworldly . . . as if one were living in a diving-bell from a different world, let down through the crass atmosphere of the twentieth century." Bishop always left there feeling happier, "uplifted, even inspired, determined to be good, to work harder, not to worry about what other people thought, never to publish anything until I thought I'd done my best with it, no matter how many years it took—or never to publish at all." Moore's world was in part a vanished sustaining maternal world transposed into another key; it nourished Bishop's writing life, yet could be contradicted with impunity. It was as if Bishop had in Moore both a model and a point of departure, an authority against which she could explore, even indulge, her more anarchic impulses.

Bishop was still in college when she met Moore in 1934. She first heard of the poet from her "more sophisticated" friend Frani Blough. There was no copy of Moore's *Observations* on the shelves of the Vassar library, so Bishop tracked down the poems to early issues of *The Dial* and *Poetry* and began a determined study not only of the verse but of reviews of Moore's work and of Moore's reviews of other poets. Almost by accident she discovered that Miss Fannie Borden, the Vassar librarian, knew Moore, had known her from the time Moore was a child, and in fact had the only copy of *Observations* at Vassar. Bishop, in telling how she met Moore, always dwelt on Miss Borden, as if she were an appropriately eccentric, somewhat Gothic herald to the story: the tall thin librarian, almost inaudible, who rode a chainless (!) bicycle, was said to be a cousin of *the* Lizzie Borden, a fact that some felt had ruined her life. Miss Borden offered to introduce Bishop to Moore, and it was arranged that the two meet one Saturday afternoon in March outside the upstairs reading room at the New York Public Library. Bishop, years later, didn't remember their conversation but she "loved her immediately." Within a few weeks she had sent Moore Father Lahey's life of Gerard Manley Hopkins, written to ask her if she might be interested in an excellent book on tattooing, and invited her to the circus.

The Moore Bishop met was forty-seven, her red hair mixed with white, her eyes pale blue, her "rust-pink eyebrows frosted with white." It was an odd moment in the older poet's life. She had ceased being editor of *The Dial* in 1929. It had been almost ten years since she had published a book of poems, and the royalties on *Observations* up to that point totaled fourteen dollars. In *Hound & Horn*—the same issue in which Bishop read Moore's wonderful "The Jerboa"—Yvor Winters was remarking, "Miss Moore, indeed, seems to have exhausted the possibilities of her style and to have abandoned writing." That image would be challenged by the appearance in 1935 of Moore's *Selected Poems,* with an introduction by T. S. Eliot. At their meeting a year earlier, Bishop observed that Moore was "poor, sick, and her work is practically unread I guess" but "amazing." Moore was "very impersonal," spoke "just above a whisper," but could "talk faster and use larger words than anyone in New York." From the very start, their correspondence shows an unexpected parity between the older woman and the younger. Nevertheless it was four years before Moore invited her to call her by her first name, something Bishop celebrated in electric capitals: DEAR MARIANNE. Her tone with Moore is always respectful, grateful, thoughtful, but even at the beginning bold—"a flicker of impudence," Moore said. Bishop is always trying to lure Moore out into the world: come to the circus, come to the movies (*Son of Mongolia,* for example), come to Coney Island (she did), come to Spain (she couldn't). Though the two women were to be friends until Moore's death in 1972, it would be the early years, 1934–1940, that were richest in implication of quirky family ties and professional challenge.

Aside from some detailed exchanges about Wallace Stevens, Bishop seems uninterested in Moore's modernist connections. Rather, what attracted her were the older poet's manners and mannerisms, her fusion of old-fashioned domesticity—the kind Bishop knew with her aunts and grandparents during her early childhood in Nova Scotia—with forthright notions about writing and style. Both Marianne and her mother ("Mother is a rabid advocate of the power of suggestions versus statement") "corrected" many of Bishop's stories and poems between 1934 and 1940. More provocative, more daunting, were Moore's poems and letters. "Why had no one ever written about *things* in this clear and dazzling way before," Bishop was to remark of Moore's work. "Although the tone is frequently light or ironic the total effect is of such a ritualistic solemnity that I feel in reading her one should constantly bear in mind the secondary and frequently somber meaning of the title of her first book: Observations." As Eliot was to say of the *Selected Poems,* "For a mind of such agility, and for a sensibility so reticent, the minor subject, such as a pleasant little sand-coloured skipping animal, may be the best release for the major emotions. . . . We all have to choose whatever subject-matter allows us the most powerful and most secret release; and that is a personal affair."

Bishop was a keen observer before she met Moore; learning that this could be a way of life identified with a way of writing was another matter. Every detail of the letters Bishop sent from Europe and Key West, every gift was "inspected"; even Bishop's postcards provided Moore "a veritable course of study" and provoked detailed comments and verbal images in return. Bishop remembered a fifth- or sixth-grade teacher who confounded her by saying that some people preferred a description of the forest to the forest itself. "I never believed her, but now I know that to send you a postcard is to get back something worth a thousand of them!" The Moores' habit of scrutiny, appropriating the exotic to their self-contained world, was challenging, intriguing, amusing—and must also have posed something of a conundrum. It was tied to a life that, even in the Thirties, was valetudinarian. Increasingly, the mother and daughter, in a manner worthy of a Victorian ménage, were bound to one another by illnesses, a tie that in the 1940s became acute. Marianne's letters are ringed with care, siege, tribulation. She is constantly in awe of Bishop's travel; apart from visits to Marianne's brother, Warner Moore, in Virginia, the Moore women always seemed too ill or beset to travel. Bishop, on the other hand, was in these years almost always on the move. After Vassar she settled in New York for almost a year, then, in July 1935, set out on her first trip to Europe. She traveled in Spain and North Africa, lived in France until the summer of 1936. She returned to France in 1937; and then after a series of yearly trips to Florida, bought, with her friend Louise Crane, a house in Key West, her first real "home" since childhood. Alongside the Moores' life of domestic economy and effort, Bishop felt herself something of a truant. The contrast, the tension, between the two ways of life, posed in sharpest relief, and in the most human terms, literary questions about place of observation and the observer. Moore's descriptions, as Bonnie Costello points out, were mostly mediated for her, a lens of print focusing her subject; she did much of her exploring through catalogues, journals, museum documents, exhibitions. On the other hand, Bishop was, in her poems, less the poised researcher, less the orchestrator of a varied ensemble of fact. In the role of traveler, she used observation as a kind of tentative anchorage, as a way of grasping for presence in the world. The "powerful and secret release" that description offered her, however much it owed to Moore, would be of a different order from the older poet's.

Bishop only slowly discovered her traveler's observations to be a poetic strength, rather than a dereliction or a self-indulgence. We are

accustomed to thinking of her lively clarity, her openness to the
world—attitudes she had mastered in her later poems—but we are
largely unaware that these blithe strengths were the product of tensions
and fears. Her commitment to the *illusion* of physical presence—her
hallmark—was hard won. She observed because she had to. Moore's
precise style ran counter to what Bishop though of as "the dreamy state
of consciousness" she lived in just after college, "the time I was writing
the poems I like best." Moore's secure bravado in dealing with the
physical world was something Bishop instinctively valued, though she
only gradually absorbed it into her writing. It was not simply the *fact* of
her response to Moore, but the miraculous and instinctive timing of it
that mattered.

Bishop's early notebooks (1934 and 1935) are in part dedicated to
concentrated descriptive exercises:

> the soft combed and carded look of the flames in the gas oven

> the rain came down straight and hard and broke into white arrow
> heads at the tips

> These last mornings the street-sprinkler goes around about 9:30.
> The water dries off very rapidly but very beautifully, in *watermelon*
> patterns—only wet-black on grey, instead of darker green on
> lighter green.

Yet her observer's instinct cuts across a more deeply rooted inclination,
an interiorizing interest. When, not long after, the passage about the
street sprinkler finds its way into a poem ("Love Lies Sleeping"), it is
with a psychological and subjective cast that Moore would not have
been likely to give it. As with so many of Bishop's poems of this peri-
od, "Love Lies Sleeping" (first called "Morning Poem") is set on the
edge of waking:

> Along the street below
> the water-wagon comes
>
> throwing its hissing, snowy fan across
> peelings and newspapers. The water dries
>   light-dry, dark-wet, the pattern
>   of the cool watermelon.
>
> I hear the day-springs of the morning strike. . .

The accuracy is of a very special sort, less after the fact, less explicit visually than the notebook entry (no colors, no adverbial stage directions). Instead, the rhythm ("light-dry, dark-wet") suggests an impression only just gathering before she finds an image for it. The protagonists of many of these early poems ("The Weed," "The Man-Moth") have trouble accommodating the claims of the world. The precision of a passage such as this one is colored by the effort of "coming back to life." Hence the provocative "hissing" and the eventually comforting context as the water wagon's "snowy fans" turn human discards—the peelings and papers— to wholeness, "the pattern / of the cool watermelon." The frailty of human arrangements and recognitions is one of the subjects of "Love Lies Sleeping," and one of its most haunting images is of the mind just barely reassembling the world but pleased with its own ingenuity:

> From the window I see
>
> an immense city, carefully revealed,
> made delicate by over-workmanship,
>   detail upon detail,
>   cornice upon façade,
>
> reaching so languidly up into
> a weak white sky, it seems to waver there.
>   (Where it has slowly grown
>   in skies of water-glass
>
> from fused beads of iron and copper crystals,
> the little chemical "garden" in a jar
>   trembles and stands again,
>   pale blue, blue-green, and brick.)

Among Bishop's notebook entries of 1934–35 are many that, if not directly indebted to surrealism, show a mind disposed to accept its lessons:

> The window this evening was covered with hundreds of long, shining drops of rain, laid on the glass which was covered with steam on the inside. I tried to look out, but could not. Instead I realized I could look into the drops, like so many crystal balls. Each bore traces of a relative or friend: several weeping faces slid away from mine; water plants and fish floated within other drops; watery jewels, leaves and insects magnified, and strangest of all, horrible enough to make me step quickly away, was one large long

> drop containing a lonely, magnificent human eye, wrapped in its
> own tear.

The monitory eye wrapped in its own tear is an appropriately riveting
image for Bishop's writing at the time: the odd combination of obser-
vation and alienation that makes her early poems, especially, different
from Moore's. She had, by the time she discovered Moore's work, an
already matured metaphysical taste, had read sixteenth- and seven-
teenth-century English lyrics; George Herbert was—and remained—
her favorite poet. Many of her best poems of the 1930s can be read as
versions of seventeenth-century poems about the soul trapped in the
body. Sometimes the predicament is comic. Her Gentleman of Shalott
accepts with a shrug being half mirror, half man. More often the ver-
sions are troubled, as with "The Man-Moth" and "The Weed." The
claims of the world come to the protagonists as an almost physical
shock, embodied in the rushing subway and the poisonous third rail of
"The Man-Moth," and in "The Weed," in the rushing waters where
the weed grows "but to divide your heart again."

   "The Weed," like "Love Lies Sleeping," takes place on the edge of
dream and waking. It is the poem in which Bishop most sees the world
through George Herbert's eyes. But unlike Herbert's "The Flower,"
for example, "The Weed" is a dream of grim release which substitutes
for heavenly joys a sense of the wild persistence of life. The call to the
physical world is involuntary and takes the speaker back not so much
from a world of grace as from a prized state of withdrawal, static and
final.

> I dreamed that dead and meditating,
> I lay upon a grave, or bed,
> (at least, some cold and close-built bower).
> In the cold heart, its final thought
> stood frozen, drawn immense and clear,
> stiff and idle as I was there.

Bishop experiences these glacial comforting states often in the early
poems and stories. Here change intrudes as a psychic explosion, "prod-
ding me from desperate sleep," in the form of a weed that divides her
cold heart's "final thought." From the "immense" clarity of this mo-
ment the allegorical scene becomes more animated. A flood of water,
then two, divide the heart, but now into "half-clear" streams. In the

strangest moment of this strange poem a few drops of water are shaken
from the struggling weed into her eyes and onto her face; so that she
sees

> (or, in that black place, thought I saw)
> that each drop contained a light,
> a small, illuminated scene;
> the weed-deflected stream was made
> itself of racing images.
> (As if a river should carry all
> the scenes that it had once reflected
> shut in its waters, and not floating
> on momentary surfaces.)

The few drops falling upon her face are like tears, and they contain
the most precise, arrested visions of the world the speaker permits her-
self. ("Illuminated" suggests not only "lit" but also bedecked and puls-
ing with the illuminist's meaning, a moment of arrested glory for the
"racing images.") But the overriding impression of the poem is the
passivity with which she undergoes both the trance-like state close to
death and the nervous gaiety with which the weed draws her back to
life. Physical vision seems twinned with separateness, loss, and some-
how with guilt. Awareness, a state to which the speaker only reluc-
tantly abandons herself, is "weary but persistent . . . stoically main-
tained," as Lowell was to say in reviewing her first book.

"The Weed," written in the summer of 1936, is obviously related
to the dreamlike notebook entry of 1934 in which, on the window
coated outside with raindrops and inside with steam, Bishop has the
hallucination of a "lonely, magnificent human eye, wrapped in its own
tear." The image is unusual enough, as is the mixture of alertness and
withdrawal it implies. ("I tried to look out, but could not," Bishop
says of her dream.) But where many young poets would have been
crippled or confused, Bishop was able, at that early stage of her writ-
ing, to make successful and moving poems of this disposition. In her
notebook, naturally, emotional contradictions are more jagged and ex-
posed. On one hand we see her as spirited and confident, full of the
modernist spunk that Mary McCarthy in *The Group* attributes to Vas-
sar women just settling in depression New York. "We were pu-
ritanically pink," Bishop writes, "and perhaps there seemed to be
something virtuous in working for much less a year than our education

had been costing our families." (She herself was briefly employed at fifteen dollars a week by the USA School of Writing, a shady sad correspondence course for hopeful—and hopeless—writers.) "I think that it is in the city alone, maybe New York alone, that one gets in this country these sudden intuitions into the *whole* of contemporaneity. . . . You catch it coming toward you like a ball, more compressed and acute, than any work of 'modern art.'" But alongside the outgoing modernism and receptivity in this, her first New York journal, are strong suggestions of guilt, reserve, and withdrawal. Contrary qualities which would much later come together as strengths in her writing were initially dispersed—and yet, in her best poems and stories of this early period, dispersal of energies was itself her subject.

Mary McCarthy once said of Bishop's writing, "I envy the mind hiding in her words, like an 'I' counting up to a hundred waiting to be found." The analogy is apt even down to the expectant concealed child. What one often hears "hiding" in Bishop's poems—especially the early ones she wrote in and about New York—is an instinctual self resisting a nervous seductive adult persona she associates with city life. "The Man-Moth" dates from her first New York stay, "Love Lies Sleeping" and "From the Country to the City" from a second stay in 1936 and 1937 after she returned from a year in France. In each of them, metropolitan excitement is transposed into a still wondering but more sinister key. The language of these early poems allows us to take them almost as Renaissance dialogues of soul and body. The prepositions in the title "From the Country to the City" are not just spatial, measuring a return from a weekend, but also suggest an epistle addressed from one realm to the other with the force of an interior drama. "Subside" is the body's erotically tinged plea against the urban brain "throned in 'fantastic triumph'" (the latter a phrase borrowed from Aphra Behn's "Love Arm'd").

"The Man-Moth" and "Love Lies Sleeping" involve similar messages and pleas from submerged figures resisting the encroachments of the febrile adulthood of the city. Except for his infrequent frustrated romantic ascents, the man-moth is doomed to ride the rushing subways always facing the wrong way. His residual purity goes all but unobserved:

> If you catch him,
> hold up a flashlight to his eye. It's all dark pupil,
> an entire night itself, whose haired horizon tightens

as he stares back, and closes up the eye. Then from the lids
one tear, his only possession, like the bee's sting slips.
Slyly he palms it, and if you're not paying attention
he'll swallow it. However, if you watch, he'll hand it over,
cool as from underground springs and pure enough to drink.

In "Love Lies Sleeping" the poet intercedes ("Queer cupids of all persons getting up") on behalf of city dwellers whose speechless representative is the dead staring protovisionary at the end of the poem:

> for always to one, or several, morning comes,
> whose head has fallen over the edge of his bed,
> whose face is turned
> so that the image of
>
> the city grows down into his open eyes
> inverted and distorted. No. I mean
> distorted and revealed,
> if he sees it at all.

Poems of this period seem to allow Bishop simultaneously to be a keen observer—the figure who "tells" the poems scrutinizes every detail to extract her meaning—and yet to identify with figures absent, withdrawn, practically lifeless. A submerged self is variously imagined and identified. But in what Bishop wrote after she left college it is clear that she was drawn to fables that gave body to a divided nature; alongside a hectic modernity one senses a shadowy space for the absent or unrealized figures of a buried or inaccessible childhood.

This is more explicit in a journal entry that connects similarly suspended states with moments of crisis in her life. On her first trip to Europe, aboard the *Königstein* in late July 1935, Bishop underwent a series of disorienting experiences. One evening she sees patches on the waves: "these are *men on rafts,* poor wretches clinging to a board or two. . . . I am *positive* I see them there, even a white body, or the glitter of their eye-balls rolled toward us." Twice at dinner she is

> overtaken by an awful awful feeling of deathly physical and mental
> (mortal?) *illness*—something that seems "after" me. It is as if one
> were whirled off from all the world and the interests of the world
> in a sort of cloud-dark, sulphurous gray, of melancholia. When
> this feeling comes I can't speak, swallow, scarcely breathe. I knew
> I had had it once before, years ago, and last night on its second

occurrence I placed it as *"homesickness."* I was homesick for two days once when I was nine years old; I wanted one of my Aunts. Now I really have no right to homesickness at all. I suppose it is caused actually by the motion of the ship away from New York— it may affect one's sense of balance some way; the feeling seems to center on the middle of the chest.

Readers who know a poem Bishop wrote about her childhood almost forty years later—"In the Waiting Room"—will recognize the collocation of feelings: the sense of being engulfed, drawn under the waves, or literally whirled off the globe, losing one's grip of discrete particulars and having to reassemble the world anew. Whether the childhood illness she refers to in her notebook (she says she was nine then) is the same one she recounts later in her poem (in which she says she was seven), the circumstances are similar, and this notebook entry made when she was twenty-four marks the moment when she begins to understand the vertigo and connect it with loss. Of course, and typically, she veers away from homesickness, says she has no "right" to it, and lays the cause to seasickness and moving away from the familiar New York. But are they indeed so different? The fainting spell of "In the Waiting Room" occurred very soon after the seven-year-old Bishop was moved away from her maternal aunts in Nova Scotia. Of the attack at age nine, she remembers that she wanted one of her aunts. The threat of abandonment and disorientation are very close in her mind; and the notebook entry suggests that she is beginning to connect her observer's powers with a constant and urgent need to fend off the something that was "after" her; that reconstructing the world was a way to combat or express what in 1936 she identifies as "homesickness."

The young woman who felt, when she sailed to Europe in 1935, that she had no right to homesickness, spent much of her life overcoming it. Anne Stevenson, the author of the first full-length book on Bishop, is correct in saying that Bishop's poems are not conventional travel poems and have much more to do with reestablishing the poet's own sense of place. Bishop was to say that she always liked to *feel* exactly where she was, geographically, on the map. A whole train of displacements had marked her youth, and the plain facts that set them in motion are recorded in several chronologies Bishop was asked to prepare for publication and in the autobiographical stories she was eventually able to write once she had settled in Brazil. She advised Stevenson to print this entry: "1916. Mother became permanently insane, after several breakdowns. She lived until 1934." Bishop went on to say, "I've never concealed this, although I don't like to make too much of it. But of course it is an important fact, to me. I didn't see her again." The shattering reserve of that comment (down to the careful comma before "to me") is a warning to critics. Bishop never traded on her losses. At least one of her close friends from the Vassar years, Louise Crane, was unaware that Bishop had a living mother until her own mother told her that Gertrude Bishop had just died. One of her college advisers, who knew that Bishop was "on her own," found her "in a perfectly polite and friendly way, very reticent. . . . When I opened a door, she would turn the talk to her work, about which she was intelligent and resourceful." Long before she ever wrote directly about her childhood, Bishop seemed aware of the fact that she would in one way or another do so. A notebook entry written just before sailing to Europe in 1935 reads:

> A set of apparently unchronological incidents out of the past have been reappearing. I suppose there must be some string running them together, some spring watering them all. Some things will never disappear, but rather clear up, send out roots, as time goes on. They are my family monuments, sinking a little more into the earth year by year, boring [?] silently, but becoming only more firm, and inscribed with meanings gradually legible, like letters written in "magic ink" (only 5 metaphors).

The little self-protective parenthesis at the end suggests that for the moment these were feelings best distanced as a *literary* problem.

Bishop had spent much of her parentless childhood in Great Village, Nova Scotia, where her mother had taken her after the death of her father. Gertrude Bulmer Bishop was twenty-nine when her husband died, only eight months after the birth of their daughter and only child, Elizabeth. They had been married three years, and the family always felt that the shock of his early death (he was thirty-nine) brought on the series of breakdowns his wife then suffered. (Bishop herself believed that, though there was no history of insanity in the family, her mother had shown signs of trouble before.) For the first five years of her life the young child was effectively in the care of her mother's parents and her aunts. Her mother was hospitalized most of the time; first in McLeans' sanitorium outside Boston and then, after a final breakdown, in a mental hospital near Dartmouth, Nova Scotia, for the last eighteen years of her life.

To an unusual degree the child's attention was deflected toward the village itself, its rhythms and familiar figures. Great Village was at least fifty years behind the times: no electricity, no plumbing. Whether the village represented external stability and safety, or whether the child's losses prodded her to scan everything habitually for clues and meanings, the smallest details of Great Village life remained with her: the tanners' pits, the blacksmith's shed behind their house, the dressmaker, the milliner, the routine of taking the cow to graze. The decisive shock of her early life must have come when she had to give up the reassurances of Great Village and her mother's family to live in Worcester, Massachusetts, with the more solidly established Bishop grandparents. Not that they were unkind. But it is from this displacement that she dates the first of the fits of vertigo she much later identified as shocking her into an awareness of her own human pain. She began to suffer the severe illnesses—bronchitis, asthma, symptoms of St. Vitus's dance, severe eczema sores—that plagued her until her late teens. The Bishops sent her to live with a maternal aunt in Boston; she could go only fitfully to school, and spent most of her young girlhood "lying in bed wheezing and reading." Years in the Walnut Hill School, a private high school, and at Vassar seem to have revived and strengthened her, but she emerged into young adulthood feeling that she had always been a guest in other people's houses.

When Bishop first used the Nova Scotia of her childhood as a setting for a short story, "The Baptism" (1937), it was with an eerie sense of a youthful life vanishing, withdrawing before her eyes. In "The Baptism" three young sisters, orphaned, face their first Nova Scotia winter on their own. The almost unspoken fact of the story is that the mother and father have only recently died. The parents' elided disappearance is taken for granted, as if it were perfectly natural for three young women to be living alone in a tiny remote village without some adult presence, some relative, to oversee them.

Lucy, the youngest, becomes increasingly obsessed with a guilt whose sources she cannot identify and almost convinces her sisters that "she must have been guilty of the gravest misdemeanors as a young girl." One night she hears the voice of Christ above her bed and another evening has a vision of God burning, glowing, on the kitchen stove. "His feet are in hell." The growing ecstasy and alienation from her sisters ends in her decision—they are Presbyterians—to become a member of the Baptist church. She is only heartsick that for total immersion she must wait until the ice leaves the river. At the first thaw she is baptized, catches cold, develops fever, and dies.

Childhood images that Bishop was to look back on with affection in later works—the religious engravings in the family Bible, the singing of hymns around the piano—turn up here in a more dangerous context. Reading one of their father's old travel books, *Wonders of the World,* Lucy becomes overstimulated by a depiction of the Nativity: "the real, rock vaulted Stable, the engraved rocks like big black thumb prints." Readers will anticipate the return of those images ten years later in "Over 2,000 Illustrations and a Complete Concordance." In that later poem Bishop remembers the engraving with yearning for simple belief in the domestic warmth it recalled. Lines of the engraving beckon magically to the eye, move apart "like ripples above sand, / dispersing storms, God's spreading fingerprint." But in 1936 and for the obsessive Lucy of "The Baptism" the "big black thumbprint" seems to mock, if not besmirch, the scene. The engravings draw her away from her family, deeper into her mania, until finally, terrifyingly, the child disappears.

Early deaths—several in Nova Scotia—are subjects to which Bishop was frequently drawn, as if scrutinizing the horizon for her own childhood. "The Farmer's Children," probably begun at the time of "The Baptism" but published ten years later, deals with two boys who die of exposure, frozen to death in a barn. "Gwendolyn" (1953) recounts the death of a valued young playmate; and the poem "First Death in Nova Scotia" is about the laying out of a child, her dead cousin Arthur. One of the books she borrowed from Moore, read and reread in 1935, was the diary of Margery Fleming, a Scottish girl, born in 1803, who wrote these journals as part of her tutelage in her sixth, seventh, and eighth years and was dead before she was nine.

In the 1930s Bishop did not think of herself exclusively as a poet. Much of her writing energy was absorbed by short stories. It was through surreal narrative such as "The Baptism" and through the fables of her early "nondescriptive" poems that she instinctively sought some way to represent her conflicts. That she understood the need to "place"

her childhood is suggested in a very grown-up essay she did as an un-
dergraduate. "Dimensions for a Novel" suggests that she was an atten-
tive reader of Proust or that some of the novels she had read prodded
her to at least an intellectual grasp of how personal loss enters into one's
writing:

> If I suffer a terrible loss and do not realize it till several years later
> among different surroundings, then the important fact is not the
> original loss so much as the circumstances of the new surroundings
> which succeeded in letting the loss through to my consciousness.

Or again:

> The crises of our lives do not come, I think, accurately dated; they
> crop up unexpected and out of turn, and somehow or other arrange
> themselves according to a calendar we cannot control.

The stories or poems she was describing were far from the ones
she would be writing the year she left college. But the essay presents
itself as a kind of literary preparation for releases that were to come
later. It draws on a reserve of patience, a faith in the indirection that
will allow urgent feelings to appear, the slow reordering of sensibility
in which events are understood not chronologically but in a new psy-
chically accurate or revealing formation. "The process perhaps resem-
bles more than anything the way in which a drop of mercury, a drop to
begin with, joins smaller ones to it and grows larger, yet keeps the
original form and quality."

When the young Bishop says that the important thing was not so
much one's original loss as the new surroundings that admit it to con-
sciousness, she seems to be deflecting her energies from narrative to
description and to anticipate the ways she would slowly, obliquely,
absorb, through her writing, feelings too painful to face head on. In
certain surroundings—Key West in the late 1930s and again in 1946 and
1947 after revisiting Nova Scotia; or Brazil after 1951—she would be
stimulated by circumstances that reminded her of her childhood in
Great Village, the intimacies and improvisations of village life, and the
parentless years she spent there. It was only in the protection of and
prompted by a life both exotic and domestic in Brazil that she wrote

directly about the losses of her childhood: two remarkable stories, "In the Village," which tells of her mother's insanity and early disappearance from her life, and "Gwendolyn," the story of the death of a young playmate.

But those stories were twenty years in the future, and a writing life is more and less than direct expression. The subject matter that allowed Bishop "the most powerful and secret release" in the thirties and forties reflected in part Marianne Moore's poetry and scrutinizing friendship. When Bishop met Moore, we know, she had already struck out on a course independent of the older poet. Moore's influence was less a passion to be outgrown—the case with many apprenticeships—and more a steady slow infusion to the bloodstream. Gradually, in response to Moore's example, Bishop's narrative ambitions were being dispelled in favor of description and observation. Not that she radiated authority the way Moore did. In Moore's poems the observations hung in the air like charged particles in her magnetic field. Or, sometimes, like dispersed flashes of a distant storm. They help us locate an intellectual or emotional impulse, a center of energy. In Bishop's poems, time and movement are most important; her observations grow out of travel and exposure to landscape. Her assertions are more provisional; the poems are "situations" that help her explore and voice her frail claim to presence in the world.

Bishop's *Complete Poems* might well have been called by the title of her first book, *North & South,* as Stevens wanted to call his life's work *The Whole of Harmonium.* In the village intimacies and domesticities of Key West and especially of Brazil, she found the "new surroundings" that both replaced and reawakened her northern childhood. "What I'm really up to is recreating a sort of deluxe Nova Scotia all over again in Brazil. And now I'm my own grandmother." In 1946 and 1947 she visited Great Village and Cape Breton for the first time in many years. The great poems that resulted—"At the Fishhouses," "Cape Breton," "Over 2,000 Illustrations and a Complete Concordance" among them—revived her sense of the ancient emptiness, the dwarfed intimacies of their human communities, as if relearning a forgotten harmonic scale. We have to learn to read these "observations" as, for Bishop in the writing and at the time, more potent than narrative and preceding it. It was a skill for which Moore had prepared her, but she put it to uses different from Moore's. Bishop's eye for detail, as Howard Moss suggests, is a dramatic eye: she often experiences traditional dramatic problems—character, comic or tragic action—by fitting out a stage for them, a stage on which the protagonists will not necessarily appear.

In 1935, with very little evidence to go on—Elizabeth Bishop had written only a few poems and published fewer—Marianne Moore wrote a prophetic note (an anticipatory defense against feminist critics as well?).

> Some feminine poets of the present day seem to have grown horns and to like to be frightful and dainty by turns; but distorted propriety suggests effeteness. One would rather disguise than travesty emotion; give away a nice thing than sell it; dismember a garment of rich aesthetic construction than degrade it to the utilitarian offices of the boneyard. One notices the deferences and vigilances in Miss Bishop's writing, and the debt to Donne and to Gerard Hopkins. We look at imitation askance, but like the shell which the hermit crab selects for itself, it has value—the avowed humility, and the protection. Miss Bishop's ungrudged self-expenditure should also be noticed—automatic apparently, as part of the nature.

The occasion was an anthology called *Trial Balances* in which thirty-two young poets between the ages of twenty and twenty-five were introduced by more established poets. Louise Bogan presented Roethke, Stephen Vincent Benet introduced Muriel Rukeyser. Moore's presentation of Bishop was an act of extraordinary vision. Faced with a young poet of dissimilar temperament and needs, she sensed that a kinship of method would eventually liberate Bishop's energies and define her difference from Moore. Moore put her faith in a thoughtfulness that is also oblique, does not bluntly purvey ideas, and is not "like the vegetable shredder which cuts into the life of a thing."

NOTES

This essay first appeared in more extended form in *Grand Street* (Autumn 1983).

Excerpts from the writings of Elizabeth Bishop used by permission of Alice Methfessel, Literary Executor of the Estate of Elizabeth Bishop.

Excerpts from the writings of Marianne Moore used by permission of Clive E. Driver, Literary Executor of the Estate of Marianne C. Moore.

At Home with Loss: Elizabeth Bishop and the American Sublime

Joanne Feit Diehl

In a wryly discursive letter to Anne Stevenson, her first biographer, Elizabeth Bishop comments directly upon her relationship to the American literary tradition. "But I also feel," she writes, "that Cal (Lowell) and I in very different ways are both descendants from the Transcendentalists—but you may not agree."[1] Bishop, despite the characteristic demurral, thus acknowledges that her work derives from that early manifestation of American self-consciousness known as transcendentalism. The particular slant she takes toward American Romanticism, her swerve from Emerson and his heirs (different as it is from Lowell's) substantially depends upon her gender, upon the fact of Bishop's being a woman. In what follows I sketch the outlines of a reading of Elizabeth Bishop that attempts to account both for the influence of gender and the importance of tradition in her work, her awareness of origins and the origins of her difference. That Bishop continues to define herself in terms of the American Romantic imagination is perhaps less a conscious decision than an unavoidable burden affecting all our poets, male and female, who cannot, of course, evade their literary predecessors. Yet a consideration of the relationship between eros and poetics suggests the possibility that the woman poet can win a certain measure of freedom from literary indebtedness and thus acquire in the very weakening of those traditional ties a restitution born of loss.

If, as Wittgenstein writes, "to imagine a language means to imagine a form of life," then contemporary women poets are inventing, through their poems, new forms of constitutive identity; in remaking language, they strive to reinvent themselves. The impetus for this reinvention derives from the woman poet's need to reassert authority over experience, establishing an unmediated relationship with the natural world and, beyond it, with the powers of the word. Dickinson is the first woman poet to attempt such a transformation, and, although Bishop expresses a certain disdain for the self-pity she perceives in Dickinson's poems, she acknowledges not only her forebear's genius but her historical significance as well. "I particularly admire her having dared to do it all alone," Bishop remarks.[2] And the relationship between Dickinson and herself may be closer than the urbanely disingenuous Bishop might reveal. In any case, I preface this discussion with a brief excursus into an earlier struggle for origins in order to delineate an alternative poetic tradition which begins with Dickinson and finds its most powerful contemporary display in the works of Elizabeth Bishop.

In her response to Emerson's vision of the poet as central man, Dickinson provides the groundwork of an alternative poetics for future women who would stake out a new territory for the Sublime as she engages the fundamental issues that characterize the psychodynamics of the poet's quest for authority over experience. How Dickinson conceptualizes the American poetic tradition and her strategies for dealing with its imminent manifestations in terms of her struggle with her forebears thus becomes the primary, compelling instance of the ambitious nineteenth-century woman poet fighting for her individual authority. In the Romantic pattern of the Sublime which Dickinson inherits, the process of inspiration is inseparable from the drama of poetic influence. At the sublime moment, an external power floods into the poet, causing the self momentarily to fall away. This creates an intense, if temporary, anxiety on the part of the subject alleviated solely by the foreknowledge that the infusing power shares its fundamental identity with the experiential self, an identity chiefly expressed in terms of gender, or, in the dynamics of the family romance, as a paternal relationship.[3] Dickinson, as woman poet, experiences no prior assurance either that this male-identified influx of power shares her identity or that the Sublime encounter, once completed, will not render her vanquished—sexual anxiety shadowing, as it must, the poetic encounter. If there is no recognizable continuity between the patriarchal power and the female experiential self, then the poet may be unable to resolve the conflict between ravishing other and receptive self, thereby rendering her unable to retrieve the requisite power to write the Sublime poem. Instead, she responds to his power with a grim version of Emersonian compensation.

Your Riches—taught me—Poverty.
Myself—a Millionaire
In little Wealths, as Girls could boast
Till broad as Buenos Ayre—

You drifted your Dominions—
A Different Peru—
And I esteemed All Poverty
For Life's Estate with you—

(299)

The priceless gift proves just that—no compensation can make up for the sense of indebtedness the speaker experiences. The gift becomes a potentially debilitating one because it demonstrates that as woman and as poet, Dickinson cannot make this wealth her own, nor can she preserve (once transgressed) her former illusion of self-sufficiency. In terms of poetic influence, then, the lack of a recognizable continuity between the patriarchal power and the female experiential self renders the poet unable to resolve the conflict between the ravishing other and the receptive self in her favor, thereby potentially barring the poet from retrieving the power to write the Sublime poem.

Consequently, Dickinson and the women poets who follow her witness a profound discontinuity when faced with the masculine-identified experiential sublime, their ontogenetic development as poets, and more to the point here, their poems, reflecting this discontinuity. In the wake of such discontinuity, Dickinson conceives of the process of poetic influence in both homo- and heterosexual terms, and this transference of gender identity serves as a measure of the extent to which she envisions the masculine as imposing a threat while the feminine offers, if only intermittently, a vision of poetic influence freed from a possibly crippling anxiety. When Dickinson confronts her inherited male power, the poems incorporate a defense against the potentially catastrophic nature of these encounters by responding to the necessity of receiving such an influx, by privileging the process of abstention, by making renunciation the foundation of her counter-sublime. With an aplomb that checks desperation, Dickinson asserts, "Art thou the thing I wanted? / Begone—my Tooth has grown!"[4] Only when Dickinson envisions the workings of poetic inspiration in terms of a female-to-female transference as in poem 593, "I think I was enchanted," does one witness the abatement of anxiety and the celebration of poetic renewal. Yet

there are in Dickinson's poems no more than a few instances that de-
scribe such a benign process; more characteristic of the poems that deal
explicitly with the process of influence are those which describe it in
agonistic terms, where the poet fights for her/his very life. Dickinson's
legacy of the counter-sublime might best be summarized as a tactical
audacity that, in its confrontations with an emergent and potentially
dangerous Emersonianism, challenges the very tenets of syntax, the de-
velopment of a poetics that fractures so as to bestow meaning.[5] By thus
obscuring her meaning, Dickinson rehabilitates the subversive thoughts
she might otherwise be forced, because of internal and external stric-
tures, to suppress.

Separated as she is from Dickinson both by time and temperament,
Elizabeth Bishop nonetheless faces an allied if somewhat extenuated
version of the Emersonian Sublime, and, once again, the crux of the
poetic problem relates to gender. But Bishop, even more than Dickin-
son, defends against the challenge to her poetic autonomy by usurping
the very terms in which it is made. In other words, Bishop compen-
sates for the recognition of her loss of poetic authority in Emersonian
terms by an erasure of the sexual dialectic upon which his vision funda-
mentally depends.[6] Although Dickinson experiments with a similar
strategy, substituting the male for the expected female pronoun or re-
ferring to her youthful self as a boy, she moves beyond gender only at
intervals; it remains for Bishop to provide a sustained rhetoric of asex-
uality in order to find an adequate defense against the secondariness to
which the American Sublime would sentence her. What distinguishes
Bishop's work from the canonical American Sublime, I would suggest,
is a loss equivalent to restitution, the enactment of Bishop's "I" as the
eye of the traveler or the child, able to recapture an innocence that only
apparently evades intimate sexuality or the assertion of gender.[7] One
finds in Bishop's poems a map of language where sexuality appears to
yield to an asexual self, making possible a poetry that deceptively frees
her from the gender-determined role into which she would be cast as a
female descendant of the American Sublime. The prevailing absence in
her poems of the overtly sexual Whitmanian self becomes a means of
reestablishing woman's unmediated relationship to the world she would
make her own. Thus, her poems are a kind of brilliant compensation, a
dazzling dismissal of the very distinctions that might otherwise stifle
her.

In her late poem, "One Art" (whose title suggests that mastery

sought over loss in love is intimately related to the control she main-
tains in her poetry), Bishop articulates the tension between discipline in
life and the force of circumstance. The poem speaks in the tones of the
survivor.

> The art of losing isn't hard to master;
> so many things seem filled with the intent
> to be lost that their loss is no disaster.

Renunciation, as for Dickinson, becomes the way for the poet to ac-
quire a tentative mastery over Emerson's fatal vision. By articulating
the control such renunciatory self-sufficiency implies, the poem wrests
its essential individuating authority. From its opening line, with its
echo of a folk prescription such as "an apple a day," the poem leads
into the specifics of daily loss—of keys, or time—the syntactic paral-
lelism suggesting an evaluative equation of what we immediately rec-
ognize as hardly equal realities. Such parallelism, by providing a tem-
porary distraction that draws the reader away from the cumulative
force building in the poem, functions as a disarming form of humor
that undercuts the self-pity otherwise latent in the poem's subject.

> Lose something every day. Accept the fluster
> of lost door keys, the hour badly spent.
> The art of losing isn't hard to master.

The poem presents a series of losses as if to reassure both author and
reader that control is possible—an ironic gesture that forces upon us the
tallying of experience cast in the guise of reassurance. By embracing
loss, as Emerson had that Beautiful Necessity, Fate, Bishop casts the
illusion of authority over the inexorable series of losses she must
master.

> Then practice losing farther, losing faster:
> places, and names, and where it was you meant
> to travel. None of these will bring disaster.

The race continues between "disaster" and "master" as the losses span
her mother's watch, houses, cities, two rivers, a continent, and per-
haps, in the future, an intimate friend whom, breaking out of the pat-
tern of inanimate objects, the poem directly addresses.

> —Even losing you (the joking voice, a gesture
> I love) I shan't have lied. It's evident
> the art of losing's not too hard to master
> though it may look like (*Write* it!) like disaster.

Here conflict explodes as the verbal deviations from previously estab-
lished word patterns reflect the price of the speaker's remaining true to
her initial assertion that the experience of loss can yield to mastery. In
this deceptively direct poem, with a directness that comes to predomi-
nate in Bishop's late work, she delineates the relationship between the
will and the world. Note the split of "a gesture / I love" across two
lines, the profession standing by itself as well as turning back to the
beloved gesture, as syntax reveals the pain that the poem has been
fighting, since its beginnings, to suppress.

Determined upon a course of truth-telling that will cover all con-
tingencies, the thought of losing "you" triggers an anxiety with which
the poem must wrestle to its final lines. This last time, the refrain varies
its form by assuming an evidential structure which challenges as it ex-
presses what has hitherto been taken as a fact known from within the
poet's consciousness. Coupled with the addition of "It's evident" is the
adverbial "too" (It's evident / the art of losing's not too hard to mas-
ter") which increases the growing tension within the desire to repeat
her credo while admitting growing doubts about its accuracy. In the
end, the pressure to recapitulate the by-now-threatened refrain betrays
itself in the sudden interruption of the closing lines by an italicized hand
that enforces the completion of the "master" / "disaster" couplet that
the poem itself has made, through its formal demands, an inevitable
resolution: "the art of losing's not too hard to master / though it may
look like (*Write* it!) like disaster." The repetition of "like" postpones
ever so fleetingly the final word which hurts all the more. "Disaster's"
inevitability ironically recalls the fatalism of such childhood rituals as
"he loves me; he loves me not," in which the child's first words, "he
loves me," and the number of petals on the flower determine the
game's (and the prophecy's) outcome. In its earlier evocation of folk
ritual and in its tight rhyme scheme, where prescribed verbal patterns
determine the "disaster" with which the poem concludes, "One Art"
reveals an ironic playfulness that works in conjunction with a high se-
riousness, a strategy that proliferates in Bishop's poems. With its reiter-
ated assertion of the ability to control loss, the poem rushes headlong

into increasingly intimate occasions, until, by the end, the italicized "write it" forces the poet to acknowledge disaster—to write is *to redeem* that loss.

The "you" "One Art" fears to lose is not sexually identified, and this identification, of course, makes little difference. But in "Crusoe in England," another poem of loss from the stark territory she called *Geography III,* Bishop engages the issues of same-sex friendship and life on an island where biological reproduction proves impossible. Crusoe's compensation for severely privative circumstances is an informing eye and the reproductive workings of a fertile imagination. Bishop's Crusoe is essentially a survivor, returned now to that other island, the England from which he feels even more deeply estranged. Reflecting on his earlier life amid a terrain at once forbidding and unique, hence no longer discoverable or namable ("none of the books has ever got it right"), Crusoe describes a surrealistic landscape domesticated by the powers of the isolated imagination, where conventional assumptions about biology give way before the uncanny and the strange. Here, oddly, even with a certain delirium, the imagination remakes its self-made world. On his island Crusoe witnesses a world where procreative doublings are denied.

> The sun set in the sea; the same odd sun
> rose from the sea,
> and there was one of it and one of me.
> The island had one kind of everything:

If Coleridgean echoes evoke a world of trancelike stasis, what distinguishes Crusoe's island is its profound sexual as well as geographical isolation. Drunk on homemade brew, playing his homemade flute (recall the tunes of Thoreau's solitary instrument), Crusoe whoops and dances among the goats, crying, "Home-made, home-made! But aren't we all?" And with the question he simultaneously implicates us in his world as he forces us to measure our distance from it. When the grotesque, inebriated bard quotes Wordsworth to his audience of snail shells metamorphosed by the desperate imagination into iris beds, he forgets the final word: " 'They flash upon that inward eye, / Which is the bliss. . .' The bliss of what?" "One of the first things that I did / When I got back was look it up." The word, of course, is "solitude," and with its ironically unspoken inclusion, the poem witnesses Wordsworthian consolation transformed into the burden of repressed memory. Carried to the edge of a madness that includes the nightmare of accidentally slitting a baby's throat, "of islands, islands spawning islands, / like frogs' eggs turning into polliwogs / of islands" (regeneration become hopeless replication), Crusoe blesses Friday's arrival with a simplicity that belies as it asserts the sexual burden of his description.

> Friday was nice
> Friday was nice, and we were friends.
> If only he had been a woman!
> I wanted to propagate my kind,
> and so did he, I think, poor boy.
> . . . .
> —Pretty to watch; he had a pretty body.

Crusoe breaks off, silent on the details of his relationship with Friday until the poem's close, where, examining the relics of his island experience, he finds them useless—all except the haunting memory of his friend: "And Friday, my dear Friday, died of measles / seventeen years ago come March." The plaintive, arcane "come" with its forward thrust, assures one that Friday's memory, rather than fading with time, will, in Crusoe's imagination, expand through it. A boy "with a pretty body," he dies of a childhood disease, neither able to produce new life nor himself to live. Such a recollection of lost friendship is finally the best Crusoe as survivor can do, invoking through his reminiscence a homemade world where, in the midst of stark privation, the stranded, exiled imagination philosophizes, dances, and sings. The hallucinatory quality of Crusoe's experience reveals a desperately fertile mind struggling for its very life.

In tones of wry and bitter humor, in language deceptively innocent yet expressive of deep feeling, "Crusoe in England" articulates an extenuating quality which parallels that of Bishop's own poetics. Through the narrative transposition of female to male voice, a voice that describes an asexual world in which the self longs to sustain its imaginative life, Bishop evokes a homoerotic desire equivalent to that which informs her own linguistic imagination. Spoken in the naive tones of the masculine voyager, what Crusoe's words ironically veil is the plaint of a self questing beyond the hierarchies of the heterosexual, an imagination creating a homeground in exile. Through his conversion of the harshest of geographic regions, Crusoe bizarrely celebrates the powers of the solipsistic imagination transforming the truths of isolation. Al-

though Bishop's carefully modulated ironies and cool reserve distance
her from Crusoe's desperate creativity, what her vision shares with her
daemonic persona's is a desire to convert such isolation into a region
that allows her to reconstitute the relationship between self, words, and
world—to identify, solely in her own terms, an island made new for
both poetry and friendship. The eye of the traveler and the innocence of
the voice combine here to test the wild freedom of privation as well as
to acknowledge the pain of its irretrievable loss.

As Bishop writes in "Santarém," a poem from the last year of her
life (1979),

> Even if one were tempted
> to literary interpretations
> such as: life/death, right/wrong, male/female
> —such notions would have resolved, dissolved, straight off
> in that watery, dazzling dialectic.

The alluvial dialectic we witness in "Santarém" is created not by diver-
gence but by the confluence of the Tapajós and Amazon rivers. In her
attempt to free herself from the Emersonian tradition, Bishop, as she
states here, eschews the hieratic distinctions of self-other which are its
foundation. Her literary dialectic, akin to the merging rivers which she
so admires and does not want to leave, converts her ground of loss, of
deprivation based on gender, into a source of strength. Through this
redefinition, Bishop tests the very origins of literary sexual difference
by trying on a comparison between Santarém and Eden, the canonical
genesis of guilt related to gender. The distinction between these two
sacred scenes depends, for Bishop, on the difference between diver-
gence and union. "Two rivers. Hadn't two rivers sprung / from the
Garden of Eden?" "No, that was four / and they'd diverged. Here only
two / and coming together." Arriving at the place where she "really
wanted to go no farther," Bishop describes an alternative Eden, one
that rejects the patriarchal, Judaeo-Christian origins of sexual differ-
entiation for a fusion that draws all power into the observing self. This
engrossing self differs from Emerson's imperial "I" in its very dis-
avowal of a dualism founded upon sexual differentiation; Bishop's "I"
evades by eliding the gender distinctions so pervasive in Emerson's
rhetorical world view. Nor is this an instance of androgynous merging;
instead, the very terms of the observing self reject the premises of gen-
der identification.

Turning from this moment in "Santarém" when Bishop delineates
the conditions that surround the Sublime moment—an experience she
typically defines through travel, presence, and observation (the lapidary
radicalism that informs Bishop's best poems)—I want to consider a text
vastly different in tone, but which treats rather directly, if with charac-
teristic archness, the issue of sexual transference. Aware of the on-
tological ambiguities behind the apparently innocent activity of "Ex-
changing Hats," Bishop writes:

> Unfunny uncles who insist
> in trying on a lady's hat,
> —oh, even if the joke falls flat,
> we share your slight transvestite twist
>
> in spite of our embarrassment.

The acknowledgment of shared interest in sexual shifts, the "slight
transvestite twist," is not unrelated to a plural self, as the poem's "we"
at once playfully dissociates the speaker from the poet and simul-
taneously suggests her multiple identities. The provisional status of cos-
tume itself becomes an issue as it prods the fictile imagination: "Cos-
tume and custom are complex. / The headgear of the other sex /
inspires us to experiment." Mysteries, Bishop informs us, are revealed
as much as they are hidden by such awkward experimentation. Tawdry
as the "unfunny uncle" seems, he may still be hiding "stars inside" his
"black fedora." And the "aunt exemplary and slim," (at once an ideal
and an exemplum) becomes through her "avernal" eyes at once hell-
ishly male and female, and, through the auditory associations of the
adjective "vernal," springlike, embodying change and rebirth. Bishop
underscores this second reading by speaking of change.

> Aunt exemplary and slim,
> with avernal eyes, we wonder
> what slow changes they see under
> their vast, shady, turned-down brim.

Bishop's play on "avernal" recalls, then, the abyssal eyes of her aunt
and the vernal mix of opposites, the equinoctial experience of night and
day as analogous to a male/female equivalency that remains a mystery
apparently both to itself and to the observer. The brim of the aunt's
hat, like the uncle's fedora, withholds knowledge from view as it am-
biguously protects one's identity from a too intense scrutiny.

Such a blurring of distinctions and the implications of crossing over through costume reappear in the late poem, "Pink Dog," where the poor animal is dangerously exposed (her vulnerability the result of her nakedness). The subject of Bishop's poem, a rather sickly, depilated bitch, must disguise herself so that she avoids being an object of scorn or ridicule; she must don a costume to survive the continuing "celebration" of life known as Carnival. Despite a vast difference in tone, "Pink Dog" is related to Wallace Stevens's "The American Sublime," for both poems address what one needs to survive in a place of deception.[8] Stevens, seeking what will suffice, poses the question, "How does one stand / To behold the sublime, / To confront the mockers, / The mickey mockers / And plated pairs?" His provisional answer is a stripping away of the external self so that all that remains is "The spirit and space, / The empty spirit / In vacant space." What can such a spirit draw upon for sustenance? Stevens poses this question in sacramental terms, asking where one can find a sustaining faith: "What wine does one drink? / What bread does one eat?"—lines Bishop will parodically echo at the close of her poem. "Pink Dog" similarly confronts a world of disguise and advocates a necessary defense not, however, a stripping away but the armor of costume.[9] And the difference in response, I suggest, is related to the dog's color, to her femaleness, to the biological embarrassments of being a nursing mother with scabies (a disease caused by an insect that gets under the skin and causes intense itching). Her discomfort, then, is related to a once external, now internalized agent, a discomfort that can be masked but not cured by disguise.

Immediately following the poem's opening, "The sun is blazing and the sky is blue," with its echo of another Stevens poem about transformation, "The house was quiet, and the world was calm," we meet the hairless dog. Afraid of contagion, the crowds "draw back and stare" with us.

> Of course they're mortally afraid of rabies.
> You are not mad; you have a case of scabies
> but look intelligent. Where are your babies?

The dog's raw, pink skin and her hanging teats need a defense that can only come through the use of intelligence operating as disguise. Bishop rhymes teats and wits with an apparently effortless, desperado humor, as associative gesture so assured that the identification seems, as it frequently does in her poems, to carry all the circumstantiality of truth.

> (A nursing mother, by those hanging teats.)
> In what slum have you hidden them, poor bitch,
> while you go begging, living by your wits?

Unless the "poor bitch" can now redirect her wits in aid of disguise, she will join those "idiots, paralytics, parasites" thrown into nearby tidal rivers. The practical solution, explains the level-headed sardonic voice of the poem, is to wear a "fantasia," a carnival costume.

> Carnival is always wonderful!
> A depilated dog would not look well.
> Dress up! Dress up and dance at Carnival!

The voice that proffers this advice is at once sympathetic and admonitory, insisting that the necessity of costume in such a situation is self-evident.

The woman and dog are related by their exposure, their gender, and, perhaps, their vulnerability. Wit alone can protect each of them—a wit the poet practices so as to disguise and preserve her identity. Rarely does Bishop confront masking so directly, although throughout her poems the need for protection is met by the courage of a self willing to incur the risk of exposure. In fact, the predicament of the isolated, exiled, anomalous self, whether in "Man-Moth" or "Giant Toad," keeps reappearing because it is related to Bishop's sense of herself as poet, particularly as woman poet in relation to the tradition.

Compensation (as Emerson himself came to recognize) is not only a possible boon in nature, but may be a significant human activity as well. In her creation of a poetics that seeks to disrupt the fixities of our inherited understanding, Bishop strives to assign the human map of comprehension a less rigid set of directions, an alternative geography based not upon polarities of difference but upon the dictates of the poet/geographer's painterlike understanding freed of disabling divisions: "More delicate than the historians' are the map-makers' colors." Inherited historical distinctions fade before this more vivid rendering of personal aesthetics. Bishop's eye thus evades as it questions the distinctions of both geography and gender, envisioning in their stead a world that invites a freer conception of sexual identity and a highly particular sense of place—the dissolution of all externally imposed hieratic distinctions. Such an alternative mapping creates, as in "Santarém," another version of the Sublime, one that develops from an inherited sense of loss and discontinuity, that with dazzling restraint reconstitutes the world according to its and the world's priorities. With all the audacity of Emerson, albeit·disguised by a tact made necessary by the radicalism of her vision, Bishop's poems aim at nothing short of freedom from the inherently dualistic tradition that lies not only at the foundations of the American Sublime, but at the very heart of the Western literary tradition itself.

Bishop alters her stance vis-à-vis the Emersonian Sublime by denying her secondariness in relation to the central poet. In her rejection of Emerson's assigning woman to subordination, she herself also disavows an overt sexual presence without sacrificing erotic intensity. Bishop thus manages a more complete and, in some ways, a more extreme self-metamorphosis than even Emerson achieves. By incorporating the male Not Me into the female Me and so creating a transsexual self-as-poet, Bishop does not simply present an impersonal or asexual poetic voice, but rather substitutes a comprehensiveness that extends her authority over experience. There is no depersonalization here; instead, by so eradicating the dialectical terms in which Emerson, the frustrated monist, had been forced to face his world, Bishop rejects the debilitation of the woman poet at the moment of Sublime infusion of power into the self. Imagining that incursive power as neither male nor female and experiencing herself as beyond gender, Bishop defuses the Oedipal struggle by desexualizing it. Nor does she simply play the role of passive observer in this transformation. In fact, her imaginative gestures, as in "One Art," are often those of active relinquishment, the compensatory work of the imagination we call poetry. Finally, it is in the act of reconstitution, of a moment recaptured—a moose's sudden appearance, loss of a sense of self while waiting for her aunt at the dentist's office, the death of an intimate friend—that Bishop recovers herself as center of a self-made world as independent as Dickinson's. Such sacrificial compensation may seem more severe than Emerson's, yet the extremity proves a necessary defense on the part of a woman poet who would face the Romantic imagination's insistence upon the poet as central man.

If, for Bishop, the Sublime poem must begin and end in loss, hers is a loss equivalent to restitution—no intrusive self but a world as minutely observed as it is tellingly rendered; for, between the brackets of loss stands the witness of the poem, as in "Crusoe in England," the making of a homeground so distinctive Robert Lowell once remarked

of Bishop's work, "She's gotten a world, not just a way of writing."[10]
Bishop imagines a form of life where circumstantiality merges into art,
where the rivers of Santarém run together, where breathtakingly subtle
modulations of language replace Dickinson's encoded poetics. The cos-
tume so necessary to the pink dog's survival becomes, for its creator, a
highly articulate speech that distances as it draws us ever closer to the
anomalous, isolated, yet sublimely defiant territory Bishop calls home.

NOTES
    1. Elizabeth Bishop to Anne Stevenson, quoted in the *Times Literary Sup-
plement,* "Letters from Elizabeth Bishop," by Anne Stevenson, March 7, 1980,
p. 261.
    2. "Letters from Elizabeth Bishop," p. 261.
    3. For a carefully delineated account of the relationship between the work-
ings of the literary sublime and gender interaction, see Thomas Weiskel, *The
Romantic Sublime* (Baltimore and London: Johns Hopkins University Press,
1976).
    4. Dickinson, poem 1282.
    5. The specific character of these strategies of defense are the subject of
my recent essay, "'Ransom In A Voice': Dickinson's Defensive Poetics," in
Feminist Approaches to Emily Dickinson: Reading the Poems, edited by Suzanne
Juhasz (Bloomington and London: Indiana University Press, 1983).
    6. For a discussion of the sexual complexities of Emerson's work, see Eric
Cheyfitz, *The Trans-Parent: Sexual Politics in the Language of Emerson* (Baltimore
and London: Johns Hopkins University Press, 1981).
    7. In her *Women Writers and Poetic Identity* (Princeton: Princeton University
Press, 1980), Margaret Homans discusses the "feminine tradition's" relation to
a patriarchal structure of hieratic distinctions closely related to gender differ-
entiation. For her views of contemporary women poets' abilities to reconstitute
the fundamental relationship between words and things, see especially pp. 215–
16. Although Homans does not comment on Bishop's work, my reading of the
poet suggests that Bishop does not deny but rather intensifies the ironic mask-
ing Homans considers essential to the figurative nature of poetry at the same
time that she manages to escape patriarchal dualisms—an achievement akin to
Dickinson's, although arrived at through different means.
    8. The relationship between Stevens and Bishop often assumes this par-
odic cast for reasons associated with Bishop's need for priority and a powerful
sense that Stevens's consolations cannot be her own. Bishop expresses her turn-
ing away through characteristic archness rather than a self-conscious despair.
    9. See Terrence Diggory's "Armored Women, Naked Men: Dickinson,
Whitman, and Their Successors," in *Shakespeare's Sisters,* edited by Sandra M.
Gilbert and Susan Gubar (Bloomington and London: Indiana University Press,
1979), for a discussion of the defensive strategies of nakedness and armor as
they relate to gender identity.

10. Robert Lowell in an interview appearing in *The Paris Review* and quoted by Elizabeth Spires, "An Afternoon with Elizabeth Bishop," *Vassar Quarterly* (Winter 1979).

Poetry and Political Experience: Denise Levertov

John Felstiner

"And what old ballad singer was it," Yeats asked, "who claimed to have fought by day in the very battle he sang by night?"[1] Himself a would-be reviver and recorder of his nation's genius, Yeats liked to imagine a heroic ethos uniting thought and action, aesthetic and political experience. "Our Sidney and our perfect man," he calls Lady Gregory's son Robert, a sculptor and aviator who fell in 1918 in the Great War.[2] However appropriate such an image of virtuosity may be for earlier epochs, it was ground to bits by 1918, let's say in the poems of Isaac Rosenberg and Wilfred Owen, both killed that year.

For poets such as Denise Levertov, who was born in 1923 and began publishing after the Second World War, it has hardly been given to see beauty in military prowess or to fill the heroic mold of Yeats's old ballad singer. Levertov does not claim for poets any special powers of feeling and understanding, neither the archaic kind of oracular or shamanistic vision nor the ambiguous Romantic legacy of supersensitive alienation. At the same time she has insisted, and in her own persistent political activity has demonstrated, that "the poet's total involvement in life" means involvement not only in sensations and emotions but in the world of events.[3] The gift that poets do possess, articulateness, entails more than paying lip service to their world. It means—for writers along with teachers, critics, and readers—taking active responsibility for the words in poetry, going beyond a vicarious experience of the words, allowing their dynamic consequences.

My own vivid sense of Denise Levertov originated in late 1966 when she read at Stanford from a group of poems called *Life at War*.[4] Educated as I was to the tradition of W. B. Yeats and T. S. Eliot, plus the old bards Whitman and Frost, I scarcely expected a woman, someone in a red print dress with a rose or pomegranate bursting on it, to speak with the authentic poetic voice.

Sealed inside the anemone
in the dark, I knock my head
on steel petals
curving inward around me.

The petals then open,

. . . my seafern arms
my human hands
my fingers tipped with fire
sway out into the world,

and she sings, but

the petals creak and
begin to rise.
They rise and recurl
to a bud's form

and clamp shut.
I wait in the dark.

And there, she leaves us too. I immediately began sharing this poem
"The Pulse" with students, who were astonished to learn that it had to
do with the war in Vietnam—astonished to feel how intimately the
political impinges on the personal.

Here one might ask, as many people have, whether this intimate
registering of the external world, this quick fine sensitiveness, belongs
to a woman's rather than a man's poetry. God forbid! Denise Levertov
would say. But perhaps something of the original question still holds.
How many male poets today can write with quite her intimate sense of
things? Yet God help us all if we lack it, she insists, resisting any femi-
nist stipulations about herself or her craft.

At the depth of common humanity to which Levertov would take
us, her "we" must include women and men alike. In her poem called
"Life at War" (what an expanding title!) she says, "burned human flesh
/ is smelling in Vietnam as I write."

Yes, this is the knowledge that jostles for space
in our bodies along with all we
go on knowing of joy, of love;
our nerve filaments twitch with its presence

> day and night,
> nothing we say has not the husky phlegm of it in the saying,
> nothing we do has the quickness, the sureness,
> the deep intelligence living at peace would have.

A war poem: a subjective lyric—the two worlds touch, interpenetrate.
A danger, especially with such persuasive language, might be that we
let the poet do our feeling and reacting for us, when really she means to
awaken, to inspirit "our own live will," as in another poem from *Life
at War*.[5]

To awaken—the idea occurs in Levertov's 1959 statement for *The
New American Poetry:* "Insofar as poetry has a social function it is to
awaken sleepers by other means than shock."[6] If you commit yourself
to poetry, she says on another occasion, you will not "drift through
your years half awake."[7] Probably as true a source as any other for this
sense of poetry is William Carlos Williams, whose 1923 *Spring and All*
describes a late winter landscape "by the road to the contagious hospi-
tal," with its first crisp bits of plant growth: "rooted, they / grip down
and begin to awaken."[8] Levertov has written of Williams's little-known
political poems and identified his quality of life-prizing resistance, de-
fiance.[9] At bottom I think what she values most in his lyrics, and what
has most influenced her, is an "intrinsic freshness" every lover of
Williams keeps on discovering. "But what?" Williams says abruptly,
halfway through the poem about birds finding food in winter, "To
Waken an Old Lady."[10] I find myself uttering that exclamation of sur-
prise—"But what?"—at every line break in Williams.

To startle, then cleanse, clarify, and deepen our sense of things—a
poem's political task may begin this way.

> To render it!—*this* moment,
>   haze and halos of
>   sunbless'd particulars
>
> . . . .
>
> (centuries furrowed in oakbole, *this* oak,
> *these* dogrose pallors, that very company
>   of rooks plodding
>   from stile to stile of the sky.[11]

Here she does it, startling, cleansing, clarifying, and always aware, as
Williams always remained aware, that what counts for us arises from
the saying, the naming. You can sense her care (and hear it in her

reading aloud) through the rhythm of the opening lines, the ear's plea-
sure in "haze and halos," the exactness of "furrowed" and "pallors,"
the metaphoric find of "stile to stile." So much depends upon our
seeing and saying these things—*how* much, we may gather from Lever-
tov's title for the poem: "An English Field in the Nuclear Age." Where
else save in the poem can we learn precisely to hold our breath and
realize that this moment of oakbole and dogrose and rooks, "this min-
ute at least was / not the last)."

Language, the language of peoms, shaped by yet shaping what it
has to say, can awaken us, though of course personal and public events
may do so as well. Denise Levertov has written beautifully about her
craft and about its relation to political experience in *The Poet in the
World* and *Light Up the Cave*.[12] She has also suggested where her own
idiom derived its life. Born in England, educated distinctively at home
and read to prolifically (along with her older sister Olga) by a highly
literate and active Welsh mother and Russian-Jewish father, Levertov
married the American writer Mitchell Goodman and came to the
United States in 1948, there to absorb the freshening voices of
Williams, Duncan, Creeley, and others. Her father was descended from
Hasidic rabbis but converted decisively to Christianity to spread *that*
word among Jews. Her mother's great-grandfather was the tailor-my-
stic Angell Jones of Mold. I like to think of those Welsh-Hasidic-Chris-
tian strains growing within a mid-century American idiom and the
"Here and Now" of Levertov's first book in this country, eventually to
be tested by the unremitting state of emergency we have lived in since
the fifties.

For instance, I think her lines from "An English Field in the Nu-
clear Age" implicitly thank Williams and also G. M. Hopkins (trained
in Wales) for the way

> To render it!—*this* moment,
> haze and halos of
> sunbless'd particulars.

In this poem, it's not only the naming that makes for hope, the poet
substantiating her world, it's the act of transubstantiation. Her belief
that holiness inheres in things, a belief her ancestor Hasidim could share
with Saint Francis, leads Denise Levertov into a tenacious reverence and
defense of created life. This reverence fosters a kind of saving inno-
cence, from which emerges her commitment to communal witness—
marches, sit-ins, demonstrations, rallies, mass arrests, benefits, gener-

ous friendships. Faith, hope, love—these words, these possibilities, appear more and more in her poems, though never detached from the trouble of the world around her.

> Let's try
> if something human still
> can shield you,
>   spark
> of remote light,

she says in a recent poem.[13] That simple spiritual and communal urgency has become her hallmark. It makes religious, political, and poetic experience all of a piece.

"I do not believe that a violent imitation of the horrors of our times is the concern of poetry," Levertov wrote in 1959. "Insofar as poetry has a social function it is to awaken sleepers by other means than shock."[14] She had in mind a faddish incoherence in poems of the late fifties, not a desire to exclude history from poetry. Still it seems a painful measure of our own times to remember that statement while listening, as I did in a Palo Alto church in April, 1983, to her oratorio *El Salvador: Requiem and Invocation.* Her notes ask for "an ominous harsh or cacophonous" music, joined then by a collage of voices repeating single words: "Blood . . . Rape . . . Decapitated . . . Torture . . . National Guard . . . Helicopter . . . Vomit . . . Decomposed . . . Stench." The oratorio goes on to tell of a pre-Columbian Mayan civilization dwelling at peace with its gods and its land, only to be invaded, exploited, and sown to violence:

> How did the horror begin?
> Was it a thunderclap? Did men
> blaspheme?
> . . . .
> Men from a far place,
> a few, & a few, then more,
> more—yet still
> only a few, but powerful
> with alien power—
> came seeking gold,
>   seeking wealth,
>   denying
>   the mystery of the land,
>   the sacred harmony,

breaking the rhythm
taking the earth unto themselves
to use it.

An American Indian rather than a cultural feminist sense of Mother
Earth lies behind this passage. Yet the language of it, the verse as such,
doesn't brim and quicken in Levertov's fashion—partly because the or-
atorio is not a poem but was written for music. Almost any libretto
will seem flat on the printed page. Still I wonder if the horror we be-
hold in El Salvador somewhat stymied Levertov's own authentic voice?
(One could go—she herself would go, I imagine—to the *Canto general*
of Pablo Neruda for a full sense of national and personal disaster in
Latin America.) Perhaps it's as Levertov says in "Thinking About El
Salvador, 1982": "Because every day they chop heads off / no force /
flows into language"—although using it this way, I'm demeaning a
poem that ends in powerful testimony to

the silence
of raped women,
of priests and peasants,
teachers and children,
of all whose heads every day
float down the river
and rot
and sink,
not Orpheus heads
still singing, bound for the sea,
but mute.[15]

And I should add that the oratorio *El Salvador* has a compelling
cumulative effect, ending as it does in prayer and hope.

Even against the ultimate disaster, against nuclear terror, Denise
Levertov has somehow summoned hope. I cannot forget her reading
the title poem from *Candles in Babylon*.

Through the midnight streets of Babylon
between the steel towers of their arsenals,
between the torture castles with no windows,
we race by barefoot, holding tight
our candles, trying to shield
the shivering flames, crying
'Sleepers Awake!'

> hoping
> the rhyme's promise was true,
> that we may return
> from this place of terror
> home to a calm dawn and
> the work we had just begun.

Americans might tend to miss an underlying and fragile innocence here, if they don't know the English nursery rhyme: "How many miles to Babylon? / Threescore miles and ten. / Can I get there by candle light? / Yes, and back again." The present tense of Levertov's poem holds her, holds us, in exile, awakening us—if ever poetry can—to that exile and to a stubborn hope.

NOTES

1. W. B. Yeats, *Autobiographies* (London: Macmillan, 1955), p. 151.
2. W. B. Yeats, "In Memory of Major Robert Gregory," in *Collected Poems* (New York: Macmillan, 1956), p. 131.
3. "The Poet in the World," in *The Poet in the World* (New York: New Directions, 1973), p. 114.
4. From *The Sorrow Dance* (New York: New Directions, 1967), pp. 77–90.
5. "Didactic Poem."
6. Donald Allen, ed., *The New American Poetry* (New York: Grove, 1960), p. 412.
7. Notes from "The Craft of Poetry" seminar (1965), quoted in Linda Welshimer Wagner, *Denise Levertov* (New York: Twayne, 1967), p. 19.
8. William Carlos Williams, *Selected Poems* (New York: New Directions, 1969), p. 25.
9. "Williams and the Duende" and "William Carlos Williams, 1883–1963," in *The Poet in the World*, pp. 254–66.
10. Williams, *Selected Poems*, p. 19.
11. "An English Field in the Nuclear Age," *Candles in Babylon* (New York: New Directions, 1982), p. 79.
12. *Light Up the Cave* (New York: New Directions, 1981).
13. "Mass for the Day of St. Thomas Didymus," *Candles in Babylon*, p. 115.
14. See note 6 and "A Testament and a Postscript, 1959–1973," in *The Poet in the World*, pp. 3–6.
15. *Sequoia* 26, no. 2 (Spring 1982): 37.

In Yeats's House: The Death and Resurrection of Sylvia Plath

Sandra M. Gilbert

By an absolute *fluke* I walked by *the* street and *the* house . . . where I've
always wanted to live. . . . And guess what, it is *W. B. Yeats' house*—
with a blue plaque over the door, saying he lived there!
—Sylvia Plath to Aurelia Plath, November 7, 1962

> That crazed girl improvising her music,
> Her poetry, dancing upon the shore,
> Her soul in division from itself
> . . . that girl I declare
> A beautiful lofty thing, or a thing
> Heroically lost, heroically found. . . .
> —W. B. Yeats, "A Crazed Girl"

As the thunder rolled bumping and snarling away across the sky,
they saw the figure of a man appear from the darkness. . . . A brilliant
flash lit up the white face and its frame of heavy hair. . . .
Yeats: and he lived here. . . . all the time his presence would cast
its light upon their frontage.
—Dorothy Richardson, *The Trap*

. . . in the house of a famous poet . . . my work should be blessed.
—Sylvia Plath to Aurelia Plath, November 7, 1962

> Climb to your chamber full of books and wait,
> No books upon the knee . . .
> —W. B. Yeats, "To Dorothy Wellesley"

> The panther's tread is on the stairs,
> Coming up and up the stairs.
> —Sylvia Plath, "Pursuit"

> What climbs the stair?
> Nothing that common women ponder on

> If you are worth my hope! Neither Content
> Nor satisfied Conscience, but that great family
> Some ancient famous authors misrepresent,
> The Proud Furies each with her torch on high.
> > —W. B. Yeats, "To Dorothy Wellesley"

> Well, here I am! Safely in Yeats' house!
> > —Sylvia Plath to Aurelia Plath, December 14, 1962

> In the evening, *Yeats*. Far away from the tumult; hidden, untroubled
> in his green room.
> > —Dorothy Richardson, *The Trap*

> . . . I saw the wildness in her and I thought
> A vision of terror that it must live through
> Had shattered her soul. . . .
> > —W. B. Yeats, "A Bronze Head"

> . . . I feel Yeats' spirit blessing me.
> > —Sylvia Plath to Aurelia Plath, December 14, 1962

"I am afraid of getting older" wrote the seventeen-year-old Sylvia Plath in 1949, "I am afraid of getting married. Spare me from cooking three meals a day—spare me from the relentless cage of routine and rote. I want to be free. . . . I want, I think, to be omniscient. . . . I think I would like to call myself 'The girl who wanted to be God.' Yet if I were not in this body, where *would* I be—perhaps I am *destined* to be classified and qualified. But, oh, I cry out against it. I am I—I am powerful—but to what extent? I am I."[1] "I am I": oddly, prophetically, that somewhat theatrical adolescent phrase echoes the words of a poet whose works even a precocious teenager might not yet have read—William Butler Yeats, who was to become Sylvia Plath's "beloved Yeats" and in whose house, some thirteen and a half years later, she was to die in a suicide that, as most critics see it, might have been either a cry for help or a crying out against being "classified and qualified" or, more simply, a cry of pain. For in a late verse called "He and She" Yeats had used just the phrase the young Plath used in her journal—"I am I"—and used it explicitly to examine what I will argue she was herself exploring: the relationship between male authority and female identity, or, to be more specific, between male creation and female creativity.

> As the moon sidles up [writes Yeats]
> Must she sidle up,

As trips the sacred moon
Away must she trip:
"His light had struck me blind
Dared I stop."

She sings as the moon sings:
"I am I, am I;
The greater grows my light
The further that I fly."
All creation shivers
With that sweet cry.

Tentatively, provisionally, I want in this essay to discuss the ways in which the life, the death, and ultimately the poetic resurrection of "the girl who wanted to be God" were affected by her increasingly intense consciousness that the very scene of writing is now, as never before, shared and shaped by the dialogue between a literary "He and She." I want, in other words, to explore Plath's sometimes exuberant, sometimes anxious awareness that she was born at a moment in history when her "I am I, am I" might for the first time "shiver" all creation. In addition, taking Plath as a paradigmatic precursor, I want to think about what might be some important implications of that historical awareness (as it influenced both her death and her resurrection) for those of us who share Plath's literary desire, if not her destiny.

Criticism of Plath's poetry has, of course, proliferated in recent years; in fact, her reputation, or, perhaps more accurately, her image, seems never to have undergone the "eclipse" that so often causes readers to forget a major writer in the first decades after her or his death. On the contrary, as I noted when I reviewed the 1979 criticism of contemporary poetry for the 1981 edition of *American Literary Scholarship,* Plath in that year got more attention than any other poet treated in my section of the book, a significant phenomenon, since my section surveyed writings on such major artists as Lowell, Roethke, Levertov, Rich, Ginsberg, and Ashbery. Plath's work, as I pointed out, is "still controversial. Yet even those who dislike it find it absorbing, even mesmerizing, as if this thirty-one-year-old woman who died in 1963 were in some troubling sense what Keats might call a 'figure of allegory.' "[2]

But in what sense, specifically, does Plath become allegorical for critics? Here I think that writers and reviewers like Denis Donoghue, Gary Lane, David Holbrook, Hugh Kenner, Margaret Dickie Uroff, and Marjorie Perloff would speak to very different issues. Rather extravagantly, one set—probably the majority—would praise or blame Plath's suicidal intensity, tracing an allegorical, psychodramatic, even melodramatic relationship between life and art. More conservatively, the second set would explain or analyze Plath's stylistic influences, tracing a somewhat less problematic though still allegorical relationship between art and art. To give a few examples of what the first group would say: Denis Donoghue might elaborate on his idea that Sylvia Plath was "a girl who lived mostly and terribly on her nerves," explaining in particular how "she showed what self-absorption makes possible in art"; David Holbrook might explain why he thinks Plath's "poetry seduces us to taste of its poisoned chalice"; Hugh Kenner might support his assertion that *Ariel* offers us "insidious nausea" and "bogus spirituality" fashioned "with the gleeful craft of a mad child"; and Marjorie Perloff might explain her contention that Plath "had really only one subject: her own anguish and consequent longing for death."[3] To give fewer examples of what the second set would say: Gary Lane, Margaret Dickie Uroff, and Marjorie Perloff (who is versatile enough to belong in both sets of critics) might show how Plath's poetic evolution was helped or hindered by powerful male precursors like Yeats, Thomas, Stevens, Roethke, Lowell, and Hughes, and, to a lesser extent, by powerful female precursors like Dickinson, Bishop, and Moore.[4]

The first set of critics, in other words, would moralize; the second set would analyze. Few, however, would try to consider whether there is a connection between, on the one hand, the poetic influences that shaped Plath's style and, on the other, the personal dilemma that became her subject. More specifically, few would speculate on what it meant to be a woman, born in America in 1932, reading major poetry and trying to write major poetry in the years from, say, 1952 to 1963—what it meant, that is, to be a "girl who wanted to be God" setting out, like a female Stephen Daedalus, to "forge" an identity, an "I am I," in Wellesley, Massachuetts, at Smith College, at *Mademoiselle,* at Cambridge University, in Spain, in Boston, in London, in Devonshire, and finally in Yeats's house.

But almost by itself the list of places I've just offered should suggest how new, if not unique, Plath's historical situation was. It hardly seems necessary to remind ourselves that, born a century earlier, neither Emily Dickinson nor Christina Rossetti, two of Plath's major literary foremothers, could ever have journeyed from continent to continent, college to college, city to city that way. When their precursor, Elizabeth Barrett Browning, started her dramatic travels, after all, she had to tiptoe like a thief out of that infamous house on Wimpole Street, and even so her father never spoke to her again. As for the literary constraints of which such geographic constrictions were emblematic, moreover, it hardly seems necessary to remind ourselves that those were equally severe. Elizabeth Barrett Browning looked "everywhere for [poetic] grandmothers and found none"; while Emily Dickinson, feeling "shut up . . . in prose," fell in love with "that foreign lady" Elizabeth Barrett Browning precisely because she constituted in her own person (and created in Aurora Leigh) a unique precursor.[5] By the time the seventeen-year-old Sylvia Plath took up her pen in 1949 and wrote "I want to be free . . . I want to be omniscient," however, the world had radically changed, for an event had long since taken place that, as Virginia Woolf says in *A Room of One's Own,* "if I were rewriting history I should think of greater importance than the Crusades or the Wars of the Roses. The middle-class woman began to write."[6] Beginning to write, moreover, that symbolic woman began to travel—into the universities, into the professions, into a series of surprisingly various rooms of her own all over the world. What Barrett Browning, Rossetti, and Dickinson had struggled to start became a living female tradition that was handed down to women like Virginia Woolf, H. D., Marianne Moore—and Sylvia Plath. It became a tradition, too, that had to be confronted by men like W. B. Yeats, D. H. Lawrence, James Joyce, T. S. Eliot, and Ted Hughes.

When Virginia Woof implies in "Professions for Women," therefore, that writing is in some way the most "harmless occupation" a woman can pursue, she oversimplifies the case. It is true that, as she says, "the road was cut many years ago . . . . many famous women, and many more unknown and forgotten have been before me, making the path smooth, and regulating my steps."[7] But it is also true that the new (female) road, whether it parallels or intersects the old (male) one, complicates our literary geography, for every new road makes the landscape more intricate, more problematic, even while it elaborates possibilities. Thus when Plath writes in "The Disquieting Muses" about "the kingdom you bore me to, / Mother, mother,"[8] she is hinting at an anxiety Woolf does not really explore. For the world to which Plath's mother bore her was complex indeed, as we can instantly perceive if we stop for a moment to consider who was writing half a century ago, in the year when Aurelia Plath produced her *Wunderkind.* On the one hand, Yeats, Joyce, Pound, Eliot, Faulkner, Hemingway—many of the major male (and mostly masculinist) modernists—were publishing, though a few would soon be perishing. On the other hand, Stein, H. D., Millay, Moore, Barnes, and Woolf—many of the major female (and mostly feminist) modernists were publishing, and (except for Woolf) none would soon be perishing. Among them, these representatives of both sexes created a dialectic that became an inheritance which may well have been "disquieting" to an ambitious young woman poet, a "girl who wanted to be God."

Because Plath is usually seen as either a sort of neurasthenic sorceress of syntax—a witty, wily, willful witch of words—or a diligent devotee of Roget's *Thesaurus*—a docile and decorous ephebe of fifties elegance—she isn't often understood to be what she really was: an extraordinarily conscious and at least semi-*self*-conscious student of the peculiarly new literary tradition in which she quite pivotally participated. Yet from the first, of course, as her early flirtation with her thesaurus should indicate, she was a voracious reader, and a reader who surely understood the implications of the literary history that she imbibed, she tells us, almost as if it were her mother's milk. "I recall my mother . . . reading to me . . . from Matthew Arnold's 'Forsaken Merman,'" she writes, recounting her personal myth of origins in "Ocean 1212-W," adding that "A spark flew off Arnold and shook me like a chill . . . . I had fallen into a new way of being happy."[9] If not from the first, too, at least quite early she must have understood the implications of her gender for the genre she had chosen. At Cambridge, for instance, she played the part of Phoebe Clinkett, Pope's parodic portrait of the eighteenth-century poet Anne Finch as, in Plath's own words, a "mad poetess," (*LH,* p. 190), a "verbose niece who has high flown and very funny ambitions to write plays and poetry." Mouthing the absurdities of this savagely satirized woman artist, she gave what her director told her was an "excruciatingly funny" performance, but of course it was also a performance whose deeper meaning, had she allowed herself to confront it, might have been merely excruciating, because of the message it gave to a "girl who wanted to be God" about literary men's attitudes toward literary women's aspirations. By the time she was well established at Cambridge, moreover, Plath was exactly what many of her most expert readers are: a sophisticated student of a twentieth-century literary tradition that was constituted out of an implicit if not explicit battle between highly cultured intellectual men (Pound, Eliot, Joyce, Lawrence) and their female counterparts, literary ladies who seemed either to be part of a less cultivated group like the one that Hawthorne called a "damned mob of scribbling women" (Teasdale, Millay, Olive Higgins Prouty) or part of a more cultured but also more dangerous, even presumptuous group that we might call a Black Mass of scrivening women (H.D., Stein, Woolf, Moore).

That Plath saw herself as oscillating between these two, or rather three, unprecedented male and female/female poles, becomes clear when we read the countless letters home she wrote from Smith and Cambridge. Articulating her loyalty to the male tradition out of whose figurative rib she had been born like a new Eve, for instance, she expressed her worship of her "beloved Yeats," her admiration for Lawrence, her reverence for Joyce, her respect for Thomas. At the same time, she hinted at her feelings of rivalry toward these men and, by implication, her powerful sense of her own power in comparison to theirs: "I am learning and mastering new words each day, and drunker than Dylan, harder than Hopkins, younger than Yeats in my saying" (LH, p. 243). Simultaneously too, though, she indicated her anxiety about being a "scribbling woman": her poems, she said, are "not quailing and whining like Teasdale or simple lyrics like Millay" (LH, p. 277). And again, at the same time—to complicate the plot even further—she expressed her admiration for what she considered serious female precursors, noting when she sent her mother some poems from college that "any resemblance to Emily Dickinson is purely intentional," praising the brilliance of Dorothy Krook ("a woman on the Cambridge faculty for whom I would sweat my brains out"), and observing that "I get courage by reading Virginia Woolf's Diary," that she felt "very akin to [Woolf]," that she found Woolf's novels "excellent stimulation for my own writing" (LH, pp. 305, 324), and that, indeed, "Her novels make mine possible."[10] Thus, even while she repudiated what she saw as the bitterness, sentimentality or oversimplification of one part of the female literary tradition she had inherited, or excoriated most of the women dons at Cambridge as "bluestocking grotesques," she deliberately defined herself as "a woman poet like [sic] the world will gape at. . . . One of the few women poets in the world who is a rejoicing woman . . . a woman singer" (LH, pp. 248, 256), and insisted that she wanted to be "a woman famous among women" (J, p. 260).

But what were the implications of such a self-definition, arising as it did out of divided loyalties, ambivalences, ambiguities? A casual but crucial sentence Plath tossed off in another letter suggests that one central implication was an extraordinary sense of guilt and consequent terror:

guilt over her own power; terror that she might be, should be, punished for her power. Complaining about the burden of domesticity in England, a country that had not yet at that point discovered "the Cookie-sheet, Central Heating, and Frozen Orange Juice," she commented that "if I want to keep on being a triple-threat woman: wife, writer and teacher . . . I can't be a drudge."[11] A _triple-threat woman:_ the phrase is telling, for it both explains her early fascination with "The Forsaken Merman" and foreshadows her later fascination with images of herself as an arrow, an acetylene virgin, a runaway, a queen bee, a crackling moon, a murderess, a deadly interloper, a ferocious transgressor. Arnold's poem, after all, tells a tale of the way a poetically pathetic merman is seduced and abandoned by a "cruel" earth-woman who, claiming her own place in the sun, leaves "lonely forever / The kings of the sea." As for Plath's later images of her own threatening self, they record similar cruelties, from "the upflight of the murderess into a heaven that loves her" described in "Stings," to the violently "dancing and stamping" villagers let loose in "Daddy," the "face / So murderous in its strangle of branches" encountered in "Elm," the man-eating heroine resurrected in "Lady Lazarus," and "The lioness, / The shriek in the bath, / The cloak of holes" imagined by the Clytemnestra-like speaker of "Purdah."[12]

Even while most women "fight for the father, for the son," wrote Plath in her Cambridge notebook, as if proleptically explaining such later images, most have also the power to "believe in [men] and make them invincible," along with the complementary, more terrible power of "the vampire," who expresses "the old primal hate. That desire to go around castrating the arrogant ones who become such children at the moment of passion" (_JP,_ pp. 250–51). Significantly, moreover, a moment after she made this confession, she implicitly alluded to Yeats—"How the circling steps in the spiral tower bring us back to where we were!" (_JP,_ pp. 250–51)—as if she knew how he might refer to her: as a "thing heroically lost, heroically found," a Helen for whom there was "no second Troy" to burn, as an adept of "the Proud Furies," a creature full of "wildness," one of Herodias's desirous and demented daughters, blasting through "the labyrinth of the wind."[13]

For if Pope reacted with comic rage against Anne Finch's poetic presumption by satirizing her as Phoebe Clinkett, Plath's more recent masters, male modernists like Yeats, Joyce, and Lawrence, had responded even more censoriously to what they perceived as "the old primal hate" of the "vampire" women who seemed to want to usurp not only (like Olive Higgins Prouty) the literary marketplace, but even (like H.D., Woolf, and Plath) the scene of writing itself. Portraying the vulgarly virginal Gerty MacDowell in the Nausicaa section of *Ulysses,* for instance, Joyce satirized the "namby-pamby jammy marmalady drawersy" style of "scribbling women" like Maria Cummins, the author of *The Lamplighter,* at least as savagely as Pope, in his depiction of poor Phoebe Clinkett, had parodied what he took to be Anne Finch's style, while in one of his notebooks he exulted that in his misogynistic *Waste Land* "T. S. Eliot ends idea of poetry for ladies."[14] Similarly, in a ferocious verse called "The Lady Poets with Footnotes," Ernest Hemingway had attacked literary women as fat or sterile or drunk or nymphomaniac or all those reprehensible things together, while in *Miss Lonelyhearts* Nathaniel West's reporters had fulminated against lady writers with three names— "Mary Roberts Wilcox, Ella Wheeler Catheter, Ford Mary Rinehard— what they all needed was a good rape," and in "Portrait d'Une Femme" Ezra Pound had told a chaotically cultured woman that "Your mind and you are our Sargasso Sea.[15] If the messages conveyed by the life/work of Plath's "beloved" Yeats were more complicated, they must have sometimes been equally daunting, for even as Maude Gonne's erstwhile lover praised strong women like Lady Gregory, Dorothy Wellesley, and Maude herself, he deplored the way Con Marckiewicz's mind had become "a bitter, an abstract thing," denounced the "vague Utopia" of feminism dreamed by Eva Gore-Booth, observing that "she seems / When withered old and skeleton-gaunt, / An image of such politics," praised "woman / That gives up all her mind," and prayed that his own daughter might "become a flourishing hidden tree."[16] When we read her anxious insistence that she is "not a bitter or frustrated or warped manimitator" (*LH,* p. 256), therefore, we can see that Plath must have intuited and internalized the misogyny implicit or explicit in all these masculinist modernist statements.

Internalizing such misogyny, however, she did not respond as women poets from Anne Bradstreet and Anne Finch to Christina Rossetti and Elizabeth Barrett Browning did, by trying to renounce or repudiate, deny or disguise her own power. Rather, her first response, like that of many other women artists who are her contemporaries or descendants, was to affirm her strength, to revel and rejoice in it: "I am making a self, in great pain, often, as for a birth, but it is right that it should be so" (*LH,* p, 223); "by re-forging my soul, I am a woman now the like of which I could never have dreamed" (*LH,* p. 241). To be sure, some of her precursors had made similar assertions, beginning perhaps with Anne Finch, who replied to Pope's criticisms by warning "Alexander, have a care / And shock the sex no more, / We rule the world our life's whole race, / Men but assume that right . . . ."[17] But all too often such women, like Finch herself, succumbed to spleen or melancholy, and imagined flying only "with contracted wing."[18] Between Plath and those foremothers, however, a new age of literary equality had intervened, an age that made possible her sharing, as she put it, of "her husband's dearest career" (*LH,* p. 276), an age that brought this couple up as a representative "He and She" to "romp through words" together (*LH,* p. 235), an age that let her live in Yeats's house.

It was, of course, an age that had been defined in the first part of this century, long before Plath was born—and it was defined by male historians like John Langdon-Davies as well as by female prophets like Virginia Woolf. "Once both sexes use their reason equally," wrote Langdon-Davies in a passage Plath underlined in his 1927 *History of Women,* ". . . then women cannot fail to dominate. Theirs is the stronger sex once nature and art cease their cruel combination against them, because it possesses a greater singleness of purpose and a greater fund of imagination."[19] And a year later, in 1928, Virginia Woolf, to whom Plath felt so much akin, predicted, as we all know, the second coming of the mythic woman poet Judith Shakespeare: "The opportunity will come, and the dead poet who was Shakespeare's sister will put on the body which she has so often laid down. Drawing her life from the lives of the unknown who were her forerunners . . . she will be born."[20]

Was she born in Sylvia Plath? Was she born when, alone and (like Judith Shakespeare) abandoned in London, Plath finally in 1962 wrote her mother that "I am a writer . . . I am a genius of a writer . . . I am writing the best poems of my life; they will make my name. . . ." (*LH,* p. 468)? I would suggest that she was, but that she had to "lay down" her body again not because, like Woolf's Judith, she had been discouraged or denied, but precisely because, encouraged as she was by history and prophecy, she had to suffer in her own person the sexual battle that marked a turning point in time. I would suggest, in other words, that, to paraphrase Adrienne Rich's poem on Marie Curie, Plath died a famous (not an obscure) woman, and died not denying but knowing that "her wounds came from the same source as her power."[21]

The connection in Plath's career among the literary history her letters ambitiously review, the power her poems ambivalently renew or repress, and the wound her death ambiguously reveals is made clearest in two short stories ostensibly about dreams but really about reading and writing, stories which enter vigorously, though very differently, into a dialogue with the twentieth-century male literary tradition represented in them by D. H. Lawrence and his north of England descendant Ted Hughes. The first, "The Wishing Box," was evidently written in 1956; the second, "Johnny Panic and the Bible of Dreams," dates from December, 1958. The first, about suicide, is slight, blackly comic, barely successful. The second, about what we might call femicide, is longer, bleakly sardonic, brilliantly successful. But despite these distinctions the two constitute in some sense a single narrative which dramatically summarizes the sense of transgression or usurpation that seems to have haunted their author when she considered the possibility (or the reality) of female creative power.

To be sure, "The Wishing Box" is at least on the surface a comic tale of female powerlessness. Harold and Agnes, a young married couple— clearly surrogates of Ted and Sylvia—meet at breakfast to discuss *his* dreams, which are always vivid, richly formulated, funny visions of aesthetic triumph. In one, he discusses manuscripts with William Blake, in another he plays the Emperor Concerto, in a third he is introduced to a gathering of American poets in the Library of Congress, and in two others (the ones that most comically and definitively relate him to Hughes) he encounters, respectively, a red fox (who presents him with a bottle of permanent black Quink) and a giant pike. Listening with pretended admiration to his accounts of these nighttime events, Agnes, who has only a few dreams herself (and those are nightmares), finds herself "wrestling with the strange jealousy which had been growing on her like some dark malignant cancer ever since their wedding night" (*JP*, p. 204), and thinks that "It was as if Harold were spending one third of his life among celebrities and fabulous legendary creatures in an exhilarating world from which [she] found herself perpetually exiled, except by hearsay" (*JP*, p. 205).

At first, in an attempt to compete, she plans to study Freud on the sly and fortify "herself with a vicarious dream tale by which to hold Harold's interest each morning" (*JP*, p. 207), a strategy that recalls both the literary seductions of Scheherezade and the occult wiles of George Yeats. But finally she gives up and confesses her inadequacy to

her husband, who sets her a series of dream exercises not unlike the
group of poetic exercises Hughes set Plath. Even these don't work,
however, and though Agnes tries to restore her "shaping imaginative
powers" (*JP*, p. 209) by reading novels, cookbooks, "home appliance
circulars . . . anything to keep from facing the gaping void in her own
head of which Harold had made her so painfully conscious," the very
letters she looks at writhe "like malevolent little black snakes across the
page in a kind of hissing, untranslatable jargon" so that finally, insom-
niac as Esther Greenwood in *The Bell Jar*, and hysterical at the "intol-
erable prospect of wakeful visionless days and nights stretching un-
broken ahead of her" (*JP*, p. 210), she consumes a "wishing box" full
of sleeping pills and dies into the only country of dreams accessible to
her.

What is frightening and crucial about this tale, it seems to me, is its
obsession with the dream competition between husband and wife, and,
more specifically, its emphasis on both the sense of creative, even sexual
inadequacy and the "dark malignant cancer of jealousy" Agnes feels
when facing the fertility of Harold's imagination. Indeed, considering
that Plath wrote the story at just the time when she was boasting to her
mother that she and Hughes "romp through words together," that he
"is my best critic as I am his," and that she was "glad his book is taken
first," proud that he is "always just that many steps ahead of me intellec-
tually and creatively so that I feel very feminine and admiring" (*LH*, p.
270), "The Wishing Box" comes as something of a surprise, for it sug-
gests that its author had, on the one hand, a deeply traditional female
anxiety that she could not keep up with the élan of the male imagination,
and, on the other hand, a deep, *Ladies Home Journal* conviction that she
should not keep up. Better death than the expression of (female) desire,
the story seems to say. Or, more accurately, death is the most appropri-
ate expression of female desire, the best dream a woman can have.

But of course Plath knew, in the truest part of herself, that she
could and did keep up with Hughes's, and many other men's, imagina-
tive élan. Thus, "Johnny Panic and the Bible of Dreams" offers, as it
were, the other term of the painful puzzle the two tales together articu-
late. For in "Johnny Panic," a story Hughes himself saw as "moving
straight toward *The Bell Jar* and the more direct poems of *Ariel*" (*JP*,
p. 6), the female narrator—"Assistant Secretary in [an] Adult Psychi-
atric Clinic"—becomes "a dream connoisseur" (*JP*, p. 153), a dedi-
cated transcriber of the horrendous nightmares inspired by the god

"Johnny Panic," and "this," she says with the sardonic pride of a Lady Lazarus, "is my real calling." By comparison with the comically ambitious or innocently poetic dreams recounted in "The Wishing Box," however, the nightmares of "Johnny Panic" are intricate, metaphysical poems; more, they are exactly the Plathian nightmares—"dark glowing landscapes peopled with ominous unrecognizable figures" (*JP*, p. 205)—that Agnes had rejected as inadequate in that story.

In some sense, then, the narrator of "Johnny Panic" is a prophetically visionary version of the poet herself, an impassioned imaginative woman whose powerful ambition is to record all the dreams contained in the old books of the clinic, books that were begun when "the clinic started thirty three years ago—the year of my birth, oddly enough." But when finally, after much plotting and scheming, she does undertake that task, contriving to spend all night in the hospital copying the contents of the "dream book [that] was spanking new the day I was born" (*JP*, p. 164), she quickly and traumatically learns that her inspired transcription is an awful transgression. Finding her among the files at dawn (Plath's own regular writing time), the clinic director marches her off to a sadomasochistic place of punishment where a terrible nurse and "five false priests in white surgical gowns and masks" ritually strip her, annoint her, robe her in "sheets virginal as the first snow," extend her full length on a white cot, and place a "crown of wire" on her head, a "wafer of forgetfulness" on her tongue" (*JP*, p. 166). The shock of the sacrificial shock treatment she then undergoes elicits a vision that does indeed influence and, in a searing blue light, illuminate both *The Bell Jar* and *Ariel*.

> At the moment when I think I am most lost the face of Johnny Panic appears in a nimbus of arc lights on the ceiling overhead. I am shaken like a leaf in the teeth of glory. His beard is lightning. Lightning is in his eye. His Word charges and illumines the universe.
> The air crackles with his blue-tongued lightning-haloed angels.

Coupled with "The Wishing Box," in fact, this story also illuminates the problem that Suzanne Juhasz has called (and that Plath must have seen as) the "double bind" of the woman poet: if she empties her head of her own dreams, she dies into (as Forster put it) "panic and emptiness"; but if she ambitiously studies and records what are, symbolically speaking, her own dreams, she is shaken and shocked by a panic that also, inevitably, produces emptiness. Worse still, her panic is energized not only by her Pandora-like curiosity about the secret facts of her own history that are recorded in the clinic's musty dream books, it is also activated by her consciousness that her identification of *her* history with these sacred tomes constitutes a fearful usurpation of literary history itself. In other words, Plath is aware that when the clinic director shocks her transgressive dream connoisseur out of her mind he is doing so because this scribbling woman's appropriation of the dream books offers a challenge to his authority over them, his mastery of the mystery of their material.

Plath's awareness of this specific point is most dramatically revealed, I would suggest, by the fact that "Johnny Panic" is very clearly a revision of one of D. H. Lawrence's most ferociously misogynist tales, "The Woman Who Rode Away," a story that recounts the miserable misadventure of a thirty-three-year-old, nerve-worn, white woman who escapes from her boringly bourgeois marriage only to be seized by a band of male Indians, ritually annointed, stripped, splayed out on a flat rock by five priests, and offered as a sacrifice to their sun god so that they can recapture "the mastery that man must hold, and that passes from race to race."[22] For, says Lawrence in a concise statement of the story's central theme and a statement which would surely have proffered Plath a terrifying summary of male modernist reactions to the transgression implicit in the dream transcriptions of her poems, his heroine knew that "Her kind of womanhood, intensely personal and individual, was to be obliterated again, and the great primeval symbols were to tower once more over the fallen individual independence of woman. . . . Strangely as if clairvoyant, she saw the immense sacrifice prepared."[23] And why must such an immense sacrifice be prepared? Precisely because it is the white woman's power—the power, let us say, of feminist-modernists like Lawrence's rival Katherine Mansfield and his patroness Mabel Dodge Luhan—that has debilitated not only the white men but the Indian men and the traditionally dutiful Indian women. The moon, says one of Lawrence's noble savages, must be told that "*the wicked white woman can't harm you any more.*"

As we saw, Hughes noted that Plath's revision in "Johnny Panic" of Lawrence's fiction of female sacrifice leads directly to *The Bell Jar* and *Ariel,* a point that he seems to have intended as a comment on the exuberantly colloquial style of this early tale. But it is worth remembering that, like the narrator of "Johnny Panic" and the speaker of many of the *Ariel* poems, Esther Greenwood in *The Bell Jar* defines herself as a "wicked"—that is, a wickedly ambitious—woman, a woman who wants to "shoot off in all directions" herself instead of being the passive "place the arrows shoot off from."[24] Not surprisingly, then, Esther's emotional crisis is directly precipitated by a confrontation with male modernism (and ultimately, through it, male literary history) like the one to which "Johnny Panic" indirectly alludes. As you may recall, home for the summer and shut out of a creative writing course she hoped to take, this fashion magazine prize-winner plans to write her Honors Thesis on *Finnegans Wake*. But when she opens Joyce's magnum opus—a "thick book [that] made an unpleasant dent in my stomach"—Esther is overwhelmed by the horror of interpretation and, implicitly, by the horror of what she must interpret. "My eyes sank through an alphabet soup of letters to the long word in the middle of the page," she says, describing her encounter with the fatal fall of HCE. "Why should there be a hundred letters? . . . Haltingly I tried the word aloud. It sounded like a heavy wooden object falling down-stairs" (*BJ,* p. 102). Then, when she tries to read on, as in "The Wishing Box" the alphabet itself becomes alien and alarming: "The letters grew barbs and ram's horns [and] associated themselves in fantastic, untranslatable shapes . . ." (*BJ,* p. 102). Finally, therefore, she decides to "junk" her thesis, the Honors program, and even (because it would require her to take a course in the eighteenth century) her college English major. For, says this surrogate self of the Cambridge student who claimed to have so much fun playing the part of Pope's Phoebe Clinkett, "I hated the very idea of the eighteenth century, with all those smug men writing tight little couplets, and being so dead keen on reason" (*BJ,* p. 102).

Given the ferocious alphabet in which she seems to have felt ensnared, what way out could there have been for Plath? Certainly everything I have said so far about the literary battle of the sexes that she internalized as a war in her own mind would seem to have precluded her writing at all. Yet, as we know, write she did, and, as I have hardly had time to note, she wrote great poems. How? Why? I want in an attempt to come to some sort of conclusion to suggest that, for her, paradigms of poetic (if not personal) survival came from a woman novelist—Virginia Woolf—who did not herself personally survive, and, paradox-

ically, from one of the male poets—W. B. Yeats—whose awe of
female power facilitated Plath's art even while, as we saw, his anger at
female intellectual energy repressed and depressed her ambitions. As
early as 1956, after all, Plath was telling her mother proudly that "all
the scholarly boys [at Cambridge] think of me as a second Virginia
Woolf" and not much later she confided that "I get courage by reading
[Woolf's *Diary*]" because "I feel very akin to her" (*LH,* pp. 230, 305).
By the time she wrote her radio play, "Three Women," in 1962—a
text that, like "Johnny Panic," Hughes sees as a crucial transition work
from the style of *The Colossus* to the mode of *Ariel*—that kinship was
manifesting itself in the very texture and tempo of Plath's verse as well
as in its increasingly brilliant illumination of the complex "I am I" that
constitutes human consciousness. Specifically, I would argue that the
cadences of the three introspective women speakers in Plath's verse play
evolved out of the cadences that define the voices of the three introspec-
tive women speakers whose lives Woolf explored in what she called her
"play-poem" *The Waves.*[25] In addition, the prototypical female person-
alities Plath's three women represent seem significantly analogous to
the female paradigms represented by Woolf's Susan, her Rhoda, and
her Jinny, for the first voice, like Susan's, is that of a fiercely nuturing
mother, the second, like Rhoda's, is that of a woman who feels herself
almost metaphysically "lacking" in appropriate femaleness, and the
third, like Jinny's, is that of a woman who wills herself to live seduc-
tively but "without attachments."

Significantly, as I discovered after I began to speculate along these
lines, Plath's copy of *The Waves,* now held by the Smith College Rare
Book Room, is the most heavily underlined of all her books, with the
exception of a few texts in which she took notes when she was an
undergraduate or graduate student. Even without such documentary
evidence of influence, however, we can see, if we juxtapose a few sam-
ple passages from *The Waves* with some representative lines from
"Three Women," how the reveries of Plath's women are not only sub-
stantively but stylistically shaped by the meditations of Woolf's hero-
ines, for both Woolf's and Plath's "dramatic soliloquys"—the phrase is
Woolf's but applies equally well to Plath's verses—rely heavily on self-
defining metaphors, on incantatory incremental repetition, and on in-
terpolated rhetorical questions, to characterize their speakers. Compar-
ing school (where she is) to home (where she wants to be), for exam-
ple, Woolf's earth motherly Susan thinks that "something has grown in
me . . . [at home] gradually I shall turn over the hard thing that has

grown here in my side.''[26] Similarly, Plath's first voice, entering labor, thinks that "A power is growing in me, an old tenacity. . . .''[27] Later, Susan declares that·"I am the field, I am the barn" (*Waves,* p. 242) and still later, become a mother, she defines herself as "spun to a fine thread round the cradle, wrapping in a cocoon made of my own blood the delicate limbs of my baby" (*Waves,* p. 294). Similarly, Plath's first voice resolves to be "a wall and a roof protecting . . . a sky and a hill of good" (*Women,* p. 180) and, become a mother, she imagines herself as "a river of milk . . . a warm hill" (*Women,* p. 183). Guarding her children, Susan asks "Where can the shadow enter" (*Waves,* p. 308), and similarly, resolving to guard, Plath's first voice wonders "How long can I be a wall keeping the wind off?" (*Women,* p. 185). The parallels between their lives and their words, their realities and their rhetoric, seem obvious.

In the same way, where Woolf's Susan and Plath's first voice are singleminded and even—as Woolf puts it—"fell" in their femaleness, Woolf's Rhoda and Plath's second voice are faint with the failure of identity, aching with emptiness. Rhoda imagines her defiance of life as "a thin dream . . . a papery tree" (*Waves,* p. 213), while the second voice—a secretary who has miscarried—fears that "the streets may turn to paper suddenly" (*Women,* p. 187); Rhoda approaches a puddle and confesses that "I could not cross it. Identity failed me. We are nothing, I said, and fell" (*Waves,* p. 219), while the second voice insists that "I am found wanting"; after the mythic Percival's demise in India, Rhoda broods on death, elaborating upon her male double Louis's assertion that "Death is woven in with the violets . . . Death and again death" (*Waves,* p. 273), while the second voice, bleeding away her embryonic child, declares "This is a disease I carry home, this is a death. / Again, this is a death" (*Women,* p. 177).

To turn, finally, to Woolf's Jinny, a femme fatale who lives the purely passionate "life of the body," she is perhaps less akin to Plath's third voice than Susan is to the first and Rhoda to the second, but even between these last two figures there are significant resemblances. Jinny claims, for instance, that "I do not settle long anywhere; I do not attach myself to one person in particular" (*Waves,* p. 296), while the third voice, a student who has given her illegitimate child up for adoption, insists that "It is so beautiful to have no attachments! / I am solitary as grass" (*Women,* p. 186); again, Jinny sees "every blade of grass very clear" (*Waves,* p. 206) and gives herself to "a tree . . . the river . . . afternoon" (*Waves,* p. 351) while the third voice is haunted by "Hot

noon in the meadows [where] the buttercups / Swelter and melt . . . "
(*Women*, p. 186). The options for women, say Woolf's novel and
Plath's play in a kind of antiphonal chorus over time, are threefold: the
qualified power of maternity, the absolute powerlessness of meta-
physical consciousness, and the pseudo-power of seductive indifference.
But when exploring those limited options, women can and should
speak in a style marked by unlimited metaphorical energy, a style of
liberated self-analysis that persistently and insistently explores the cru-
cial "I am I" of female identity. The woman writer, or so Woolf taught
Plath, may indeed be destined to "be classified and qualified" but she
still has the imaginative power to articulate the tension between the self
that "wants to be God" and the classifications which would constrain
that self.

The explosion of *Ariel* is thus a breakthrough into further and even
more powerful Woolfian self-analyses, a breakthrough accomplished
when the poet remembers that "I have a self to recover, a queen." Not
surprisingly, therefore, many of the *Ariel* poems continue to echo key
passages from *The Waves*, including a few spoken by Woolf's male
characters. Plath's confession in "Tulips" that "I have no face. I have
wanted to efface myself," for instance, recalls Rhoda's frightened,
twice-repeated recognition that "I have no face" (*Waves*, p. 203);
Plath's "I think I am going up, / I think I may rise" in "Fever 103"
echoes Rhoda's "I am above the earth now . . . I mount; I es-
cape . . ."(*Waves*, p. 193); Plath's "I am dark-suited and still, a member
of the party" in "Berck Plage" recalls Louis's "I become a figure in the
procession, a spoke in the huge wheel" (*Waves*, p. 198); Plath's "Now I
break up in pieces that fly about like clubs" in "Elm" parallels Rhoda's
"I am broken into separate pieces; I am no longer one" (*Waves*, p. 248);
Plath's "I / Am a pure acetylene / Virgin" echoes Rhoda's "I am un-
sealed, I am incandescent" (*Waves*, p. 214); Plath's continual visions of
smiling or sinister "hooks" recall Rhoda's "I feel myself grappled to
one spot by these hooks [people] cast . . ." (*Waves*, p. 337); Plath's gal-
loping words with their "indefatigable hooftapes" echo Neville's
"words and words and words, how they gallop . . ." (*Waves*, p. 232).
Even the hard-won processes of composition through which both these
women artists achieved such powerfully self-defining cadences are sig-
nificantly similar, moreover. Woolf, who suspected she had "not yet
mastered the speaking voice," rewrote *The Waves* by "reading much of
it aloud, like poetry"[28] while, as Hughes reminds us, Plath began
around the time she wrote "Three Women" to "compose her poems

more to be read aloud," and indeed to compose them, often, by read-ing aloud. The female voice, such a process of composition suggests, must not be silenced; it must and will be *heard,* even, in Plath's case, broadcast to an audience of thousands. Neither "Roget's trollop" nor the silent furtive transgressor of "Johnny Panic," the woman poet can speak out and up for herself.

Yet when Plath was speaking her last potent self-analyses in that strong bitter late voice many of us have heard on records and tapes, she was speaking, of course, in and from Yeats's house. Given the cen-soriousness of the tradition this "beloved" poet must at least in part have represented for her, how, even with the help of Virginia Woolf, could she have achieved such acts of linguistic audacity? In answer to this question, I want finally to suggest that in the end Plath felt "Yeats's spirit blessing" her, as the apparition of Yeats blessed Dorothy Richardson's Miriam, because, despite his ambivalences, Yeats, among all the male modernists, had the most reverence for female power. Indeed, in plays like "Cathleen ni Houlihan" and "The Only Jealousy of Emer" and in sequences of "dramatic soliloquys" like "A Woman Young and Old" and the "Crazy Jane" poems, he himself tried to capture the unique inflections of the female voice, with its pride in sexuality, its ambivalence toward patriarchal authority, its impassioned assertion of identity, and its amused contempt for male pretensions. By dwelling on Yeats's writ-ings, then, while literally dwelling in his house, Plath may have ultimate-ly learned to resurrect rather than reject the subversive strength he pre-dicted for the woman poet when he told Dorothy Wellesley to expect a visit from "that great family / Some ancient famous authors misrepre-sent, / The Proud Furies, each with her torch on high."[29] Like Dorothy Wellesley, no "common" woman, Plath took on the revisionary role of such a Fury, rising ferocious as "God's lioness" from the earth in which those great and greatly misunderstood figures were shut up at the close of the Oresteia. In doing so with Yeats's implicit approval, moreover, she found a poetic father—a liberating male muse rather than an inhibit-ing male master—to match the poetic mother she had discovered in Virginia Woolf.

I am saying, in other words, that with what must have felt like the tacit encouragement of Yeats and Woolf, Plath gave herself up to *herself* and acknowledged her own ambition to be "a woman famous among women." To be sure, her engagement with such powerful precursors did at times involve her in a kind of Bloomian struggle for authority: not only did she boast (with some anxiety) that she was "younger than

Yeats in [her] saying," she also claimed that she would find "images of life: like Woolf found. But . . . *I will be stronger*" (*J*, p. 165, emphasis added). Nevertheless, together these literary parents became not primarily antagonists but, rather, sacred facilitators: Plath felt Yeats's "spirit blessing" her and spoke with awe of Woolf's "blessed diary"(*J*, p. 152). Thus it was with what she perceived as the sacramental benedictions of Yeats and Woolf that she became the person she most feared and desired to be—most terribly, the lion-red queen with her wings of glass, the voraciously resurrected Lady Lazarus, the glamorously guilty murderess boasting that "If I've killed one man, I've killed two"; and most triumphantly, the fierce virgin whose fallen selves peel away from her as she ascends to a heaven of her own invention, shivering all creation with her purified "I am I, I am I." If her body could not sustain such a difficult flight out of "the mausoleum, the wax house" of a literary history that wanted to kill her, her spirit could and did, for she is, after all, resurrected every day as a crucial member of the visionary company who continue to inhabit the twentieth-century poetic tradition we might call "Yeats's house." Because (as her 1981 Pulitzer prize shows) she does victoriously inhabit that house, moreover, her unquiet ghost continues to haunt not just the women readers and writers who look to her words for strength but the male readers and writers who look at her work with mingled admiration and anxiety.

As the most peculiarly privileged of these readers, Ted Hughes, speaking in strikingly Plathian cadences in a poem called "Cadenza," articulates the ambivalence all of them must feel, an ambivalence that may well explain the hostilities of critics like Denis Donoghue, Hugh Kenner, and David Holbrook.

> And I am the cargo
> Of a coffin attended by swallows.
>
> And I am the water
> Bearing the coffin that will not be silent.
>
> The clouds are full of surgery and collisions,
> But the coffin escapes—as a black diamond,
>
> A ruby brimming blood,
> An emerald bearing its shores.[30]

Even when she is dead, says Hughes's poem, this woman poet is irremediably alive: her coffin will not be silent; her voice has changed the field of our hearing forever. Past the "snow blitz," past the gas, past the cries of "Johnny Panic" and his armies of critics cursing the "poisoned chalice" of her poetry and the acclaim of disciples blessing her anguish, her coffin goes on singing its ambiguous messages to us— warning us of the perils of power even as it praises the possibilities of power. Half a century after her birth, we who are Sylvia Plath's contemporaries and descendants must still listen to the questions she hammered out in such great pain: her askings are, in the words of "Words," "Axes, / After whose stroke the wood rings," "indefatigable hooftaps" of a puzzled Pegasus let loose on a new road, prayers that "fixed stars" may not forever govern our lives.

NOTES

In a slightly different form, this essay was first delivered as a keynote address at a conference on Women Writing Poetry in America that was held at Stanford University in April, 1982. I am grateful to the organizers of the conference, especially to Marilyn Yalom and Diane Middlebrook, for advice and encouragement. In addition, I am indebted throughout the paper to the ideas of Susan Gubar. I am grateful also to Ruth Mortimer of the Smith College Rare Book Room for facilitating my work with the collection there. An expanded version of this essay will become a chapter in *No Man's Land: The Place of the Woman Writer in the Twentieth Century*, a sequel to *The Madwoman in the Attic*.

Epigraphs: Sylvia Plath, *Letters Home*, edited by Aurelia Schober Plath (New York: Harper and Row, 1975); W. B. Yeats, *Collected Poems* (New York: Macmillan, 1955); Dorothy Richardson, *The Trap*, in *Pilgrimage*, vol. 2 (New York: Alfred A. Knopf, 1938).

1. Sylvia Plath, *Letters Home*, edited by Aurelia Schober Plath (New York: Harper and Row, 1975), p. 40. Hereafter cited in the text as *LH*.

2. James Woodress, ed., *American Literary Scholarship 1979* (Durham, N.C.: Duke University Press, 1981), p. 221.

3. *New York Times Book Review*, November 22, 1981, pp. 1, 30; David Holbrook, *Sylvia Plath: Poetry and Existence* (London: Athlone Press, 1976), p. 131; Hugh Kenner, "Sincerity Kills," in *Sylvia Plath: New Views on the Poetry*, edited by Gary Lane (Baltimore: Johns Hopkins University Press, 1979), pp. 43, 44, 42; Marjorie Perloff, "Sylvia Plath's 'Sivvy' Poems: a portrait of the poet as daughter," in *Plath: New Views*, p. 173.

4. Gary Lane, "Influence and Originality in Plath's Poems," in *Plath: New Views*; Margaret Dickie Uroff, *Sylvia Plath and Ted Hughes* (Urbana: University of Illinois Press, 1979); Perloff, "'Sivvy' Poems."

5. *The Letters of Elizabeth Barrett Browning*, edited by Frederick G. Kenyon, 2 vols. in 1 (New York: Macmillan, 1899), 1:230–32; Thomas Johnson, ed., *The Complete Poems of Emily Dickinson* (Boston: Little, Brown and Co., 1960), #613.

6. *A Room of One's Own* (New York: Harcourt, Brace and World, 1929), p. 68.

7. *The Death of the Moth* (New York: Harcourt, Brace and Co., 1942), p. 235.

8. *The Colossus* (New York: Vintage Books, 1968), p. 60.

9. Sylvia Plath, *Johnny Panic and the Bible of Dreams: Short Stories, Prose, and Diary Excerpts* (New York: Harper and Row, 1980), p. 21. Hereafter cited in the text as *JP*.

10. *The Journals of Sylvia Plath,* edited by Ted Hughes and Frances Mc-Cullough (New York: Dial Press, 1982), p. 168. Hereafter cited in the text as *J*.

11. Lois Ames, "Notes Toward a Biography," in *The Art of Sylvia Plath,* edited by Charles Newman (Bloomington: Indiana University Press, 1971), p. 166.

12. All in *The Collected Poems* (New York: Harper and Row, 1981).

13. Yeats, "To Dorothy Wellesley," "No Second Troy," "Nineteen Hundred and Nineteen," all in *Collected Poems* (New York: Macmillan, 1955).

14. Richard Ellmann, *James Joyce* (New York: Oxford University Press, 1959), pp. 487, 510.

15. Hemingway, "The Lady Poets with Footnotes," in *88 Poems,* edited by Nicholas Gerogiannis (New York: Harcourt Brace Jovanovich, 1979), p. 77; West, *Miss Lonelyhearts* (New York: New Directions, 1946), p. 14; *The Selected Poems of Ezra Pound* (New York: New Directions, 1957), pp. 16–17.

16. Yeats, "On A Political Prisoner," "In Memory of Eva Gore-Booth and Con Marciewicz," "On Woman," and "A Prayer for My Daughter," all in *Collected Poems* (New York: Alfred A. Knopf, 1938).

17. Katharine M. Rogers, ed., *The Selected Poems of Anne Finch, Countess of Winchilsea* (New York: Frederick Ungar, 1979), p. 82.

18. Ibid., p. 7.

19. Quoted in Aurelia Plath, "Introduction," *Letters Home,* pp. 32–33.

20. *A Room of One's Own,* p. 118.

21. Adrienne Rich, "Power," in *The Dream of a Common Language* (New York: W. W. Norton, 1978), p. 3.

22. *The Complete Short Stories of D. H. Lawrence* (New York: Viking Press, 1961), 2:581.

23. Ibid., p. 569.

24. *The Bell Jar* (New York: Bantam Books, 1972), p. 68. Hereafter cited in the text as *BJ*.

25. Woolf, *A Writer's Diary,* edited by Leonard Woolf (New York: Harcourt, Brace and Co., 1953), pp. 107, 134.

26. Virginia Woolf, *The Waves,* in *Jacob's Room and the Waves* (New York: Harvest Books, 1959), pp. 211–12. Hereafter cited in the text as *Waves*.

27. "Three Women," in *Collected Poems,* p. 180. Hereafter cited in the text as *Women*.

28. *A Writer's Diary,* p. 153.

29. Yeats, "To Dorothy Wellesley," in *Collected Poems,* pp. 301–2.

30. Ted Hughes, *Selected Poems* (New York: Harper and Row, 1972), p. 58.

Sylvia Plath, *The Bell Jar,* and Related Poems

Marilyn Yalom

In the spring and summer of 1961, Sylvia Plath wrote her first and only novel, *The Bell Jar.*[1] Published in 1963 in England, it was destined to become almost immediately a classic in the literature of madness. While she was immersed in *The Bell Jar* and during the preceding months of February and March when the novel was in gestation, Plath wrote nine poems[2]; some of these are among her best, ushering in the new voice that was posthumously recognized as "her later appalling and triumphant fulfillment" in the 1966 publication of *Ariel.*[3] Most of these poems are concerned with sickness and health, breakdown and recovery, death, birth, and rebirth—the core themes of *The Bell Jar.* Although *The Bell Jar* derives its content from Plath's mental breakdown in 1953 and the poems from a series of medical events that began seven years later, both the novel and the poems are rooted in a common psychological subtext underlying the texts that command our attention.

The wounded "I" of the poems—an "invalid" (no. 134), a "nobody" (no. 142), "a half-corpse" (no. 141) haunted by sleepless visions of loss, barrenness, death, and the divided self—is twin sister to the "I" of the novel, exhaling the same medicinal breath. "Face Life" (no. 137), "In Plaster" (no. 141), and "Tulips" (no. 142) take place explicitly in hospital settings, the first inspired, according to Ted Hughes, by "the experience of an acquaintance" and the second and third by Plath's appendectomy[4]; even the poems that are not set in medical wards are studded with images of patienthood.

> The wind stops my breath like a bandage. (no. 134)
>
> . . . the people idle/
> As if in hospital. (no. 135)
>
> The moon lays a hand on my forehead,/
> Blank-faced and mum as a nurse. (no. 139)
>
> Now the pills are worn-out and silly, like classical gods. (no. 144)

The vision of sickness projected into these poems, compounded from Plath's experiences of childbirth, miscarriage, and appendectomy which had occurred between April, 1960, and March, 1961, and *The Bell Jar* description of her 1953 psychotic break, suicide attempt, and prolonged institutionalization have certain psychological similarities. These center around the poles of death anxiety and an obsession with maternity which, as Judith Kroll has demonstrated, formed the literary cornerstones of a personal myth of death and rebirth.[5] What concerns me in this study are the existential dimensions of Plath's fear of death and her obsession with childbirth and babies. Because these concerns are more nakedly evident in *The Bell Jar,* I shall focus predominantly on the novel rather than the poems, in the belief that such an analysis will be illuminating for both.

In examining the psychological studies that have already considered Plath's life and work, I find the writing of certain psychopolitical thinkers in the radical psychiatric camp to be especially valuable. They have focused for the most part on the interplay between "our schizoid civilization" and "the schizoid individual." Following R. D. Laing, they have assumed, like the English psychologist David Holbrook in his perceptive study of Sylvia Plath, that "schizophrenia is the inevitable result" of contemporary society.[6] Holbrook's book recalls the earlier work of A. R. Jones, who, in a short piece on Plath's poem "Daddy," stated that "the tortured mind of the heroine reflects the tortured mind of our age."[7] One of the failings, however, of these psychopolitical writers is that they do not take sufficiently into account the gender-specific strands of mental disease. In the case of Plath, they do not take seriously enough her fundamental bitterness and rage against a life situation in which she found that being female and being fully human were mutually exclusive. This is the core meaning of the statement found in her journals that "Being born a woman is my awful tragedy."[8]

Feminist critics, on the other hand, tend to see in *The Bell Jar* nothing but its gender-charged aspects. They read it as the work of a pre-feminist consciousness at odds with and crushed by a world of masculine malevolence, "a world where"—as Plath averred—"in spite of all the roses and kisses and restaurant dinners a man showered on a woman before he married her, what he secretly wanted when the wedding service ended was to flatten her out underneath his feet like Mrs. Willard's kitchen mat" (p. 69). Such critics as Barbara Hill Rigney[9] and

Phyllis Chesler[10] place the blame for women's mental illness squarely in the male camp with its program designed to dominate and deform the "second sex."[11]

While acknowledging my debt to each of these theoretical schools and especially to recent feminist scholarship, this study is equally rooted in other sources. It draws its insights from psychoanalytic and existential theoreticians, who are not always in agreement with each other. Its basic assumption is that the experience of madness, for women as well as for men, emanates from a confrontation with the brute existential facts of life— from such givens of the human condition as freedom, isolation, aging, and, most significantly, death. But at the same time, it attempts to demonstrate that the *forms* of madness women undergo have specifically female parameters.

Thus, in *The Bell Jar,* it is necessary to consider the existential dimensions of the author-heroine's experiences: the protracted and early death of her father that flooded her with lifelong anxiety; the rite of passage into adulthood necessitating choice and forcing the discovery of her own aging process; and the escape into madness as a reaction to intolerable internal and external stress. But it is also necessary to recognize female specificity in the recurrent images of dead babies, jarred fetuses, and other forms of aborted maternity that spring from a female consciousness shaped by the biological, cultural, political, and psychological forces germane to women.

To illustrate the first—the broadly human and deeply existential substructure of *The Bell Jar*—let us examine the parable of the fig tree offered early in the book as a condensed representation of the narrator's sense of being in the world. In the parable, each fig on the tree represents a different possibility for self-realization, both in the private domain mediated through husband, children, and lovers, and in the public world where she might become a professor, editor, or world traveler. The vivid fig tree, with each fig offering a life choice, is grafted upon other legendary biblical trees—the tree of life, the tree of knowledge, the tree of Jesse. The tragic irony of Plath's vision is that she conjures up a twentieth-century nightmare, a Kafkaesque paralysis of starving to death before, indeed within, the tree of life.

I saw my life branching out before me like the green fig tree in the story.

From the tip of every branch, like a fat purple fig, a wonderful

future beckoned and winked. One fig was a husband and a happy
home and children, and another fig was a famous poet and another
fig was a brilliant professor, and another fig was Ee Gee, the amaz-
ing editor, and another fig was Europe and Africa and South
America, and another fig was Constantin and Socrates and Attila
and a pack of other lovers with queer names and offbeat profes-
sions, and another fig was an Olympic lady crew champion, and
beyond and above these figs were many more figs I couldn't quite
make out.

I saw myself sitting in the crotch of this fig tree, starving to
death, just because I couldn't make up my mind which of the figs I
would choose. I wanted each and every one of them, but choosing
one meant losing all the rest, and, as I sat there, unable to decide,
the figs began to wrinkle and go black, and, one by one, they
plopped to the ground at my feet. (pp. 62–63)

The figs initially described as "fat" and "purple" are traditional
symbols of female fecundity. Esther is not only within reach of these
figs—she is sitting *in* the tree, in its "crotch." Both "crotch" and
"fig," though ostensibly attributes of the tree, are even more sug-
gestive of the person within the tree, and specifically of the female
organ, denoting generative powers that wither and die for want of
being exercised.

Lest we have any doubts about the meaning of the parable, the
author provides a textual interpretation: Esther is depicted as "starving
to death" because she can't make up her mind which of the figs she
should choose. "I wanted each and every one of them, but choosing
one meant losing all the rest. . . ."

Never was the existential dilemma of choice presented more graphi-
cally, nor the neurotic personality's inability to choose and thus to live.
The reasons for this inability are also clearly stated: any choice implies the
exclusion of another choice. Choosing means that certain possibilities will
be closed off forever: it brings us closer to an awareness of death, which
Heidegger defined as the "impossibility of further possibility." It means
moving inexorably with the stream of life, and inevitably toward one's
end. Refusing to choose is a way of freezing time, of keeping alive the
illusion of the availability of all possibilities.

Why is the narrator so fearful of choice? Why is she so terrified of

growing toward death that anything, even madness, is preferable? A
hint of the source of terror is offered a few pages before the parable of
the fig tree. There the narrator refers back to the death of her father
when she was about nine years old. She tells us that she was only
"purely happy" before she was nine and that she "had never been really
happy again" (pp. 60–61). She recognizes that this key loss in child-
hood (drawn from the author's personal history like almost everything
else in the book) is somehow linked to the crisis of identity and late
adolescent psychosis experienced in her twentieth year.

Several of Plath's poems written between February, 1961, and her
suicide two years later perseverate around these two tragedies of child-
hood and early adulthood. In "Face Lift," an early, less aesthetically
successful version of "Lady Lazarus" (no. 198), the "I" of the poem
recalls her ninth and twentieth years as landmarks in a personal history
of sickness and renewal.

> When I was nine, a lime-green anesthetist
> Fed me banana gas through a frog mask. The nauseous vault
> Boomed with bad dreams and the Jovian voices of surgeons.
> Then mother swam up, holding a tin basin.
> O I was sick.
> ....
>   . . . I'm twenty,
> Broody and in long skirts on my first husband's sofa, my fingers
> Buried in the lambswool of the dead poodle; (no. 137)

In both references Plath departs from the facts of life, allowing the poet
imaginative liberties which the novelist does not enjoy. The nine-year-
old's experience of sickness (this time her own, rather than her father's)
reads like a surrealist dream of underwater creatures, and the poet at
twenty has acquired an imaginary first husband. Perhaps the words
"Broody" and "first husband's sofa" (a transformation of "first psychi-
atrist's sofa?") recall her psychotic break at twenty, but only for the
reader familiar with biographical information external to the poem. The
closest connection to *The Bell Jar,* both linguistically and connotatively,
is found in lines that suggest the death of the old self discarded in the
aftermath of a face lift or successful psychotherapy: "they've trapped
her in some laboratory jar. / Let her die there. . . . "

In "Daddy" (no. 183) the poet refers again to the crucial ninth and twentieth years, although nine is now changed to ten in order to achieve a more symmetrical structure of cyclical rebirth every decade.

> I was ten when they buried you.
> At twenty I tried to die
> And get back, back, back to you.

Written in the wake of her separation from Ted Hughes in October, 1962, which reactivated Plath's sense of abandonment and unleashed the full tide of her negative feelings toward the male imago, "Daddy" gives us access to some of the powerful emotions she harbored toward her long-dead father. Here Plath's persona views her earlier suicide attempt as a desire for union with the father, and her ill-fated marriage to the poet Ted Hughes as a later endeavor to replace the lost father figure with a husband made in his image. Freudian thought, which had penetrated all levels of American culture in the fifties and sixties, had given Plath a theoretical framework by which she was able to comprehend her father's lasting importance in her psychic life. As early as 1958 when she was in therapy in Boston with Dr. Ruth Beuscher, she had begun to try to untangle the web of turbulent emotions she experienced for one parent who had "deserted" her at an intolerably early age and the other—the mother—whom she irrationally blamed for her father's death.[12] Her reading of Freud's *Mourning and Melancholia* led her to entertain the thesis that her "reasons for suicide" were rooted in a "murderous impulse" transferred from her mother onto herself. Today one is inclined to wonder to what extent the fifties mother-as-scapegoat school of thought, epitomized by Lidz's "schizophrenogenic mother," colored Plath's psychotherapy with Dr. Beuscher and her subsequent portrayal of family psychodynamics in *The Bell Jar*.[13]

In the novel Plath bracketed out her negative feelings for her father; she remembers him only with the nonjudgmental love of a small child, forgetting the morbid tyranny of his long illness, suppressing the rage that found release in her late poetry, and reconstituting her past so as to create an idealized picture of daughterly solicitude.

Without entering into traditional psychoanalytic theories about the father-daughter relationship (which Lynda K. Bundtzen does, pertinently, in *Plath's Incarnations*[14]), I wish to suggest a somewhat different line of approach—that the death of a parent of either sex, especially when the child is at an early age, is a traumatic event of massive proportions. As the psychiatrist Irvin Yalom has written, "The loss of a parent brings us in touch with our own vulnerability; if our parents could not save themselves, who will save us?"[15] Unlike Freudian theory, which translates death anxiety into the fear of abandonment by a parental figure, existential theory posits that the fear of one's own death is a primal source of anxiety. The recognition of the finitude of life, difficult enough to assimilate when one is an adult, may prove intolerable when confronted prematurely. Thus the child's loss of a parent leads to intimations of its own mortality, generating a fund of anxiety that may be crucial in the shaping of character structure. Despite the fact that death anxiety goes underground—i.e., that it is repressed and remains subterranean in one's later years—the child's dread of death, especially if one has been exposed to it too early and too intimately as in the case of Plath, continues to produce internal stress throughout one's life. When combined with the external stress of a major life transition, such as Plath experienced on the brink of adulthood, the two forces were of such intensity as to render her helpless, out of control, and ultimately mad.

Why, we may ask, should a life transition involving choice and decision, such as most human beings experience on the threshold of adulthood, evoke in Plath's case such debilitating anxiety? The insights offered in the parable of the fig tree and in Irvin Yalom's analysis support each other and offer a reasonable explanation. "Individuals in their late teens and early twenties are often acutely anxious about death."[16] Faced with irreversible decisions, they become anxious, paralyzed, even psychotic precisely because these decisions exclude other possibilities. Thus passage into adulthood, necessitating momentous decisions concerning one's professional and personal life, may simultaneously unleash unconscious fears of growth toward death; if these fears come to dominate an individual's psychic life, they may precipitate what appears to be wholly irrational behavior.

The Bell Jar tells the story of a young woman facing the rite of passage into adulthood signified by the last year of college. Outwardly, she has all the conventional earmarks of an individual destined for success—an outstanding college record, contact in the world of fashion writing, even a conventional boyfriend. Inwardly, however, she is terrified of the future and of any decision that implies growth toward maturity and the autonomy of becoming one's own parent. One way of avoiding growth is to become imprisoned in neurotic indecision. This is what the narrator suspects when she tells Buddy Willard that she wants to live both in the country and in the city. She states explicitly,

> I *am* neurotic. I could never settle down in either the country *or* the city. . . . If neurotic is wanting two mutually exclusive things at one and the same time, then I'm neurotic as hell. I'll be flying back and forth between one mutually exclusive thing and another for the rest of my days. (P. 76)

A feminist interpretation of this passage reminds us of the mutually exclusive demands of marriage and career, and of the double bind experienced by women today caught between a "feminine" and a "feminist" mystique.[17] Like many of us, Plath's autobiographical heroine was caught in the squeeze between societal expectations that she herself had incorporated and attempts at self-determination that would have allowed a more authentic self to emerge. If we ask ourselves whether Plath/Greenwood would have been "saved" had she been born a generation later and come to maturity in a more favorable climate for women, what can we answer? I am inclined to believe that her life would have been easier, that she would have felt less alone, but I am hard put to convince myself that she would have avoided the experience of madness after her junior year of college. By the time the author/narrator of *The Bell Jar* had reached her twentieth year, her inner anguish before death and fear of life bore little resemblance to the cheerful façade she presented to the outside world. The outside world, feminist or otherwise, would probably have been at a loss to comprehend, much less alter, the self-destructive forces at play in the process of her psychotic break.

Yet it is because feminist concerns have sharpened our perception of female specificity that we now recognize the gendered expression of Plath's disequilibrium; both the poems and the novel attest to uniquely female forms of apprehension. Let us consider first the author/narrator's phobic attitude toward motherhood and babies, and then her suicide attempt from the perspective of paternal and maternal figures.

Plath's obsession with childbirth and babies is apparent in a substantial portion of her poetry, and she was never more preoccupied with the theme of maternity than during the composition of *The Bell Jar*. "Parliament Hill Fields" (no. 134) presents the musings of a mother who, like Plath, has had a miscarriage and who comforts herself with the thought of her live baby at home. "Morning Song" (no. 138), the least ambivalent of Plath's "mother poems," celebrates the birth of her daughter Frieda born a year earlier (April, 1960). "Barren Women" (no. 139) and "Heavy Women" (no. 140) are companion pieces, the first an elegy on female sterility ("Empty, I echo to the least footfall") the second an ironic eulogy of female fecundity ("Irrefutable, beautifully smug / As Venus, pedestaled on a half-shell").

The following year (March, 1962) produced "Three Women" (no. 157), a long verse drama set in a maternity ward. In it, three female voices articulate the varied emotions inspired by the experiences of pregnancy, childbirth, and motherhood; miscarriage, stillbirth, and the death of a child. The first voice conveys the archetypal earth-mother's ripeness and sense of fulfillment in cadenced lines reflecting the easy rhythms of nature.

> I do not have to think, or even rehearse.
> What happens in me will happen without attention.

A second voice conveys the fears of a woman who has miscarried.

> When I first saw it, the small red seep, I did not believe it.

A third voice conveys the ambivalence of a woman who has conceived against her will.

> I should have murdered this, that murders me.

Together the three women sing out the poet's repertoire of maternal notes with the strains of anxiety predominating. Yet if there is little unambivalent joy in the lot of woman as genetrix, there is open disdain for the "flatness" of men who would go mad if they were forced to endure the mother's bodily knowledge of miscarriage ("O so much emptiness"), of parturition ("I am breaking apart like the world"), and the awesome fruits of the womb—the "furious boy," "terrible girl," "these miraculous ones."

With the exception of "Morning Song," Plath's poetry of joy-bringing babies is, for the most part, unimaginative, even banal: "pink and smooth" (no. 137), "pink and perfect" (no. 157), "pink-buttocked infants" (no. 140). But when she translates her private death-ridden nightmares into images of aborted maternity, deformity, and non-human creatures, the results are both original and terrifying. Her range of dead and unnatural babies extends from the "square baby" (no. 177) to the "Dwarf baby" (no. 181) to the "Hothouse baby" (no. 188) to the "babies . . . in their hospital/Icebox" (no. 205). In a poem entitled "Stillborn" (no. 124) written a year before *The Bell Jar,* Plath compares her poems to stillborn babies. The mother's surprised voice makes the diagnosis and spells out the poetic conceit in ironic images of lower-order creatures.

> O I cannot understand what happened to them!
> They are proper in shape and number and every part.
> They sit so nicely in the pickling fluid!
> . . . .
> They are not pigs, they are not even fish,
> Though they have a piggy and a fishy air—

The poet-mother's authentic, nonironic despair at her lifeless baby-poems is communicated in the penultimate line: " . . . they are dead, and their mother near dead with distraction."

In another poem from the same year, the poet's persona, a distraught hospital inmate who "appears to have suffered a sort of private blitzkrieg," is herself compared to "a foetus in a bottle." Both poems, "Stillborn" and "A Life" (no. 132), prefigure the foetus-jar leitmotif of the novel.

In *The Bell Jar* the narrator's obsessive maternal fears can hardly go unnoticed. Esther is haunted by visions of babies in various stages of existence: "bald babies, chocolate-colored babies, Eisenhower-faced babies" (p. 181), "big glass bottles full of babies that had died before they were born" (p. 51), babies in the process of coming into the world, cadaverous babies strung throughout her consciousness like a dance of death. It is important to recognize that although Esther's obsessions may spring from personal pathology, they lead to visionary insight. With foresight into the feminist politics of a later generation, the narrator understood that marriage and children constitute for some women, like herself, the ultimate entrapment. Thus we must understand Esther's obsessive maternal fears both as a symptom of mental illness and as a reasonable reaction to the genuine threat that motherhood entails for creative women.

Initially the narrator's attitude toward motherhood is simply sarcastic. Women who embrace maternity are depicted as dupes of male treachery, unaware of what they have abandoned in the process. Esther is acutely aware of the danger that motherhood presents to her creative self. Her boyfriend's naive comment that after she became a mother, she "wouldn't want to write poems anymore" leads her to reflect that having children "was like being brainwashed, and afterward you went about numb as a slave in some private, totalitarian state" (p. 69).

A living example of maternal mindlessness is found in the figure of Dodo Conway, the mother of six, on the verge of a seventh, who parades her baby carriage up and down the street before Esther's home. Esther's reactions to Dodo are highly revealing.

> Dodo interested me in spite of myself.
> . . . .
> I watched Dodo wheel the youngest Conway up and down.
> She seemed to be doing it for my benefit.
> Children make me sick.
> (Pp. 95–96)

On the one hand, Dodo incarnates the bovine immanence of woman as flesh, acquiescing to the dictum that biology is destiny. On the other hand, Esther confesses to being "interested" in her and believes, at some irrational level, that Dodo's activities are carried out for her express benefit. Such an idea of reference suggests that Dodo is one of the many doubles for the protagonist; she represents a split-off maternal self, publicly repudiated yet unsuccessfully repressed. Esther feels compelled to duck down below the window of her room, in the abject position of a crouching animal, so as to escape Dodo's accusatory gaze.

From a feminist perspective, Dodo embodies those patriarchal values with which most women collude in becoming mothers. Esther, alone in her determination not to become brainwashed like her female contemporaries, is nonetheless not above feeling their reproach and a sense of ostracism from the fold. Certainly this sense of being different, even if the difference is consciously assumed, contributes to Esther's increasing state of alienation.

Her withdrawal from the world around her is summed up in the image of the bell jar—an image of being cut off from the rest of the world, shielded from outside stress but also imprisoned within her own "sour air." The bell jar is, however, not only a metaphor for isolation and psychosis; it is closely associated with the earlier images of dead babies in glass jars—and hence linked to the heroine's infantophobia. A convergence of these two images—that of the bell jar and that of the dead baby—produces one of the most telling expressions of the narrator's anguish: "To the person in the bell jar, blank and stopped as a dead baby, the world itself is the bad dream" (p. 193). Here the narrator is no longer an outsider observing someone else's baby; she *is* the dead baby. She conjures up the dead baby as her personal emblem because she fears that she too is a still-birth, "stopped," not yet fully born. The revulsion she has felt at babies in bottles and babies in prams and babies with or without teeth is in part the revulsion she feels toward herself; maternity presents the most fearful of all threats, not only because of the societal implications it has for all women, but because the author at her profoundest level of being fears she has not yet given birth to herself. How then can she give birth to another?

While having babies is a "normal," "healthy" activity for many women despite the problematic nature of motherhood as an institution, it is certainly not questionable to assume that annihilating oneself is an abnormal, unhealthy act. The narrator's attempted suicide can be seen only as flight from life, an unequivocal rejection of one's person and potential progeny. Here too gender issues are salient in the psychodynamics of her near-fatal act.

Just before Esther determines to take her life she makes a visit to her father's grave—a grave she had never before seen. In a touching gesture of rapprochement with the dead father, she bemoans the tragedy of a parent's death and the cruel indifference of the universe. "I laid my face to the smooth face of the marble and howled my loss into the cold salt rain" (p. 137).

Immediately following this scene Esther almost kills herself. Up to this point the reader has been made to feel that she was only toying with the idea of suicide. But immediately after the graveyard scene, without any transitional passage, she says "I knew just how to go about it" (p. 137). What is left unsaid is the connection between the embrace of her dead father and the ability to take her own life. Clearly the encounter with father triggers her will toward death, but we can only speculate why. Did the suicide attempt issue from a macabre desire for union with the father, a desire that Plath herself described as the longing of "a girl with an Electra complex?"[18] Was it, as Holbrook contends, the logical consequence of a regressed ego craving a return to the original stasis of non-being?[19] Was it, as Judith Kroll has argued, a quasi-volitional act in a personal mythology of death and rebirth?[20] I should like to suggest yet another possibility. The rediscovery of her father's death may have forced upon Esther the stark discovery of her own mortality. Paradoxically, one way of denying the absolute reality of death is by taking control of it—i.e., by killing yourself before death kills you. Esther is so afraid of death that she plans to kill herself in a "calm, orderly way," thereby gaining an illusion of control. She describes the meticulous steps that led from her mother's strongbox containing a bottle of fifty sleeping pills to the cellar crevice into which she squeezed her body and where she carefully swallowed, one by one, the lethal pills. For our purpose it is important to recognize that while the reasons for her suicide will always be open to speculation, the *form* of the attempt was specific and has its own meaning. To choose to die by ingesting sleeping pills is, among other things, a form of suicide statistically more prevalent among women than among men. The form itself implies less active physical violence than, for example, shooting oneself—a more prevalent form among men, as the narrator herself noted (p. 127).

This specifically female cast of her suicide is true not only of her inner space invaded by deadly drugs but also of the outer space in which Plath/Greenwood chose to situate her body. She squeezed into an "earth-bottomed crevice" in her mother's basement, "crouched at the mouth of the darkness, like a troll," and on her "knees, with bent head, crawled to the farthest wall" (p. 138).

The symbolic return to the maternal matrix becomes at the same time the conduit to a second birth. The breakthrough from complete darkness, through the "black water" and "tunnel" into the slit of light that "opened, like a mouth or a wound" and finally into full light is a masterpiece of double entendre, presenting at once a realistic description of being removed from a dark enclosure and a metaphoric description of childbirth. If we have any doubts as to the second level of meaning, they are dispersed by the words with which the passage ends: ". . . through the thick, warm, furry dark, a voice cried, 'Mother!'" (p. 139).

One of the little-noticed ironies of *The Bell Jar* is that it is the mother-daughter bond which represents the life force and the father-daughter bond that represents the death force—ironic because mother is the target of such venomous satire and father the recipient of daughterly nostalgia. Unlike the father who died when Esther was a child and persisted unchanged in the temple of the heart, mother became subject to adult criticism. She is filtered through the eyes of a highly judgmental daughter who does not spare her mother, just as she does not spare herself. This difference in overt attitude between mother and father may lead us astray in perceiving the underlying psychodynamics: we should not forget that the graveyard encounter with father acts as a catalyst for suicide, whereas the link with mother saves the narrator from total self-destruction. Unconsciously Esther craves life as much as death and places herself in a womblike setting where the mother's generative powers have the possibility of being effective a second time.

The Bell Jar and related poems offer insights into human pathology in general and female pathology in particular. They teach us that Plath, like all human beings, was sensitive to parental loss, the stresses of young adulthood, the burden of choice, and the idea of her own mortality. In Plath's case, these existential concerns were exacerbated by the early death of her father, producing a lifelong psychic fissure. The mother, who tried to be both mother and father, "a man and woman in one sweet ulcerous ball,"[21] succeeded in bringing her daughter back to life from her first suicide attempt; but in spite of, and, ironically, perhaps because of, her symbiotic devotion to Sylvia, she too undoubtedly contributed to her daughter's vulnerability. [See following essay by Mossberg.—Ed.]

Existential factors and parental influences were, in this reader's view, primary in Plath's mental fragility. Yet gender issues were by no means insignificant. In addition to the common anxieties that all human beings are heir to, Plath carried the specifically female burdens of maternity and motherhood. Her obsession with stunted forms of life reflects both her fundamental self-image and the fears of countless women whose sense of self is intertwined with the awesome challenge of producing and sustaining human life.

NOTES

1. Sylvia Plath, *The Bell Jar* (London: Faber and Faber, 1963; New York: Harper and Row, 1971; New York: Bantam Books, 1971). All page references are to the Bantam paperback edition.

2. These include "Parliament Hill Fields," "Whitsun," "Zoo Keeper's Wife," "Heavy Woman," "In Plaster," "Tulips," "I am Vertical," "Insomnia," and "Widow." Each poem will be identified according to its number in *The Collected Poems of Sylvia Plath,* edited by Ted Hughes (New York: Harper and Row, 1981).

3. Sylvia Plath, *Ariel* (New York: Harper and Row, 1966), Foreword by Robert Lowell, p. ix. "Morning Song," "Tulips," and "The Rival" appeared in *Ariel.*

4. Plath, *Collected Poems,* p. 291.

5. Judith Kroll, *Chapters in a Mythology: The Poetry of Sylvia Plath* (New York: Harper and Row, 1976).

6. David Holbrook, *Sylvia Plath: Poetry and Existence* (London: Athlone Press, 1976).

7. A. R. Jones, "On 'Daddy,' " in *The Art of Sylvia Plath: A Symposium,* edited by Charles Newman (Bloomington and London: Indiana University Press, 1970), p. 236.

8. *The Journals of Sylvia Plath* (New York: Dial Press, 1982), p. 30.

9. *Madness and Sexual Politics in the Feminist Novel* (Madison: University of Wisconsin Press, 1978).

10. *Women and Madness* (New York: Doubleday and Co., 1972).

11. Surely no work has been more influential for those of us who grapple with feminist concerns than Simone de Beauvoir, *Le deuxième Sexe,* vols. 1 and 2 (Paris: Gallimard, 1949).

12. Plath, *Journals,* p. 280.

13. For a discussion of psychiatric theories that scapegoat the mother, see David Spiegel, "Mothering, Fathering, and Mental Illness" in *Rethinking the Family: Some Feminist Questions,* edited by Barrie Thorne and Marilyn Yalom (New York: Longman, 1982), pp. 95–110.

14. Lynda K. Bundtzen, *Plath's Incarnations: Woman and the Creative Process* (Ann Arbor: University of Michigan Press, 1983).

15. Irvin D. Yalom, *Existential Psychotherapy* (New York: Basic Books, 1980), p. 168.

16. Ibid., p. 171.

17. See Linda Gray Sexton, *Between Two Worlds: Young Women in Crisis* (New York: William Morrow and Co., 1979).

18. A. Alvarez, "Sylvia Plath," in *The Art of Sylvia Plath,* p. 65.

19. Holbrook, *Sylvia Plath: Poetry and Existence.*

20. Kroll, *Chapters in a Mythology.*

21. Plath, *Journals,* p. 267.

Sylvia Plath's Baby Book

Barbara Antonina Clarke Mossberg

The predictable result of Sylvia Plath's "Ottomania" in her writing is that her father Otto is seen as the archetype of her muse, understood as the "Colossus," in such recent studies as Mary Lynn Broe's *Protean Poetic* (1980) and Margaret Dickie Uroff's *Sylvia Plath and Ted Hughes* (1979). Does Plath not say she wants to get "back, back, back to you"—to an audience of one "Daddy"? Yet while Plath addresses her father here, there is evidence that in her creative life it is her *mother* she is trying to get "back, back, back" to—get back to, and get back *at*.

Among Sylvia Plath's papers sold to the Lilly Library in Bloomington, Indiana, in a box next to her paper doll collection, is the baby book kept by Sylvia Plath's mother, along with unpublished, unedited first mother-daughter letters and Plath's earliest writing. What we see in this "precosia" is how early Plath's voice began, and in such earnest—that it ripened still green. At eight, Plath was disciplined, self-conscious, and professional about her writing, concerned with publication; at sixteen, she already feels possessed, driven by her muse: "You ask me why I spend my life writing?" "I write only because / There is a voice within me / That will not be still." It is in the effort to identify the origin of this insatiable tyrant muse that the "precosia" at the Lilly may be most useful, particularly in helping to establish the role that Plath's mother may have played in Plath's literary development, in what I call her "baby talk."

I am not referring to her talk about babies, or her literal talk as a baby, as recorded in the baby book; nor am I suggesting an infantile quality to her voice as a poet. But I am suggesting an infantile *use* of her voice: that the why as well as the how of her prodigious, prodigal use of language is tied inextricably to her relationship with her mother and the psychological matrix in which she first acquired and began to practice language skills. The Lilly "precosia" provides evidence that Plath's experience as a child in which she first conceived the importance of her ability to use language was aesthetically as well as emotionally so crucial for her that she could not walk on two legs as a *poet* (to use the Sphinx's definition of adulthood) without fearing abandonment and rejection by her muse. There is a certain significance in the fact that Plath's voice never gets gray, a function not of early death, but of Plath's aesthetics, in which she felt it was "four legs" or nothing, if she wanted to write. The Lilly materials enable us to trace the development of her compulsion to produce words for a "voice which will not be still," what I will argue is essentially a "mummy" muse, and aesthetics which require walking on "four legs" in a perpetual morning of the creative psyche.

At first glance the baby book, where Plath's "voice" is first heard, seems rather difficult to evaluate, information which can have significance only to a mother, more a portrait of a mother than a child, an exercise in conscientiousness, and even more, I think, an attempt to grasp or make real something ineffable, elusive: another being's growth. Notations of weight and height at various weeks and months seem more a code for incredulity, or pride. Instead of a philosophical treatise on life's self-sufficiency out of the womb, there is "grew two inches" or simply "33 inches" and a date. Baby books may well be an undiscovered genre of women's writing, relatively conflict-free, circumscribed, ghost-writing and autobiography of a life within and without, possessed and unpossessed. How it reveals a mode of maternal sensibility becomes an issue when the baby later writes poetry about maternity, especially when we keep in mind that being a good—nay, great— mother was crucial to Aurelia's identity. She cut short her own career in English to become "totally imbued with the desire to be a good wife and mother." Sylvia as first child was the recipient of redirected full-time energy, conscience, and aspirations.

Therefore this baby book is literally her "production." Aurelia titled it "The Record of Sylvia Plath by her 'mummy,'" and wrote "Sivvy" on the side, symbolically establishing both their identities (Mummy-Sivvy) and her role in this relationship of subserving herself to the historically important Sylvia Plath, a creature of her own making. She is the "author" of child and book, and thus of Plath's first syllables, words, and expressions which she records—as well as her first habits, concerns, ideas, and modes of behavior. Plath "speaks" here through her mother, in her mother's voice, comes alive as a personality in her mother's words—"grows" in the pages.

The baby book contains clippings ("Professor Becomes Father," says one), a picture of Plath at 11-1/2 months holding a doll, birth data, who sent what gifts, who sent flowers, teething facts, her height and weight at various months and years, her first shoes (bought at Filene's, size 4, the "Five-toe Moccasin")—and Plath's response ("Don't like them! They taste horrid and I can't shake them off!"). The book is part memorabilia, part perfunctory entries, and part a literary autobiography where Mrs. Plath self-consciously invents, creates history in the telling. Under "Baby's First Birthday," she provides a setting in the form of a dialectic between interior and exterior experience, the warm, women-made creative, controlled scene, and the irrelevant outside world: "Outdoors—warm & cloudy/ Indoors—Bright & festive." The narrative follows.

> The tiny cake with gleaming candle was made by her loving "grammy." As it was a sponge cake and unfrosted, Sylvia had a taste of a dried piece of it next day. Auntie Dot sent a beautiful dress, pink and white baptiste, hand-embroidered, with tiny puff-sleeves. Miss Cocoran came, bringing a china porridge dish, mug, and sectioned plate.

After telling who came and who sent greeting cards, she writes,

> It is hard to realize that my baby is so rapidly emerging from her state of precious babyhood! She looks *so* grown-up in the knitted suit which I recently bought her!
> Well, her daddy and I agree that the whole world doesn't hold another one-year-old so wonderful—and so sweet!—at least, it doesn't for us!
> We wanted Sylvia to "poof" her candle, but she eagerly reached toward the flame, becoming vocally indignant when not allowed to grasp it!

In other words, this is not just an objective account, but an attempt to impose on the occasion a certain value for posterity; of course, this is partially a function of audience confusion in keeping such a book. Is it to account, or to justify, or to create nostalgia? And for whom? Herself? the family? an adult Sylvia? "the record?" And why?—questions we must ask when we read such a book, I think, keeping in mind that we usually assume *our* scrapbook is not going to be perused later by scholars (or do we assume our progeny, and hence our role as "author," will become famous?). Aurelia's "book" is very self-conscious, aware of a later judging or approving eye. What makes her qualify her innocent and natural enthusiasm in thinking Plath the world's most wonderful baby? This seems overly fastidious in such a context.

In any case, Sylvia is glimpsed through observant, scrupulous, fond eyes: at eight months squealing with glee and hopping up and down when someone goes "bye-bye," noticing "everything," and "best of all to her little mind, other babies. She wants to touch other babies, and stretches out her arms to them, shouting with excitement." But these eyes are most concerned with language.

At the age of six weeks Sylvia imitated vowel sounds—ah, oo, au; at the age of eight weeks she repeated "ga" and also said "a-goo." She coo-d frequently and enjoyed doing it. Six months—said "Gully, gully" whenever bottle was offered him [*sic??*] I tho't it was a imitation of "goody-goody" which I always said when giving the bottle to her. Eight months: mama, dada, bye-bye, tick-tick . . . .

Sept. 1 Ragman passed calling "Rags" and Sylvia called "Ags!"

Oct. 1 "Aw-gaw" (all gone! means, bottle is empty.)

. . . Sounds are made for the dog, the duck, the cow, horse, wind, *sheep;* she says "car" whenever she hears an auto pass. She has been making replies to such queries as: What does the sheep say?— "Ba," etc. for 2 months.

Aurelia added a category, "Baby's Sayings and Antics," about idiosyncrasies of her developing vocabulary.

When placed on the pottie, she immediately calls out—"Aw-done! Aw-done!" (She fibs already!)

Sylvia has misunderstood the word "dry." I once praised her when taking off her didies and said, "good Sylvia, you are all dry." It has become her announcement of a damp event. She will call out anxiously, "Aw-dwy, Aw-dwy!" and a second later a tell-tale circle of dampness shows at the seat of her pants.

Sylvia will point to her eyes, nose, mouth, ears and hair when asked. She says "eye" very plainly, and learned about it when poking in the eye of a dead fish./ She gets excited about plants and

flowers and wants to smell them immediately. [She tries to eat seed
pods.]

If Sylvia wants attention, she announces "ga-ga" (which means
'nasty' & 'forbidden'). She may then go determinedly to the fire-
place and lick the bricks with her tongue, or pop some microscopic
speck of thread or dust into her mouth. It is done in good humor,
and the rush for the "ga-ga" on the part of either parent is met by
giggles from Sylvia. Her end is then achieved!

When she is just three, she comforts her mother over her abcessed
breasts: "You're a good mummy, you are! You know what I'm going
to give you? Two new breasts—without holes in them!" She is pre-
cocious both in language and filial sensibility: they are revealed to be
the same thing.

There are detailed records of her diet, health, toys, first Christmas
(as the center of attention), and playmates, "big boys." When we re-
construct her biography, names of family friends may be invaluable;
and when we study her later themes, it may be interesting to know
how she teased or feigned endangering herself to provoke concern and
notice, or her reported initial fascination for babies, or older boys, or
her liking to be the center of attention (or her mother's liking her to
be), and there are juicy tidbits for psychologists (when she hears loud
noises she says "Daddy"). What we learn from this record primarily is
Aurelia Plath's consciousness, pride, and concern in watching her first
child develop. References to Warren are added in the margins.

From the beginning Aurelia sets out to nurture Sylvia's artistic and
intellectual potential. As both have proclaimed, it was Aurelia's own
intense interest in—and perhaps frustration about her ability to pur-
sue—literature that stimulated Plath. Sublimating her own ambitions,
Aurelia derived vicarious satisfaction from her daughter's development,
a mother and daughter team effort: Sylvia's social life Aurelia would
"taste . . . as if it had been my own"; when Plath miscarried, she
promised to produce her mother another baby; when she wanted to
commit suicide, she cried, "let's die together!"; when there was news
of a grant, she announced, "we're applying." In retrospect, Plath at-
tributes her literary awakening to her mother, dates her incentive to
write poetry (in "OCEAN W-1212") back to her childhood, explicitly
connecting her poetry and her relationship with her mother, as a baby,

and over a baby. It was literary Aurelia's reading aloud Mathew Ar-
nold's "The Forsaken Mermaid" that gave Plath a "new way of being
happy" for what language could do. And it was maternal Aurelia's hav-
ing her second child that gave Plath a sense of estrangement from her
mother's previously undivided love. In the former case, "I wanted to
cry; I felt very odd." In the latter, "I hated babies. I who for two and a
half years had been the center of a tender universe felt the axis wrench."
This birth, she says as an adult looking backward, as a *mother* of babies,
is the trauma of her life. Of course Plath inflates natural sibling rivalry
into a melodramatic catastrophe for humorous, self-mocking effect, but
it is important to remember that her own sense of her literary develop-
ment is tied to an event, *the* event, which separated her from her mater-
nal matrix, and that she dwells on this birth, as well as her father's
death, for what went wrong—or right—in her life. And her accom-
panying sudden feeling of "otherness," being "separate," became a life-
long preoccupation and major characteristic of her creative psyche. Syl-
via Plath's work is strewn with baby iconography, the fallout of an
acute ambivalence to maternity: dead fetuses floating in formaldehyde
limbo, snail-nosed babies, bald babies, crying babies; baby "crap"; the
general baby her narrator loathes and fears; the specific baby brother
whose birth traumatizes her. Even Plath's metaphor for mental torture,
the bell jar, is a variation of the fetus in the jar, the unborn baby in the
womb. (We remember she wrote this when she had a baby of her
own.) Her wounded self is addressed as "O my homunculus"; she is
her own baby, "mother to myself." Her poems are still-born babies.
Leaf through *Ariel* or *Crossing the Water*—hardly a poem goes by with-
out a baby's image.

Plath's adult essay shows that she thinks her poetry derives from
her sense of maternal rejection and alienation, and Aurelia's accounts
support this. When her baby brother nursed, Sylvia "wanted to get
into my lap," a jealousy Aurelia defused by having Sylvia play at her
feet with a newspaper to learn the alphabet. Thus words initially served
quite literally as a substitute for what the child then perceived and the
adult still remembers as lost maternal nurture. Plath's precocious lan-
guage abilities (she could read at two) are developed specifically within
the context of her desire for maternal nurture, and maternal encourage-
ment to use them.

Plath was aware of being more than conscientiously mothered; of
being nurtured on maternal self-sacrifice, devotion, and ambition. Au-

relia's efforts and desire to stimulate her daughter's literary promise are
quite clear in the early mother-daughter correspondence, which shows
the origin of Plath's sense of the imperative of her ability to speak, to
write, and to create. Aurelia writes that she found it easier for "mother
and daughter" to communicate their love with the written word rather
than orally—a statement with crucial bearing, I think, on understand-
ing the significance of the role Plath adopted for herself as the poet, and
the early age at which she did so. Plath first received a letter from her
mother when she was six, at her grandmother's because her brother
was ill and her mother was nursing him.

Dear Sylvia,
   I am going to write you a poem I read when I was a little girl. It
tells about another girl who loves her doll, whom she has named
Rebecca. This is the poem:

> I have a doll, Rebecca,
> She's quite a little care,
> I have to press her ribbon,
> And comb her fluffy hair.
>
> I keep her clothes all mended,
> And wash her hands and face,
> And make her frocks and aprons,
> All trimmed in frills and lace—
>
> I have to cook her breakfast,
> And pet her when she's ill;
> And telephone the doctor
> When Rebecca has a chill.
>
> Rebecca doesn't like that,
> And says she's well and strong,
> And says she'll try—oh! very hard,
> To be good all day long.
>
> But when night comes, she's nodding,
> So into bed we creep
> And snuggle up together
> And soon are fast asleep.
>
> I have no other dolly,
> For you can plainly see,

> In caring for Rebecca,
> I'm busy as can be!

Now I wonder how your sweet little Nancy and Sally Jane are. Are you such a kind mother to them as this little girl was to her doll, Rebecca?

This letter promulgates a maternal sensibility; it is both a boast and a complaint about maternal duty, care, sacrifice—everything the mother has to do for a troublesome baby, who takes all her time: she can only have one (and at this point in time, Mrs. Plath can have only Warren, not Sylvia); excluded from her mother's care, Plath is advised to mother her own babies. Aurelia's question, "Are you such a kind mother as this little girl was . . ." is ironically prophetic, then, of Plath's conflict over having her own babies. Who is she doing it for, and why? Will she let her mother down in the raising of her children? Could she be as self-sacrificing? as successful? We know she felt she failed her mother when she had a miscarriage.

As in the case where Plath is made to soothe her distress at maternal separation when her brother is being nursed by learning the alphabet (words as nurture), Aurelia sets a pattern for their mother-daughter correspondence: the sending of poems, the artful use of language itself, to ease as well as commemorate separation from the maternal matrix. Responding to maternal expectation and even pressure, Plath specifically and pragmatically uses her writing to win the approval and love of her mother: writing is a primary way of being good, making her mother proud through her literary achievement, and hence of being loved. Consider the juxtaposition in the following letter: "You are a good girl to send us such a fine letter. You are a lucky girl to be with grandmother. She takes better care of you than I could now. You see, Warren is still in bed and needs me all the time. . . . You are my good little girl . . . Mummy." Again, April 8, 1939: "My sweetheart, I am a proud and happy mother just now. Can you guess why? Well, I looked at your report card and saw all A's again. This is splendid, dear, and I shall give you a big hug for it when I see you." Plath was seven. A compulsive achiever, Plath wanted to please. Her letters to her mother now and throughout her life show off, list her accomplishments, stress and reiterate how "good" she is being, how worthy of her mother's love (and care, and sacrifice), the voice of the dutiful daughter, the bait used to rejoin a maternal matrix, to lure maternal *nurture*. Indeed,

Plath's constant pleas for her mother's words describe them as food: "Meaty," "fat," "satisfying." She is mother-hungry: that is why these letters stress what she eats when she is away, as if she is insatiable: "Dearest mother, Oh! camp certainly is wonderful. On Sunday afternoon we had ham and cheese just to start off the season with. I had two helpings along with four cups of milk! . . . At lunch I stuffed myself like a hog." (She goes on to list what she ate.) She even projects herself as food for her mother: "If you're hard up on ration points when I come home you can have toe [*sic*] slaughter me and you can eat me for pork," a motif that reemerges in later poems ("mother of otherness, Eat me"). She records her progress in publishing ("I turned in my two poems to the newspaper") and includes new poems: "Dear Mother, today is Saturday and this morning I got up and had a good breakfast. Then I went upstairs with Grammy, and had a bath and shampoo. I have made up some poems, here they are. [Plath is 10.] I would like to give all these things to you [her poems describe her unique "fairy" gifts of perception] but I know I can make it up by being good." She is always seeking the Maternal Pat. "In music I did the fingering just like you told me to and I kept saying to myself 'this is what mother would want me to do' so I got along very well, ate all my breakfast very well, and did not tease Warren. You will see a great difference in my character."

From the first, then, we see Plath's desire to be nurtured, and Aurelia's desire to nurture her daughter's artistic and intellectual skills. In the same letter which praises her seven-year-old report card, Plath is given creative chores: stories to illustrate ("Color them carefully. Remember that the little girl has golden [yellow] hair."), clay figures to model, a painting of Whistler's mother to study: "He loved his mother so much, that he made this picture of her. Can you find little curved lines in the picture?" Thus artistic and literary techniques are connected with the ideals set forth for maternal and filial love—set forth, again, as a function of the mother's absence. It is probably more than coincidental that one of her first poems, at age eight, is "Mother Love" (1940), and begins, "I love my mother / My mother loves me." The second quatrain equates maternal love, nurture, and a daughter's good works.

> If I were good all day
> I'd not require milk or spice
> A hug or kiss
> Would be quite nice.

This "precosia" illustrates the function writing will continue to have in Plath's life: a means to gain and sustain maternal love and approval, and prove herself worthy of her mother's diligent love. Writing, mother, and nurture are integrally related concepts, a fact which Plath symbolically underscores when she places her poems at the table, at mealtime, hidden beneath her mother's napkin or butter plate.

It is at this time that her father is dying. Plath's account of her childhood ends with a cryptic code of loss: "My father died, we moved inland." This was true, but it was more complicated and traumatic than that. Sylvia's mother returned to full-time teaching, her grandparents came to take care of them, and they moved to Wellesley. At this point, Plath found a literary mate for her mother, seeking recognition from publishers and editors who could confirm, extend, and fertilize her *mother's* approval. At age eight and a half, she published in the *Boston Sunday Herald,* describing "what I see and hear on hot summer nights." ("Hear the crickets chirping / In the dewy grass / Bright little fireflies / Twinkle as they pass.")

At ten, her letters are heavy with poems. One is a recipe for creation.

> Plant a little seedling
> Mix with rain and showers
> Stir them with some sun-shine,
> And up come some flowers

Another proclaims her unique perceptive gifts: one has to have her "fairy ears" to hear the bluebells ring, her "fairy eyes" to see "the pot of gold / That lies beyond the rainbow," a theme that continues. In "Silver Thread" (1946) she expresses her confidence in her unique abilities that will enable her to realize her dreams; "Fireside Reveries" (1947) end, "My thoughts to shining fame aspire / For there is much to do and much to dare." But she also is weary, at fifteen; "Oh, to leave behind this human form . . ./ Would that I were clear of mortal dust— / Freed at last from these confining bars." In "Fog" she seeks obliteration, and her last lines foreshadow the bell jar: "Let a haze of ocean fog / Blur my vision, stop my ears / Mute my voice and still my fears." And in "The Ideal" (1948) she has no substance and dissolves upon contact, "vacant and empty." In "Not Here" (1948) her duplicity in her confident public image, fostered by maternal pressure and encouragement, alienates her. Though she smiles and chatters, she is "Not here / never / though they think it," her body "but a ruse / To make them overlook / The absence of myself." Her poetry is now a way to deal with her anger at being forced behind a mask of pleased, pleasing conformity, a way to achieve a distance from the world she is at odds with: "All I ever ask of late / Is to be alone / So that I may carefully write / My emotions down" ("Obsession," 1948); in her art, she is the "supreme conqueror." "Only there I am able to be magnanimous and forgive you. Once there I am able to pity you." ("I have found the perfect world," 1948). Cranky, isolated, impatient, resentful, violated, and superior, this private poet self by sixteen is getting back at, as well as to, the "you" she tries to forgive: her mother, not just an abstract "world." Her writing, which she originally used to commune with her absent mother, allows her to mediate her ambivalent feeling toward her, for she drives her to words, and to withdrawal. Plath wrote poems away from the maternal matrix, but within it, she can only separate herself physically, by going upstairs and sneering at the folks below (the "mean" tone we see in later works), and through anger. Even now Plath is ambivalent toward her mother and her devoted alliance, resentful of the pressure, the duty to achieve, to justify her mother's efforts on her behalf.

A very interesting poem written when she is fifteen is "Female Author," in which Plath sets out the conflict which may lie behind her ambivalence to her mother: her sense that she must choose, as her mother had to choose, between a career—a career her mother has nurtured—and becoming a mother herself, which her mother defines as all-sacrifice. Whichever she chooses, she rejects and must be abandoned by her mother. In this poem, she suggests something sinister in the woman writer's power and preoccupations, a relation between literary creation and death. The author has breasts, but nurses chocolate fancies, not a child; "lost in subtle metaphor" she "retreats / From gray child crying in the streets." Her satire is aimed at a woman who lacks true maternal instincts.

By the end of this "precosia," several things are clear. These poems and writings should not be dismissed, for they reveal the great extent to which Plath's later themes and imagery come out of her childhood experience. Second, two voices have developed: the nuzzling little "Sivvy" who wants to be loved, and the angry woman sulking upstairs, finding her mother's world intolerable: "And I could scream . . . ." I think that this material clarifies in what ways Plath, as a child and as an adult, uses language as a baby does, to commune with, break away from, and finally revenge herself upon what appears to be a maternal muse—identified in poems such as "A Birthday Present," "Medusa," and "The Rival." In "The Disquieting Muses," Plath dates her relationship with her muse to when she was still in the crib. She is not using language the way her mother wants her to—a rebellion attracting her teacher mother's pride in their relationship; her mother's attempts to teach her have failed: "I learned, I learned elsewhere, / From muses unhired by you, dear mother." Yet it is her mother's fault: "this is the kingdom you bore me to."

Leaving aside the issue that the mother cannot win here, we see that in one way it makes sense that Plath both credits and blames her mother for her conflict as a writer in using the word. First bewailing and then striving to effect maternal separation in her use of words, there is not such a distance between her use of "aw-gaw" to indicate her empty bottle and one of her last poems, called "Words," which begins, "Axes." Her words are as driven by anger against this maternal muse as they are by need of this muse's nurture—an anger against dependence, or the necessity of being, as Plath described herself in "Who," "all mouth." Of course other poems offer sensational examples of this anger against her maternal needs, as well as acknowledgement of them: "Mother, you are the one mouth I would be a tongue to. Mother of otherness / Eat me." "The mother of mouths didn't love me." "Mother, keep out of my barnyard." Or,

> Did I escape, I wonder?
> My mind winds to you
> Old barnacled umbilicus, Atlantic cable,
> Keeping itself, it seems, in a state of miraculous repair.
>
> In any case, you are always there,
> Tremulous breath at the end of my line,
> Curve of water upleaping
> To my water rod, dazzling and grateful,
> Touching and sucking.
>
> I didn't call you.
> I didn't call you at all.
> Nevertheless, nevertheless

> You steamed to me over the sea,
> Fat and red, a placenta
>
> ....
> . . . your wishes
> Hiss at my sins.
> Off, off, eely tentacle!
>
> There is nothing between us.
>
>   ("Medusa")

And:

> Your dissatisfactions . . .
> Arrive through the mailslot with loving regularity,
> White and blank, expansive as carbon monoxide.
> No day is safe from news of you,
> Walking about in Africa maybe, but thinking of me.
>
>   ("The Rival")

In "A Birthday Present," she wants her *mother,* I think, to release her, and now, not in sixty years when she will have been destroyed. Again and again, she speaks hunger, appealing to her muse's maternal diligence, and anger, trying to separate from the maternal nature of her muse.

In high school, Plath told her mother she was looking for a man whom she did not have to mother: "There is time enough for being maternal." But there wasn't. Her mother provided her with such supra-adequate nurturing that she felt she could never be a similar mother and still do what she had to do to win her mother's love through her writing. She had to be "all mouth" to keep the poems coming, satisfying that "inner voice." One of the reasons her "true" angry voice emerged at last was that she directly confronted this muse she was daring to shock and defy on the battleground where she had always dealt with her mother, in love and anger—on the page.

"I Tapped My Own Head": The Apprenticeship of Anne Sexton

Diane Wood Middlebrook

In April 1960, Anne Sexton for the first time wrote "poet" rather than "housewife" in the "occupation" block of her income tax return. Married since 1948, mother of two daughters, Sexton had been publishing poetry for three years. The change in her status as citizen was significant for Sexton and for American literature. No poet before her had written so frankly of the female realm of family life, nor of its pathologies. And few poets, women or men, achieved success so expeditiously: nine years from drafting her first poem to being awarded the Pulitzer Prize.

Sexton's unprecedented metamorphosis from suburban housewife into major poet appears, at first glance, a fairy tale. The real interest of its improbability, though, lies in Sexton's exemplary struggle against two seemingly unrelated handicaps: that of being a suburban wife and mother without a college education and that of being, at recurring intervals, certifiably mad. At age twenty-eight, Anne Sexton quite unexpectedly began turning herself into an artist. During the years of her apprenticeship, in which she produced two highly regarded books, Sexton's good fortune included working with several established younger poets—W. D. Snodgrass, Robert Lowell, James Wright—who immediately recognized her originality and with the Boston poet-teacher John Holmes, who censured it. Friend and adversary, Holmes measured Sexton's work by the literary standards and conventions of an older generation. The chronicle of their relationship provides numerous insights into the development of Sexton's self-awareness as an artist.

1956–57: Discovering "Language"

Sexton began writing poetry at home. Following her hospitalization for suicidal depressiveness in 1956, Sexton's two young children had been removed to the care of grandmothers; Sexton found herself with no occupation but psychotherapy and convalescence. Her doctor suggested that she use her free time to improve her education. "One night I saw I. A. Richards on educational television reading a sonnet and explaining its form," she told an interviewer. "I thought to myself, 'I could do that, maybe; I could try.' So I sat down and wrote a sonnet. The next day I wrote another one, and so forth."[1] She measured progress by changes in the furniture supporting her work. At first she used a card table "because I didn't think I was a poet. When I put in a desk, it was in our dining room. . . . Then I put up some book shelves—everything was tentative."[2]

This "tentative" rearrangement of the household was symbolic of Sexton's changed relation to domestic life in 1957. Postpartum depression following the birth of Sexton's first daughter, Linda, led in 1954 to her first psychiatric hospitalization. On her own birthday in 1956 she had made the first of many suicide attempts. And though family members were initially reluctant to acknowledge how serious Sexton's psychological problems had become, they were generous with support once she entered regular treatment. Husband Kayo's father, George Sexton, paid for Sexton's psychotherapy; after Sexton's second major breakdown, in 1955, Kayo's mother took infant Joy into her home for three years, while Anne's sister Blanche periodically cared for Linda. Anne's mother, Mary Gray, paid for regular housekeeping, and Kayo took over the shopping and cooking when Anne could not manage.

Working alone at home, free from other responsibilities, Sexton found writing an effective therapy. "My doctor encouraged me to write more. 'Don't kill yourself,' he said. 'Your poems might mean something to someone else someday.' That gave me a feeling of purpose, a little cause, something to *do* with my life."[3] "I was quite naive. I thought he knew everything. Of course, he wouldn't know a good poem from a bad poem, but luckily I didn't think of that."[4]

Sexton marked her development as a poet, rather than convalescing mental patient, from the evening she enrolled in a poetry workshop offered by the Boston Center for Adult Education. The teacher was John Holmes, a member of the senior faculty at Tufts University, who supplemented his income by offering instruction in writing to the "nontraditional" types who enroll in adult education courses. Holmes was warm and unintimidating as a teacher. What Sexton derived from the class, however, was not simply how to tell a good poem from a bad poem. Attempting to characterize this period of her life for an interviewer, Sexton drew an analogy between Holmes's poetry class and the mental hospital.

> I started in the middle of the term, very shy, writing very bad poems, solemnly handing them in for the eighteen others in the class to hear. The most important aspect of that class was that I felt I belonged somewhere. When I first got sick and became a displaced person, I thought I was quite alone, but when I went into the mental hospital, I found I wasn't, that there were other people like me. It made me feel better—more real, sane. I felt, "These are my people." Well, at the John Holmes class that I attended for two years, I found I belonged to the poets, that I was *real* there, and I had another, "These are my people."[5]

Working out the implications of this association between the hospital and class provides a way of understanding some of the social significance of Sexton's art.

Until diagnosed as mentally ill, Sexton had been regarded by her exasperated family as childish, selfish, incompetent. Her mother-in-law remembered the shock with which she first watched Sexton throw herself, pounding and screaming, on the floor because she was enraged at being asked to do an errand.[6] Later, Sexton's anger sometimes threatened the safety of her young children; Linda Sexton indicates that the poem "Red Roses" (in the posthumously published 45 *Mercy Street*) recreates such an incident.[7] But in the hospital, removed from the dynamics of family life, Sexton assumed another identity. As a madwoman she was a member of a distinct social class. Even the forms of her suffering, symptomatic of the disease she embodied, were not unique but generic. Most important for her later development, in the hospital she was given a hearing by therapists trained to decode her symptoms and clarify their function in her life. And she found herself in a social group that used language in a special way, to communicate indirectly.

Years after this first hospitalization, Sexton described the discovery—"I thought I was quite alone, but . . . I found I wasn't"—to a psychiatrist friend.

It is hard to define. When I was first sick I was thrilled . . . to get
into the Nut House. At first, of course, I was just scared and cry-
ing and very quiet (who me!) but then I found this girl (very crazy
of course) (like me I guess) who talked language. What a relief! I
mean, well . . . someone! And then later, a while later, and quite a
while, I found out that [Dr.] Martin talked language. . . . By the
way, [husband] Kayo has never once understood one word of lan-
guage. (*Letters,* p. 244)

By "language," Sexton seems to mean forms of speech in which mean-
ing is condensed and indirect and where breaks and gaps demand as
much interpretation as what is voiced. Schizophrenics use language this
way, and so do poets: "figurative language" is the term Sexton might
have used here, except she meant to indicate that the crucible of forma-
tion was urgent need. Being permitted to communicate in "language"
made her feel "real"—unlike the speech transactions of family life,
which made her feel doll-like.

> Someone pretends with me—
> I am walled in solid by their noise—
> or puts me upon their straight bed.
> They think I am me!
> Their warmth is not a friend!
> They pry my mouth for their cups of gin
> and their stale bread.[8]

Psychotherapy following hospitalization, further developing the
sense of liberation achieved in the hospital, provided Sexton with a
form of education. Intensive scrutiny of her illness introduced her, hap-
hazardly but usefully, to the theory of psychoanalysis, techniques of
association, and an arena in which to display her verbal cunning. Equal-
ly important, it freed her from confinement in the family. Demonstra-
bly unfit for the occupation of housewife and mother, Sexton turned to
other work. And because she had the good fortune to live in Greater
Boston, she found her way, merely by enrolling, into another social
group that spoke "language": "I found I belonged to the poets, that I
was *real* there."

Boston in the late 1950s was full of poets. "Being a 'poet' in
Boston is not so difficult," Anne Sexton wrote Carolyn Kizer in Febru-
ary 1959, "except there are hoards of us living here. The place is

jammed with good writers" (*Letters*, p. 56). Such abundance offered numerous advantages to the apprentice. Many well-known writers taught workshops that carried no academic prerequisites. In few places outside Boston might a professor of poetry like I. A. Richards have found an audience for lectures on the sonnet, or a TV station to air them. Both the teacher and Sexton's fellow students at the Boston Center for Adult Education reflected the exceptional literacy of Greater Boston. In John Holmes's class Sexton met Maxine Kumin, a Radcliffe graduate who had decided after some years of motherhood to return to serious writing. Kumin's career was to flourish in tandem with Sexton's, each eventually receiving the Pulitzer Prize in poetry.

It was part of Sexton's transformative good luck, I think, that she found both the instruction and, later, the academic credentials she needed without passing through the advantaged but in important ways—for poets—repressive educational systems that shaped the early work of her Boston cohorts, Adrienne Rich and Sylvia Plath. Rigorous academic training of the period led young poets to imitate the masters of the British tradition, particularly the metaphysical poets and the intensely intellectual modernists. The early writings of both Plath and Rich indicate that they were excellent students, striving for correctness in these modes. As strong poets, and like men who became strong poets under the same academic influences, Plath and Rich survived this academic phase by growing out of it; in their characteristic mature work, the mannerisms of their early models have disappeared. In the realm of the university, however, not only were their literary models intellectual men, but their teachers and lovers were too, and the best women students tended to marry them and then vanish into the underclass of academic life.

Sexton avoided this common predicament of her contemporaries, paradoxically, by marrying young. Having no further academic ambitions after finishing high school, she went on to the Garland School in Boston, where girls were taught home management. She eloped within a few months. Her struggles to mature during the early years of marriage and motherhood took place almost completely within an extended family; her husband was frequently absent on business, and both parents and in-laws were important, frequently intrusive, presences. The illnesses from which she suffered throughout her adult life burgeoned in this context of censorious parental scrutiny. Problematic as her family relations were, however, they formed a different universe of concern from the one she entered as an apprentice to poetry and did not impede her development once she found her way out of the house. She turned from sufferer into poet, a social role different altogether.

1958–59: Becoming Visible

Transforming the insights won in therapy into the poetry she wrote between 1958 and 1960, Sexton was like the miller's daughter, in her own poem "Rumpelstiltskin," who acquires the gift of spinning straw into gold. Developing this gift took about three years. From the time she enrolled in John Holmes's course at the Adult Education Center, Sexton worked hard at learning the craft. The day following the first class meeting, Maxine Kumin ran into Sexton at the Newton public library, where Sexton was trying to locate the contemporary poetry shelves.[9] Here began a collaboration that was to last until Sexton's suicide. Kumin knew her way around a library but, like Sexton, initially felt intimidated by the literary world. Two housewives, they pooled cars and other resources, converted house and garden into workspace, and conducted an ongoing informal seminar in the craft of poetry over the telephone.

Sexton and Kumin were apprentices together, but Kumin possessed credentials Sexton had to acquire another way. Following the Boston Center course, Sexton spent several weeks during the summer of 1958 at the Antioch College Writer's Conference. Attracted by the poem "Heart's Needle," she went expressly to work with W. D. Snodgrass. This peculiarly American institution—the writer's workshop, the writer's conference—suited Sexton because it assumed no common denominator but a gift (or the delusion of a gift) and provided the valuable attention of professionals. Working with Snodgrass at Antioch was decisive. Sexton was already quite a capable writer; under Snodgrass she began to abandon certain of the conventions she had picked up in the poetry workshop—such as attaching the poem to an elevating literary allusion or founding the poem on an abstraction. "Heart's Needle," a poem about Snodgrass's separation from his daughter through divorce, came at a moment when American poetry had grown dull and academic. The poem had a large impact on Robert Lowell, for one, who said "Heart's Needle" had encouraged the production of his *Life Studies.* Snodgrass's influence on Sexton is visible in two of the finest poems of *To Bedlam,* "Unknown Girl in a Maternity

Ward" and "The Double Image"—poems that raise troubled questions about the relation of mother to child. Whereas Lowell had taken from Snodgrass courage to write about the general anguish of family life, Sexton grasped in his model license to explore her sickness as it pertained to her roles as daughter and mother. Working with Snodgrass, Sexton acquired the distinctive voice of her early poetry.

Back in the Boston suburbs with a cache of new manuscripts and encouragement from Snodgrass, Sexton was accepted by Robert Lowell in September 1958 to audit his graduate writing seminar at Boston University. George Starbuck and Sylvia Plath joined this class in the winter. The three—Sexton, Starbuck, Plath—formed an intense triangle whose emotional dynamics are encoded in Sylvia Plath's journal from the period and in Sexton's hilarious and tender memorial essay to Plath, "The Barfly Ought to Sing."[10]

Within a year from her first session in a poetry workshop, then, Sexton had acquired enviable visibility and respect in the poetry world. She did so by working demonically. "She would willingly push a poem through twenty or more drafts," Maxine Kumin remembers. "She had an unparalleled tenacity in those early days."[11] Despite an acute personal shyness, she also became an active self-promoter: cultivating contacts shamelessly; submitting poems anywhere she could expect editorial advice, if not publication; accepting profuse invitations to give public readings. During 1958–59, Sexton lost both her parents, within months of each other, to severe illnesses, and was hospitalized for psychiatric treatment several times herself. Nonetheless, she continued the discipline of long days at the typewriter and regular meetings with groups of poets in which she tested her developing skills.

At least as important as the Lowell class was Sexton's participation in the meetings John Holmes convened in the fall of 1958 to continue working with his star poets from the Boston Center, Sexton, Kumin, and Sam Albert. George Starbuck also joined the group. After Starbuck's departure for Italy in September 1961, the workshop had a shifting population of visitors, but until then it was a remarkably stable collective. Altogether, what came to be known as "the John Holmes workshop" met for three and one-half years, twice monthly until Holmes died of cancer in 1962. During this time Sexton, Kumin, and Starbuck produced widely noticed first books, and Holmes brought out *The Fortune Teller,* nominated for a National Book Award in 1962. Most of the poems in these four books had been "workshopped" into shape during long evening sessions at one or another of the participants' homes.

The structure of the workshop was informal: each poet in turn became first among equals as a poem was dissected and interrogated. Holmes, however, assigned himself the presiding role. He was senior in age; he also held a respectable position in the literary establishment peculiar to Boston. President of the New England Poetry Club, for a time poetry critic at the *Boston Evening Transcript,* anthologist and teacher of poetry, Holmes eventually received appointment to the American Academy of Arts and Sciences; but his writing had an old-fashioned quality, an Arnoldian judiciousness that made him an odd contemporary for the younger writers.

With Maxine Kumin and George Starbuck, Holmes was confiding and affectionate; he squired them around to meet other literary people and proposed them for teaching positions. Sexton, however, set his teeth on edge. In life as in art, Sexton possessed a commanding physical presence. Photographs from one of the workshop evenings show her sitting on the floor, a glamor girl with long legs extended, her bright red lipstick and sweater in startling contrast to the subdued coloration of her companions. When the workshop met in the Holmes's living room, Holmes's widow Doris Eyges remembers, Sexton's raucous cries penetrated to the upstairs study: "YOU'VE GOT TO HEAR THIS! IT WORKS! IT WORKS!—FANTASTIC!" The loud voice demanded and got a large share of the group's attention. Too much, Holmes grumbled to Maxine Kumin: Anne "is on my mind unpleasantly too much of the time between our workshops. . . . I'm impatient with her endless demands."[12]

1959–61: Sexton and the Censor

During her years of apprenticeship, Sexton was to have two deeply significant confrontations with John Holmes, whose role in her life, was, I believe, to disclose to her, in opposing him, her definitive strengths as a poet. The first conflict occurred in February 1959. Writing several poems a week and opening them for discussion both in the workshop and in Lowell's class, Sexton had amassed enough material to consider compiling a book. When she submitted a preliminary version for Holmes's criticism, his response revealed that his differences with her went far deeper than the mild offense his personal standoffishness had communicated.

Like a good teacher, Holmes began his critique on a positive note: "It's a book, all right, well put together." Next he suggested a change in the proposed title, for marketing reasons: "I really think booksellers and publishers would be wary." Then he went on to give the full substance of his advice, a view he had been holding silently since their earliest days of working together.

> I distrust the very source and subject of a great many of your poems, namely, all those that describe and dwell on your time in the hospital. . . . I am uneasy . . . that what looks like a brilliant beginning might turn out to be so self-centered and so narrowed a diary that it would be clinical only.
>
> Something about asserting the hospital and psychiatric experience seems to me very selfish—all a forcing others to listen to you, and nothing given the listeners, nothing that teaches them or helps them. . . . It bothers me that you use poetry this way. It's all a release for you, but what is it for anyone else except a spectacle of someone experiencing release? . . .
>
> Don't publish it in a book. You'll certainly outgrow it, and become another person, then this record will haunt and hurt you. It will even haunt and hurt your children, years from now. (February 8, 1959)

Sexton's first response was a rattled letter she drafted but did not send. "Of course I love you. . . . From true poets I want truth. Anything else would prove us unreal, after all. Thank you, John, for being real."[13] The reply she did send encloses a poem, "the condensation of it all," titled "For John, Who Begs Me Not to Enquire Further." Sexton had concluded that Holmes's motive in advising her about the manuscript was not to critique but to censor her. Useful criticism empowers creative revision, and Sexton knew how to profit from the attention of another poet. But Holmes was not saying "Revise"; he was saying "Don't publish it." Sexton's reply is a defense not only of her manuscript but of a whole genre of poetry that would come to be called "confessional."

> I tapped my own head;
> it was glass, an inverted bowl.
> . . . .
> And if you turn away
> because there is no lesson here

> I will hold my awkward bowl
> with all its cracked stars shining
> . . . .
> This is something I would never find
> in a lovelier place, my dear,
> although your fear is anyone's fear
> like an invisible veil between us all . . .
> and sometimes in private,
> my kitchen, your kitchen,
> my face, your face.

Shrewd as neurotic people often are about the concealed anxieties of others, Sexton insists to Holmes that his rejection of her poetry is in part a defense against the power of her art, which tells not a private but a collective truth and, to his horror, includes and reveals him. Sexton may or may not have heard in literary circles gossip about the gruesome suicide of Holmes's first wife or about Holmes's successful recovery from alcoholism. His life had been "ragged with horrors," as his widow put it,[14] but by the late 1950s was outwardly peaceful and secure. His advice to Sexton was possibly advice he had followed himself: "Don't publish it . . . you will certainly outgrow it and become another person." But Sexton based her work on a different understanding of suffering. In her imagery, "tapping" the head produces "stars," signs radiant with significance, uniting sufferer and beholder despite the "glass bowl" that shuts them off from other forms of contact. "Anyone's fear" of the sick inhibits this identification; the courage of acknowledgment in the poetry of *To Bedlam* comes from Sexton's lucidity about how general is the suffering that must be experienced as personal but can be grasped and expressed in metaphor.

Far from discouraging publication of the *Bedlam* poems, Holmes's reaction gave Sexton insight into what the book was really about. The poem she wrote in reply contains an allusion in its title to a letter from Schopenhauer to Goethe: "most of us carry in our heart the Jocasta who begs Oedipus for God's sake not to inquire further." The longer quotation of this letter became the epigraph of *To Bedlam and Part Way Back,* and "For John . . . " became the introductory poem to Part II, in which Sexton collected her most ambitious and self-revealing poems. Holmes had been "real"—truth-telling—in his response to her, and thus she dared be the same; moreover, his reaction provided a foil Sexton, anticipating the distaste these poems were bound to arouse, could use in her book.

Houghton Mifflin accepted the manuscript in May 1959, just as Lowell's class was ending; it appeared in March 1960 with a jacket blurb by Lowell,·which insured that the book would be widely reviewed. The reviews did not change John Holmes's opinion of the work. As Sexton workshopped poems that would shortly appear in her second collection (*All My Pretty Ones,* October 1962), Holmes's hostility deepened. "I suppose I don't want her to know how I feel," he wrote Maxine Kumin. "But I think more often than you'd ever realize that I can't stand another meeting with her there. . . . She is utterly selfish" (August 6, 1961). The objectionable characteristics of the person were equally objectionable in the poems.

> I said way back, that she was going to have a hard time to change subject matter, after the book, and it's true. I think her search for subject matter is desperate, and that we could talk to her about it, get her to try different things. . . . she writes so absolutely selfishly, of herself, to bare and shock and confess. Her motives are wrong, artistically, and finally the self-preoccupation comes to be simply damn boring. . . . [W]asn't it once understood that the whole intent of writing the bedlam poems was to get rid of them, and to cure herself, to grow up, to become through writing poetry a mature and rich person? . . . As it is, she merely reinfects herself, and doesn't seem to know any better than to enjoy it. (August 16, 1961)

Holmes took a proprietary interest in the workshop. In February 1960 he had circulated a two-page memo listing four ways to improve its efficacy; many times he would follow up a meeting with letters to one or another of the poets that expanded on his first-sight critiques. Thus in the name of straightening out a problem, he engaged Sexton in a second open confrontation in January 1961. Galled by what he referred to as Anne's "greedy and selfish demands" at one of the workshop sessions, Holmes wrote letters to each of the participants venting his spleen. To Anne he was most tactful, but he made his points.

> I was sort of upset about the workshop, as a matter of fact. . . . [Y]ou gave Sam an awfully rough time, I felt, too much of it, and hard for a man to take, and he took it like a good sport. But it went on and on. Also I thought you took too much time, more

than anyone else got, and also, for the first time I've ever minded, I thought you and Max had too much to drink, and that it took the meaning and responsible thinking away from the poems. (January 25, 1961)

Holmes wanted the workshop to work; Sexton thought it was working. Certainly it was working for her: she could audition drafts of poems within a circle of intimates she trusted to know what effects she was after. "What kind of workshop is this?" she fumed to Holmes in her reply to his letter. "Are we mere craftsmen or are we artists! . . . I resent the idea that an almost good poem isn't worth any amount of time if we can make it better and first the actual writer has got to be able to HEAR" (*Letters*, p. 118). As Sexton realized, however, the conflict was not merely over workshop manners; it involved behavior indistinguishable from poetics. For Sexton, the unbridled excitements of the group process frequently led to inspired revision. "This is a great strength and a great, but mutual, creative act each time it happens," she argued (*Letters*, p. 118); to repress the process would be to kill the work. Moreover, she knew the issue was not merely a disproportion in amounts of attention meted out in the workshop. She was not privy to Holmes's judgment in his letter to Sam Albert that she was "like a child and three times as selfish" (January 24, 1961), but Sexton's reply indicates that she had felt symbolic family roles being acted out in the group.

> In the long pull, John, where you might be proud of me, you are ashamed of me. I keep pretending not to notice . . . But then, you remind me of my father (and I KNOW that's not your fault.) But there is something else here . . . who do I remind you of? (*Letters*, p. 119)

The group went on meeting, its format unchanged, until Holmes developed cancer a year later. Holmes's disgust with Sexton increased. He seems to have diffused the problem by inviting others to confide their mistrust and dislike of Sexton and to confirm his judgment that she was a bad influence with reference to both art and manners. "I have heard lately two lengthy judgments of her, exactly like my bitterest feelings, and the impression is shared by others that she does you harm," he warned Maxine Kumin on August 6.

For Sexton, however, the exchange of letters in February had a clarifying significance, elaborated in a dream she reported to her therapist a few days after writing the letter.

> AS: This perfect voice was enunciating very carefully as if to tell me exactly how it was—and yet he was kind and patient about it—very irritated but patient all at once—and this was terrible because whatever he was telling me I was seeing the reverse. . . . [H]e'd talk reasonably, reasonably, and he wouldn't stop telling me, you know, just nicely . . . it would become so frightening that I would pound on the floor . . . maybe screaming stop it, stop it, . . . that would be the feeling: LISTEN! and then I'd try something else. PLEASE. Like HE COULDN'T HEAR ME.
>
> Dr: There is one thing I have trouble understanding; that is, what you wanted when you had to pound on the floor.
>
> AS: Well, associate. If you're pounding on the floor then you must be down on the floor. You don't stand up. Crouched . . . more like a child or an animal or someone very afraid. It's kind of crazy to be on the floor—and yet it's kind of afraid, really. . . . He keeps telling me what's so and probably he's right but it isn't so for me so I've got to try again to make the same thing so for both of us so we can make sense to each other. Otherwise, I'm crazy. I'm lost.
>
> Dr: If you can talk to one person, you're not crazy?
>
> AS: Right. . . . One sane person, that is.[15]

Like the poem "For John . . . " with which Sexton had replied to his letter the year before, this dream is also a "condensation of it all." The unnamed masculine speaker, a composite censor, blends several identities—teacher, critic, father, mother, doctor, senior poet: those in charge of telling "exactly how it is" and unable to "HEAR." Present only as "this perfect voice," his identity may include some of the prestigious reviewers of Sexton's first book: possibly James Dickey ("one feels tempted to drop them furtively into the nearest ashcan, rather than be caught with them in the presence of so much naked suffering"); possibly Geoffrey Hartman ("With such a theme, . . . did the poet have to exploit the more sensational aspect of her experience?").[16] "Kind of patient, telling me about it just nicely," he devastates her.

The doctor asks—reasonably, reasonably—what she *wants* pounding on the floor, a question Sexton answers rather indirectly. Is the only way to stop the senior poet's voice an act of violence performed in fear, "like a child or an animal"? No: Sexton wants in the dream what she wanted from the workshop, what she had described in her letter to Holmes, the "mutual intuitive creative act" by which the individual poets merged their strengths through disciplined listening. "Probably he's right," but this only makes him distant and self-absorbed. Disengaging from the craziness and fear inspired by being ignored ("you remind me of my father"), Sexton acknowledges—almost in spite of herself—the powers she can marshal against the censor: "I've got to try again . . . so we can make sense to each other."

The dream images, like the "awkward bowl / with all its cracked stars shining," radiate outward into other significant relationships formed around words. Among those unable to HEAR, by this date, are Sexton's father and mother, both dead in the spring of 1959, the same spring Houghton Mifflin accepted *To Bedlam and Part Way Back*. They did not live to read Anne Harvey Sexton's words in a book nor to see the world confirm her as a poet. As in her dream, their impenetrability inspired stubborn efforts to "make the same thing so for both of us"; from *All My Pretty Ones* through *The Awful Rowing Toward God*, Mother and Father remain in Sexton's poems the powerful withholders of confirming attention, now cleverly dead and beyond appeal.

Out in the real world, however, Sexton's bond with Maxine Kumin involved much reciprocal listening. Kumin has described how each had a special phone installed in her study: "we sometimes connected with a phone call and kept that line linked for hours at a stretch . . . ; we whistled into the receiver for each other when we were ready to resume."[17] The relationship, fruitful for both, helped Sexton engage her critical faculties once she had completed the process she referred to as "milking the unconscious."[18] Describing it to an interviewer, Sexton said "all poets have a little critic in their heads. . . . [Y]ou have to turn off the little critic while you are beginning a poem so that it doesn't inhibit you. Then you have to turn it on again when you are revising and refining,"[19] Whistling into the receiver for Maxine was a way of calling up the inner critic by paging an external one. Sexton made use of such a model throughout her life: as playwright; as member of the chamber rock group "Her Kind" that performed her poems to music; as a teacher herself; and, of course, in the workshop.

If John Holmes is one of the identities of the censor in Sexton's dream, then her struggle was not with Holmes the man but with Holmes the Man of Letters: paragon of correctness, arbiter of taste, warden of the literary tradition. The rather playful, even daughterly, tone of Sexton's reply to Holmes's attack suggests that she had already detected the sense that might be made of their mutual hostility. Holmes's distaste for Sexton's work was not based on a judgment that she was a second-rate poet. "What you have is a genius," he had written her in the letter rejecting the *Bedlam* manuscript, "an unaccountable, unconscious, startling gift with words, and emotions, and patterns for them." His quarrel was with her subject, "your time in the hospital and the complications that took you there" (February 8, 1959).

What took Sexton to the hospital was a preference for suicide over the role of mother as she had construed it from her own glamorous, intelligent, repressive, and punitive mother—in the world's eyes, a competent, well-bred woman. The disturbing subject of the *Bedlam* poems is Sexton's experience of the female roles of mother and daughter as in themselves a sickness, and not merely her sickness. Thus in poems like "The Double Image," she writes of her horror at passing on femaleness itself.

> . . . this was the cave of the mirror,
> that double woman who stares
> at herself, as if she were petrified
> . . . .
> I, who was never quite sure
> about being a girl, needed another
> life, another image to remind me.
> And this was my worst guilt; you could not cure
> nor soothe it. I made you to find me.

Sexton resisted Holmes's judgment that *To Bedlam* contained "so self-centered and narrow a diary that it would be clinical only," just as she later resisted the label "confessional" for her poetry. Speaking in the name of art ("Her motives are wrong, artistically") and asking another woman writer to agree that Sexton's subject matter was an extension of her intrusive social behavior ("she writes to bare and shock and confess"), Holmes insisted that the sick woman was discontinuous with the poet. But Sexton knew the poetry was a revelation and a critique, faithful to the female unconscious; it reflected the high cost of socializing women into feminine roles. Hers were truths that had not been put

into poetry before, or with quite the same emphases, by a woman writ-
er. "There's something else here . . . who do I remind you of?" Sexton
was asking the question of an entire tradition largely devoid of the
voice of female consciousness—though it was a voice the auditor might
be expected to recognize, having heard it at home, or in his own bad
dreams.

Coda: Assimilating "Female" to "Poet"

All of Sexton's poems about the hospital and the complications that
took her there were published and proceeded to make her reputations:
first as a "confessional" poet and then as a woman poet—a category
that was newly developing in literature at the time of her death. The
large audiences for her work included mental patients, psycho-
therapists, and great numbers of women, most of whom did not share
Holmes's point of view concerning Sexton's subject matter. The ex-
change of letters in 1961 was, apparently, the last open confrontation
between them; however, it remained for Sexton, who outlived John
Holmes after all, to write the interpretive coda to their relationship, in
an elegy written shortly after Holmes's death in 1962. Titled "Some-
where in Africa," the poem takes up the themes of reasonableness and
wildness expressed in her dream and in her letter to Holmes and syn-
thesizes them in a new way.

> Must you leave, John Holmes, with the prayers and psalms
> you never said, said over you? Death with no rage
> to weigh you down? Praised by the mild God, his arm
> over the pulpit, leaving you timid, with no real age,
>
> whitewashed by belief, as dull as the windy preacher!
> Dead of a dark thing, John Holmes, you've been lost
> in the college chapel, mourned as father and teacher,
> mourned with piety and grace under the University Cross.
>
> Your last book unsung, your last hard words unknown,
> abandoned by science, cancer blossomed in your throat,
> rooted like bougainvillea into your gray backbone,
> ruptured your pores until you wore it like a coat.
>
> The thick petals, the exotic reds, the purples and whites
> covered up your nakedness and bore you up with all
> their blind power. I think of your last June nights
> in Boston, your body swollen but light, your eyes small

as you let the nurses carry you into a strange land.
. . . If this is death and God is necessary let him be hidden
from the missionary, the well-wisher and the glad hand.
Let God be some tribal female who is known but forbidden.

Let there be this God who is a woman who will place you
upon her shallow boat, who is a woman naked to the waist,
moist with palm oil and sweat, a woman of some virtue
and wild breasts, her limbs excellent, unbruised and chaste.

Let her take you. She will put twelve strong men at the oars
for you are stronger than mahogany and your bones fill
the boat high with fruit and bark from the interior.
She will have you now, whom the funeral cannot kill.

John Holmes, cut from a single tree, lie heavy in her hold
and go down that river with the ivory, the copra and the gold.[20]

In Sexton's elegy reasonableness and wildness became two gods:
one male, identified with institutions; one female, identified with poet-
ry. The formal art of the piece reinforces the ceremonial tone, yet its
argument insists that poetry belongs to the territory of wildness: libido,
darkness, fertility, beauty, strangeness. The poem seems to tap all Sex-
ton's ambivalent love for Holmes. It praises his integrity ("cut from a
single tree") and claims him for the paradise reserved for the tribe of
poets, but it also distinguishes the censor from the artist in him. Sepa-
rating the dead poet from the authority figures in the poem—"mild
God," "windy preacher"—Sexton conveys her understanding that the
conflict between her and Holmes was not merely a conflict between
two temperaments. It was a successful struggle, on her side, against the
conventions and "standards" John Holmes affirmed, which Sexton ex-
perienced as powers that could repress, even extinguish, the growth of
her art. Criticizing her work, Holmes invariably used the words
"childish" and "selfish"; he saw the poems only as referring to the
person, whom he deplored, not as radiant signs. It was fortunate for
Sexton that neither she nor Holmes was willing to abandon the struggle
until it had forced her to clarify this difference for herself. Holmes nev-
er failed to assert his standards—which were highly acceptable ones in
literary Boston and elsewhere—as part of a process of taking her se-
riously. Under his gentlemanly disapproval she acquired knowledge of
herself as a poet of damage and resistance.

By the time she wrote "Somewhere in Africa," Sexton had
achieved genuine separation from all her early mentors—Snodgrass,

Lowell, James Wright—who were also, of course, censors; she had ac-
quired a public persona and voice that was distinctively female. And if
the female subjects of her poems were dismembered, bruised, unchaste,
and self-vilifying, the female god of art in her elegy is none of these. In
Sexton's apprenticeship, femaleness itself was an aspect of identity that
had, with great difficulty, been assimilated to the sense of authority
necessary to mastery. "Somewhere in Africa" identifies femaleness as
one of the poet's powers; with all the strength of the known but forbid-
den, the poet carries her censor and teacher to his final resting place in
her hold, on her terms.

NOTES

1. "The Art of Poetry: Anne Sexton," interview by Barbara Kevles, in
Anne Sexton: The Artist and Her Critics, edited by J. D. McClatchy (Bloom-
ington: Indiana University Press, 1978), p. 4.

2. Transcript of soundtrack, "Her Kind," from the series *NET Presents:
USA Poetry,* 1966.

3. "Art of Poetry: Anne Sexton," p. 4.

4. Unpublished paragraph in typescript of Kevles interview, in the Anne
Sexton Archive, Humanities Research Center, University of Texas, Austin.

5. "Art of Poetry: Anne Sexton," p. 7.

6. Interview with Sexton's mother-in-law, Wilhelmina Sexton Knight,
Weston, Mass., March 17, 1983.

7. *Anne Sexton: A Self-Portrait in Letters,* edited by Linda Gray Sexton and
Lois Ames (Boston: Houghton Mifflin Co., 1977), pp. 22–23. Further refer-
ences to the *Letters* will be included in the text.

8. Anne Sexton, "Self in 1958," in *The Complete Poems,* edited by Linda
Gray Sexton, with a foreword by Maxine Kumin (Boston: Houghton Mifflin
Co., 1981). This edition of the *Poems* is used throughout.

9. Interview with Maxine Kumin, Warner, N.H., November 11, 1982.

10. See *The Journals of Sylvia Plath* (New York: Dial Press, 1982), pp. 302,
310–11, and Sexton's essay in *The Art of Sylvia Plath,* edited by Charles New-
man (London: Faber and Faber, 1970), pp. 174–81.

11. Kumin, foreword to Sexton's *Complete Poems,* p. xxv.

12. Unpublished letters of John Holmes: to Maxine Kumin, August 6,
1961. I am indebted to Maxine Kumin, Samuel Albert, and the Humanities
Research Center at the University of Texas, Austin, for access to the letters of
John Holmes included here, and to Doris Holmes Eyges for permission to
quote them. In further references these letters will be identified by recipients
and dates, in the text.

13. Correspondence of Anne Sexton with John Holmes, February 11,
1959 (misdated by Sexton 1958), Anne Sexton Archive, Humanities Research
Center, University of Texas, Austin; permission to quote courtesy of Linda
Sexton.

14. Interview with Doris Holmes Eyges, Cambridge, Mass., October 8, 1982.

15. Holograph transcript of psychotherapy session, February 7, 1961, Anne Sexton Archive, Humanities Research Center, University of Texas, Austin. I am indebted to Linda Sexton for permission to quote from this recollected dream.

16. Reviews of *To Bedlam and Part Way Back,* reprinted in *Anne Sexton: The Artist and Her Critics,* pp. 117, 119.

17. "A Friendship Remembered," in *Anne Sexton: The Artist and Her Critics,* p. 103.

18. "Art of Poetry: Anne Sexton," in *Anne Sexton: The Artist and Her Critics,* p. 5.

19. "The Excitable Gift: The Art of Anne Sexton," interview by Brigitte Weeks, *Boston,* August 1968, p. 31.

20. Anne Sexton, "Somewhere in Africa," in *The Complete Poems* (Boston: Houghton Mifflin Co., 1981), pp. 106–7. Quoted by permission of Linda Sexton and the Sterling Lord Agency.

Lucille Clifton: A Changing Voice for Changing Times

Andrea Benton Rushing

Women of African descent started publishing poetry in the United States with Lucy Terry's little-known collection of poetry in 1746 and Phillis Wheatley's more renowned collection in 1784. The literary descendants of these early writers include the nineteenth-century abolitionist Frances Harper and the twentieth-century Pulitzer Prize winner Gwendolyn Brooks. During the twenties "New Negro" Renaissance, no female poets shared popular and critical acclaim with such male giants as Sterling Brown, Countee Cullen, Langston Hughes, and Claude McKay. In contrast, during the Black Arts movements of the sixties and seventies, Nikki Giovanni, Carolyn Rodgers, and Sonia Sanchez nearly rivaled the popularity of Etheridge Knight, Le Roi Jones (Imamu Amiri Baraka), and Don L. Lee (Haki Madhubti). Furthermore, women poets like Mari Evans, June Jordan, and Audre Lorde also figured as authoritative voices during this recent era of African-American cultural and political nationalism.

Literary scholar Erlene Stetson discerns a tradition of African-American women's poetry stretching from 1746 to 1980 and contends that the tradition makes extensive use of African-American music; reflects African-American women's continuing experiences with the pernicious arpeggio of poverty, racism, and sexism; and parallels Euro-centered literature by women in its use of imagery about masks, homes, and flowers. While Stetson's formulation may shed light on the work of many African-American women poets, it does little to illuminate Lucille Clifton's intentions and accomplishments. Like all the other contemporary African-American women poets, Clifton was deeply affected by the Black Arts movement of the sixties and seventies. Although subsequent experiences like the women's movement and her own heightened religious consciousness have also left their imprint on her, we must consider that soul-changing crusade the crucible which most searingly shaped her art.

A concomitant of the separatist Black Power campaign, the Black Arts movement enlisted such cultural workers as musicians, visual artists, and writers to address the masses of African-Americans about the liberation struggles which confronted them. Propelled by slogans like "I'm Black and I'm proud" and "Black is beautiful," artists pronounced European and Euro-American critical norms inadequate yardsticks for African-American creations and viewed African-American arts as cultural tools with which to destroy three centuries of racial oppression and degradation.

While many bourgeois Euro-American and African-American readers and critics deplored the rage, obscenity, and violence of "New Breed" poetry, respected African-American critics like Bernard Bell, Hoyt Fuller, Addison Gayle, and George Kent recognized its merits. More importantly, young African-Americans in pool rooms and bars (as well as on street corners and college campuses) read it attentively and imitated it widely. In the landmark essay which opens *Understanding the New Black Poetry*, literary scholar Stephen Henderson sets forth criteria which help us identify some of Clifton's aims and effects. His first and most straightforward category is theme; the others are structure and saturation. According to Henderson both oral and written African-American poetry clusters around the motif of political, sexual, and spiritual liberation. In analyzing structure, Henderson terms it the poetry's reflection of spoken language and performed music. "Whenever Black poetry is most distinctively and effectively Black, it derives its form from . . . Black speech and Black music."[1] Saturation is Henderson's rubric for "the communication of Blackness in a given situation and the sense of fidelity to the observed and intuited truth of the Black Experience."[2]

Clifton's early verse clearly indicates the influence of the Black Arts movement. In accord with its dictates about how poetry should raise the cultural and political consciousness of "the Black community," Clifton dedicates *Good News About the Earth* to those killed in student uprisings at Orangeburg, South Carolina, and Jackson, Mississippi. It contains an apology to the militant Black Panther Party.

> i became a woman
> during the old prayers
> among the ones who wore
> bleaching cream to bed
> and all my lessons stayed

i was obedient
but brothers i thank you
for these mannish days

i remember agin the wise one
old and telling of suicides
refusing to be slaves

i had forgotten and
brothers i thank you
i praise you
i grieve my whiteful ways[3]

The volume also features verse to Angela Davis, Eldridge Cleaver, and Bobby Seale. In addition to treating these political subjects, Clifton mirrors the tenets of the Black Arts movement by directing herself to a general African-American audience using the grammar, vocabulary, and rhythm of idiomatic African-American speech. Interestingly, none of Clifton's verse on these vivid figures parallels so many of the tributes to them in relying on typographical quirks, like capitalized words and slashes, or haranguing either African-American or Euro-American readers.

In light of Clifton's later poetry, it is crucial to indicate the ways in which her early work diverges from the creations of her contemporaries. Many of the women poets who came to prominence during the sixties and seventies shocked readers. Despite their slight stature and (in a few cases) bourgeois upbringing, they mirrored the strident stance, profane language, and violent imagery of urban, male poetry. Part of my interest in Clifton's lyrical verse arises from my admiration for the acumen with which she found her own voice during a turbulent period when so many poets sounded the same chords of outrage and militancy. Rather than merely imitating the sarcasm and fury of male poets, Clifton anticipated the concern with women's issues which is—like opposition to the war in Vietnam, support of homosexuals' rights, and the crusade for environmental protection—in deep, though often unacknowledged, debt to the strategies and moral vision of the Civil Rights and Black Power campaigns. Furthermore, while other poets have tended to focus on historical figures such as Harriet Tubman, Sojourner Truth, Frederick Douglass, and Malcolm X, Clifton anticipated Alex Haley's *Roots* in personalizing history and using her own natal family as a symbol of the anguish and triumph of the African-American experience. Moreover, in an era when many African-American nationalists were harshly critical of their accommodating "Uncle Tom" and "Aunt Jemima" elders, the "opiate" of African-American Christianity, and the Anglo-Saxon proper names which are a living legacy of chattel slavery and cultural assimilation, Clifton wrote in a different key. While others complained of their elders' failures, she celebrated her ancestors, while others converted to Islam, she wrote about the life-giving power of African-American religion; and, though others assumed African and Arabic names, Clifton justified her own.

> light
> on my mother's tongue
> breaks through her soft
> extravagant hip
> into life.
> Lucille
> she calls the light,
> which was the name
> of the grandmother
> who waited by the crossroads
> in Virginia
> and shot the whiteman off his horse,
> . . . .
> mine already is
> an Afrikan name.[4]

Beginning with an allusion to the origins of the name "Lucille" in the Latin for "bright light," Clifton goes on to affirm a throbbing connection between Africa, the slave experience, and her own twentieth-century life.

Despite the considerable achievements of *Good Times,*[5] *Good News About the Earth,* and *Generations,*[6] it is with the publication of *An Ordinary Woman* (1974) and *Two-Headed Woman* (1980) that Clifton strides to center stage among contemporary African-American poets. These two fine collections parse the female sector of African-American life and give vivid testimony to the terse brilliance which alerted readers of her early work to Clifton's enormous potential. Not only do they explore a broad swath of rarely examined experience; they do so in an appealing personal voice with an attractive infusion of self-revelation and wit. By now, all the major contemporary African-American women poets have written verse about women's lives: the mother-daughter dyad, heterosexual relations, oppressive standards of female beauty, and loneliness are common themes. The verse is often autobiographical, its saturation in African and African-American culture is explicit, and its tone varies from aggrieved to nostalgic to exultant. Several things set Clifton's work apart from the strophes of others. First, she has written more poems about women's lives than any other African-American poet except Gwendolyn Brooks. Second, she has consistently done so in the African-American demotic with sinewy diction, a confiding voice, and stark imagery.

With the Kali poems in *An Ordinary Woman,* Clifton makes a bold innovation in poetic presentation of African-American women. Rather than limning heroic embodiments of female power and triumph, or depicting lifelike women victimized by parents, racism, poverty, and sexism, Clifton invokes an aboriginal ebony-faced Indian goddess associated with blood, violence, and murder. Since the paternal slave ancestor Clifton celebrates in her memoir, *Generations,* came from Dahomey, with its well-known tradition of heroic women, Clifton could have crafted poems around an African-based tradition. In turning to Kali, however, she frees herself from the feminist tendency to see women as hapless victims and explores the psychic tensions of an introspective modern woman negotiating the dramatic changes in contemporary attitudes about culture, race, and gender at the same time that she juggles the roles of daughter, sister, artist, wife, and mother. Written in standard English, these lyrics differ from Clifton's earlier work in syntax and diction; they are also tighter and more forceful. Like her earlier work, however, they also employ short lines, few rhymes, brief stanzas, and recurring images of women's blood and bones. The three Kali poems are striking enough to be quoted at length.

> Kali,
> queen of fatality, she
> determines the destiny
> of things. nemesis.
> the permanent guest
> within ourselves.
> woman of warfare,
> of the chase, bitch
> of blood sacrifice and death.
> dread mother. the mystery
> ever present in us and
> outside us. the

terrible Hindu Woman God
Kali.
who is Black.[7]

The Coming of Kali

it is the Black God, Kali,
a woman God and terrible
with her skulls and breasts.
i am one side of your skin,
she sings, softness is the other,
you know you know me well, she sings,
you know you know me well.[8]

Calming Kali

be quiet awful woman,
lonely as hell,
and i will comfort you
when i can
and give you my bones
and my blood to feed on.
gently gently now
awful woman,
i know i am your sister.[9]

In these poems, Clifton juxtaposes archetypal imagery about female generative and destructive power and insists on the tense mystery implicit in that union of opposites. Furthermore, she combines awe about Kali's violence and power with a fierce, almost protective, tenderness toward the fearful figure she refers to as "sister."

The thematic connections between *Two-Headed Woman* and Clifton's previous verse are immediately apparent. The opening "Homage to Mine" section demonstrates her continuing attention to family and friends and religious themes. In other ways, however, Clifton's latest volume of verse marks some sort of threshold experience for her. Unlike most other African-American women poets of the sixties and seventies, Clifton's marriage has been stable, and she has had six children. None of her verse articulates either the strains between men and women or the loneliness which often characterizes the work of other female poets, and her sons and daughters have been sources of pleasure and affirmation for her. A pivotal poem in *Two-Headed Woman* indicates new timbres in her life.

the light that came to lucille clifton
came in a shift of knowing
when even her fondest sureties
faded away. it was the summer
she understood that she had not understood
and was not mistress even
of her own off eye. then
the man escaped throwing away his tie and
she could see the peril of an
unexamined life.[10]

Here the poet's children grow up, her husband "escapes," and (despite all the introspective verse she has written) she terms her life "unexamined." One indication of the difference between the texture of *An Ordinary Woman* and *Two-Headed Woman* is that while the former invokes Kali to personify the furious tensions between women's creative and destructive powers, the latter concentrates on the smaller (though equally intense) landscape of one woman's searching psyche.

see the sensational
two-headed woman
one face turned outward
one face
swiveling slowly in.[11]

Another indication of the difference appears in the religious verse in the volume. On the one hand, Clifton uses a lower-class Caribbean accent rather than the African-American idiom in which she usually writes. On the other, she concentrates on the near ineffability of the interface between divine call and human response. Many of her religious poems are about Mary. Rather than depicting her as the wise poised figure of Renaissance painting, Clifton portrays her as an uneducated young girl inexplicably chosen for miraculous experience. Two brief poems make Clifton's strategy clear.

holy night

joseph, i afraid of stars,
their brilliant seeing.
so many eyes, such light.
joseph, i cannot still these limbs,
i hands keep moving toward i breasts,
so many stars. so bright.[12]

island mary

after the all been done and i
one old creature, carried on
another creature's back, i wonder
could i have fought these thing?
surrounded by no son of mine save
old men calling Mother like in the tale
the astrologer tell, i wonder
could i have walk away when voices
singing in my sleep? in one old woman
always i seem to worrying now for
another young girl asleep
in the plain evening.
what song around her ear?
what star still choosing?[13]

Clifton's focus on Mary not only reflects her heightened concern with extraordinary religious experience but also resonates with the emphasis on motherhood which has characterized poetry about her family.

One comes away from Clifton's powerful recent verse knowing that while it shares its lyric qualities, lucidity, and compression with her earlier work, it also marks significant steps beyond her past achievements. Using many of the same tools which molded the stanzas of *Good Times* and *Good News About the Earth* and maintaining her interest in female experience, Clifton has broadened her range and deepened her perspective.

NOTES
1. Stephen Henderson, *Understanding the New Black Poetry* (New York: William Morrow, 1972), p. 31.
2. Ibid., p. 12.
3. Lucille Clifton, *Good News About the Earth* (New York: Random House, 1972), p. 6.
4. Lucille Clifton, *An Ordinary Woman* (New York: Randon House, 1974), p. 73.
5. Lucille Clifton, *Good Times* (New York: Random House, 1969).
6. Lucille Clifton, *Generations: A Memoir* (New York: Random House, 1976).
7. Clifton, *An Ordinary Woman,* p. 37.
8. Ibid., p. 47.
9. Ibid., p. 57.

10. Lucille Clifton, *Two-Headed Woman* (Amherst: University of Massachusetts Press, 1980), p. 47.

11. Ibid., p. 23.

12. Ibid., p. 38.

13. Ibid., p. 40.

Answering the Deer: Genocide and Continuance in American Indian Women's Poetry

Paula Gunn Allen

In the ancient bardic tradition the bards sang only of love and death. Certainly these twin themes encompass the whole of human experience. Loving, celebrating, and joining are the source of life, but they necessarily occur against a background of potential extinction. Thus, these themes become the spindle and loom of the poets' weavings, for from the interplay of connection and disconnection come our most significant understandings of ourselves, our fellow creatures, and our tradition, our past. The American Indian women who write poetry write in that ancient tradition, for like the bards, we are tribal singers. And because our tribal present is inextricably bound to our continuing awareness of imminent genocide, our approach to these themes, love and death, takes on a pervasive sense of sorrow and anger that is not easily reconciled with the equally powerful tradition of celebrating with the past and affirming the future that is the essence of the oral tradition.

We are the dead and the witnesses to death of hundreds of thousands of our people, of the water, the air, the animals and forests and grassy lands that sustained them and us not so very long ago.

We are the people who have no shape or form, whose invisibility is not visual only but of the voice as well; we can speak, but we are not heard. As Laguna poet and writer Leslie Marmon Silko writes in *Ceremony,* "(We) can't talk to you. (We are) invisible. (Our) words are formed with an invisible tongue, they have no sound."[1]

"Blessed are they who listen when no one is left to speak"[2] Chickasaw poet Linda Hogan writes in her poem "Blessing." The impact of genocide in the minds of American Indian poets and writers cannot be exaggerated. It is an all-pervasive feature of the consciousness of every American Indian in the United States, and the poets are never unaware of it. Even poems that are meant to be humorous get much of their

223

humor directly from this awareness. American Indians take the fact of probable extinction for granted in every thought, in every conversation. We have become so accustomed to the immediate likelihood of racial extinction in the centuries since Anglo-European invasion that it can be alluded to in many indirect ways; its pervasive presence creates a sense of sorrow in even the funniest of tales.

Mary Tallmountain, Athabascan poet born in the Koyukon village of Nulato, writes of the witnessing she with a wolf companion engages in in her poem "The Last Wolf." In the poem the speaker is lying in a hospital in a devastated San Francisco, waiting for the last wolf to make his way to her through the "ruined city." She hears "his baying echoes / down the steep smashed warrens / of Montgomery Street / . . . and at last his low whine as he came / . . . to the room where I sat

> I watched
> he trotted across the floor
> he laid his long gray muzzle
> on the spare white spread
> and his eyes burned yellow
> his dotted eyebrows quivered.
>
> Yes, I said.
> I know what they have done.[3]

The question that the writers face again and again, pose in a multitude of ways, answer in a multitude of ways, is this: how does one survive in the face of collective death? Bearing witness is one of the solutions, but it is a solution that is singularly tearing, for witnessing to genocide—as to conversion—requires that there be those who listen and comprehend.

The American Indian poet is singularly bereft of listeners. The Indian people don't buy excessive amounts of modern poetry or novels; they are very busy trying to preserve the elements of culture and tribal identity that are left them, while accommodating these to the larger American society around them. But audiences for the American Indian writer drawn from the ranks of other Americans are sparse because of the many large and trivial differences in assumptions, expectations, experiences, and symbol-structures between Indian and non-Indian. The American Indian writer has difficulty locating readers/listeners who can comprehend the significance of her work, even when she is being as clear and direct as she can be, because these differences in experience and meaning assigned to events create an almost impossible barrier.

What we bear witness to is not easily admissible into the consciousness of other Americans, and that inadmissibility leads us to a difficulty in articulation and utterance signified by Hogan's plaint and by these lines from "I expected my skin and my blood to ripen" by Hopi-Miwok poet, Wendy Rose.

> I expected my skin and my blood
> to ripen
> not to be ripped from my bones;
> like green fruit I am peeled
> tasted, discarded; my seeds are stepped on
> and crushed
> as if there were no future. Now
> there has been
> no past.
> My own body gave up the beads,
> my own hands gave the babies away
> to be strung on bayonets. . .
> as if the pain of their birthing
> had never been.

Perhaps the knowledge of the real possibility of total extinction spurs one to perceptions that transcend the usual political, sociological, psychological, or aesthetic responses to pain or rage. Certainly the knowledge of continuance is difficult to cling to. We cling to it nevertheless; for as Rose writes in the end of the poem excerpted above, the speaker would have protected the baby

> if I could, would've turned her
> into a bush or rock if there'd been magic enough
> to work such changes. Not enough magic
> to stop the bullets, not enough
> magic to stop the scientists, not enough magic
> to stop the money. Now our ghosts dance
> a new dance, pushing from their hearts
> a new song.[4]

The new song our ghosts push from their hearts is a song of bitterness and grief, to be sure; but it is also a song of sanity, balance, and humor.

Humor is a widely used means of dealing with life among Indians. Indian gatherings are marked by laughter and jokes, many of which are directed at the horrors of history, at the continuing impact of colonization, and at the biting knowledge living as an exile in one's own land necessitates. Thus, Leslie Marmon Silko recounts Coyote tales that are updated to reflect modern life at the pueblo of Laguna, an eastern Pueblo that is a crossroad of southwestern Anglo, Chicano, and Indian cultures.

III

Some white men came to Acoma and Laguna a hundred years ago
and they fought over Acoma land and Laguna women and
even now
some of their descendants are howling in
the hills southeast of Laguna.[5]

This short story tells the tale that what is important at Acoma is land, and at Laguna is women (said to be some of the most attractive women around) and that mixed bloods are likely to be howling around in the hills because they are the offspring of the wily and salacious Coyote. Indeed, "coyote" in much of Hispanic-America refers to a half-breed, and that idea is also present in this poetic joke.

Coyote is a tricky personage—half creator, half fool; he (or she in some stories) is renowned for greediness and salaciousness. Coyote tales abound all over native America, and he has been taken up by contemporary American Indian poets as a metaphor for all the foolishness and the anger consequent upon it that have characterized American Indian life in the last centuries. He is also a metaphor for continuance—for Coyote survives and a large part of his bag of survival tricks is his irreverence for all that overrighteous folk take too seriously. Because of this irreverence for everything—sex, family bonding, sacred things, even life itself—Coyote survives. He survives partly out of luck, partly out of cunning, and partly because Coyote has, beneath a scabby coat, such great creative prowess that many tribes have characterized Coyote as the creator of this particular phase of existence, this "fifth world." Certainly this time frame has much that is shabby and tricky to offer, and much that needs to be treated with laughter and ironic humor; it is this spirit of the trickster-creator that keeps Indians alive and vital in the face of horror.

This stance, one of bitter irony, characterizes the poetry of Crow Creek Sioux poet Elizabeth Cook-Lynn, as this excerpt from her poem "Contradiction" indicates.

She hears the wolves at night
prophetically. Put them behind,
the legends we have found,

care not a bit,
go make a night of it! . . .
She wonders why you dress your eyes
in pulsing shades of Muscatel,
while wailing songs of what-the-hell
make essences to eulogize. . . .[6]

As one might well wonder, even though the truth of it is known. When the traditions that inform the people with life, and inform that life with significance are put behind, not much but Muscatel and "songs of hell" are left. Aside from the obvious emotional, social, and psychological considerations implied in this observation, the interesting thing about the use of humor in American Indian poetry is its integrating effect: it makes tolerable what is otherwise unthinkable; it allows a sort of "breathing space" in which an entire race can take stock of itself and its future. Humor is a primary means of reconciling the tradition of continuance, bonding, and celebration with the stark facts of racial destruction, and it is used in that way by many Indian poets, as in Nila NorthSun's poem "moving camp too far."

i can't speak of
        many moons
        moving camp on travois
i can't tell of
        the last great battle
        counting coup or
        taking scalps
i don't know what it
        was to hunt buffalo
        or do the ghost dance
but
i can see an eagle
        almost extinct
        on slurpee plastic cups
i can travel to powwows
        in campers & winnebagos
i can eat buffalo meat
        at the tourist burger stand
i can dance to indian music
        rock-n-roll hey-a-hey-o
i can
        & unfortunately
        i do.[7]

Surely this poem is a mourning song, as it is one of a stunted and trivialized vision made to fit a pop culture conception of Indian, earth, and extinction; certainly it highlights some of the more enraging aspects of American culture as they can only appear to an American Indian: a Winnebago is a tribe that lives in Iowa—that is what the word refers to among Indians; but among non-Indians it is a recreation vehicle—aptly enough. And an eagle is a symbol of the spirit, of vision, of transcendance to many American Indian traditionals, but it is also an emblem that bedecks a plastic cup which sugary colored ice is served in. And buffalo signified an entire culture, a way of life for numerous tribes once upon a time—though it now is a consumer curiosity one can purchase at some tourist foodstand.

Many of the poems written by American Indian women address the stark fact of extinction directly, and they do so with a vigor and resilience that does not merely bewail a brutal fate but directs our attention to a kind of hope born of facing and facing down the brutal and bitter facts of our recent history and present condition. This sense of hope is one that is a characteristic of the peoples whose history on this continent stretches beyond the dimmest reaches of time, winding back through history to "time immemorial"; it is a hope that comes about when one has faced ultimate disaster time and time again over the ages and has emerged from them stronger and more certain of the endurance of the people, the spirits, and the land from which they both arise and which informs both with life.

The metaphors that most appeal to American Indian poets are usually those that combine elements of tribal tradition with contemporary experience: thus the poetry of Creek poet Joy Harjo finds itself entwining ancient understandings of the moon, of relationship, of womanhood, and of journeying with city streets, rodeo grounds, highways, airports, Indian bars, and powwows so that from the meeting of the archaic and the contemporary the facets of her life become articulate, and the fact that modern American Indians are both Indian and American becomes very clear, as in the wry, laconic lines from "3 A.M."

> 3 AM
> in the albuquerque airport
> trying to find a flight
> to old oraibi, third mesa
> TWA
>   is the only desk open
> bright lights outline new york,

                                                    chicago
and the attendant doesn't know
that third mesa
is a part of the center
of the world
and who are we
just two indians
at three in the morning
trying to find a way back.[8]

A contemporary American Indian is always faced with a dual perception of the world: that which is particular to American Indian life and that which exists ignorant of that life. Each is largely irrelevant to the other except where they meet—in the experience and consciousness of the Indian. Because the divergent realities must meet and form comprehensible patterns within Indian life, an Indian poet must develop metaphors that will not only reflect the dual perceptions of Indian/non-Indian but that will reconcile them. The ideal metaphor will harmonize the contradictions and balance them so that internal equilibrium can be achieved, so that each perspective is meaningful and in their joining, psychic unity rather than fragmentation occurs.

Fortunately modern life like modern poetry provides various means of making the dichotomy clear and of reconciling the contradictions within it. Airports, traveling, powpows, burger stands, recreation vehicles, and advertising layouts all provide ways to enter the contradictions and resolve them. The increasingly common images from the more arcane aspects of Western traditions, alchemy, postindustrial science, electronic technology, and the little-changing chores of housework and wifery provide images that are common denominators in the experiences of Indian and non-Indian alike, making unitary perception and interpretation at least possible. The poetry of Oneida (Wisconsin) poet Roberta Hill exemplifies this reconciliation, as in this fragment from "Leap in the Dark."

            —Then she sealed her nimble dreams
with water from a murky bay. "For him I map
this galaxy of dust that turns without an answer.
When it rains, I remember his face in the corridor
of a past apartment and trace the anguish around his mouth,

                    . . . With the grace that remains
I catch a glint around a door I cannot enter.
The clock echoes in dishtowels; I search love's center
and bang pans against the rubble of my day, the lucid

grandeur of wet ground, the strangeness of a fatal sun
that makes us mark on the margin of our loss,
trust in the gossamer of touch, trust in the late-plowed field.
I hug my death, my chorus of years, and search
and stretch and leap, for I will be apprentice to the blood
in spite of the mood of the world
that keeps rusting, rusting, the wild throats of birds."[9]

Transformation, or more directly, metamorphosis, is the oldest tribal ceremonial theme; one common to ancient Europe, Britain, and America. And it comes once again into use within the American Indian poetry of extinction and regeneration that is ultimately the only poetry a contemporary Indian woman can write. Poets who have located a means of negotiating the perilous path between love and death, between bonding and dissolution, between tribal consciousness and modern alienation must craft a transformational metaphor to articulate their experience, as Hill does in these lines from the same poem:

. . . Oh crazy itch that grabs us beyond loss
and let us forgive, so that we can answer birds and deer,
lightning and rain, shadow and hurricane
Truth waits in the creek, cutting the winter brown hills:
it sings of its needles of ice, sings because of the scars.[10]

And, in a recent poem, "Morning: The World in the Lake," Linda Hogan uses the metaphor of transformation to celebrate the duration and persistence that are the basic characteristics of continuance and of love.

Beneath each black duck
another swims
shadow
joined to blood and flesh.
There's a world beneath this one.
The red-winged blackbird calls
its silent comrade down below. . .

And then it rises, the blackbird
above the world's geography of light and dark
and we are there, living
in that revealed sliver of red
living in the black
something of feathers,
daughters all of us,
who would sleep as if reflected
alongside our mothers,

the mothers of angels and shadows,
the helix and spiral of centuries
twisting inside.
Oh the radiant ones are burning
beneath this world.
They rise up,
the quenching water.[11]

Reconciling the opposites of life and death, of celebration and grief, of laughter and rage is no simple task, yet it is one worthy of our best understanding and our best effort. If in all these centuries of death we have continued to endure, we must celebrate that fact and the power of our vitality in the face of what seemed, to many, inevitable extinction. For however painful and futile our struggle to continue seems, we have but to look outside, at the birds, the deer, and the seasons to understand that change does not mean destruction, that life, however painful and even elusive it is at times, contains much of joy and hilarity, pleasure, and beauty for those who live within its require-ments with grace.

Recently I've been working on a series of poems about assimilation and colonization—laying these against arcane and land-centered under-standings, trying to articulate the balance between despairing reality and the hope that continued existence requires, as in these lines from "Transformations."

Out in the light or sitting alone,
sorting, straightening tangled skeins
(they're always tying lives in knots)
I would like to be sleeping. Not
dreaming, just blacked out:
no one bumping around in my brain—
no tangles, no deaths, just quiet
empty nests, just threads
lying straight and ordered and still.
Outside the window I can see
sweet winter birds
rise up from tall weeds
chattering. They fly
into sunrisen sky that holds them
in light.[12]

It seems the information and the patterns for continuance are all around us, if we will accept them for what they can signify, and use them to lend vitality and form to our life. Certainly in the long ago that's what they did, and it's what we can do now as well.

NOTES

1. Leslie Marmon Silko, *Ceremony* (New York: Viking Press, 1977), p. 15.

2. Linda Hogan, "Blessings," in *Calling Myself Home* (New York: Greenfield Review Press, 1978), p. 27. Also in *The Remembered Earth,* edited by Geary Hobsen (Albuquerque: Red Earth Press, 1979; reissued by University of New Mexico Press, 1981), p. 55.

3. Mary Tallmountain, "The Last Wolf," in *There Is No Word for Goodbye* (Marvin, S.D.: Blue Cloud Quarterly, 1981), p. 15.

4. Wendy Rose, "I expected my skin and my blood to ripen," in *Lost Copper* (Morongo Indian Reservation, Banning Calif.: Malki Museum Press, 1980), pp. 14–15. Also in *The Third Woman: Minority Women Writers of the United States,* edited by Dexter Fisher (Boston Houghton Mifflin Co., 1980), pp. 85–86.

5. Silko, "Toe'osh: A Laguna Coyote Story," in *Storyteller* (New York: Viking Press, 1981), p. 237. Also in Fisher, *The Third Woman,* p. 94.

6. Elizabeth Cook-Lynn, *Then Badger Said This* (New York: Vantage Press, 1977), p. 12. Also in Fisher, *The Third Woman,* p. 104.

7. Nila NorthSun, *The First Skin Around Me,* edited by James L. White (Moorhead, N.M.: Territorial Press, 1976). Also in Hobsen, *The Remembered Earth,* p. 380.

8. Joy Harjo, "3 AM," in *The Last Song* (Las Cruces, N.M.: Puerto del Sol Press, 1975). Also in Harjo, *What Moon Drove Me To This?* (Berkeley: Reed and Cannon, 1979), p. 43, and in Hobsen, *The Remembered Earth,* p. 109.

9. Roberta Hill, "Leap in the Dark," in Fisher, *The Third Woman,* pp. 123–24.

10. Ibid.

11. Linda Hogan, "Morning: The World in the Lake," in manuscript.

12. Paula Gunn Allen, from "Transformations," revised version in manuscript; original in *Star Child* (Marvin, S. D.: Blue Cloud Quarterly, 1981).

"I Go where I Love":
An Intertextual Study of H.D.
and Adrienne Rich

Susan Stanford Friedman

> I go where I love and where I am loved,
> into the snow;
>
> I go to the things I love
> with no thought of duty or pity.
>
> —H.D., *Trilogy*

In *The Dream of a Common Language,* Adrienne Rich initiated her quest for the common language of women by quoting these stern lines from H.D.'s *Trilogy,* an epic that presents the poet's search amid the fire-bombs of World War II for a regenerative love symbolized by the Goddess.[1] Rich's epigraph is an appropriate beginning for her own volume, which names the love between women as the life force countering patriarchy's death trip. As an important literary foremother, H.D.'s rich presence nourished the evolution of the younger woman's poetic vision toward the woman-identified, gynocentric feminism of *The Dream of a Common Language.* This essay will explore not only the nature of that influence but also the insights gained through the juxtaposition of their lives and texts.

H.D.'s influence on Rich occurs within the larger context of Rich's compassionate and noncompetitive reading, both as poet and as critic, of other women writers. Rich's work expresses a feminist theory of reading in which her drive to create a "common language" that connects women intensifies the underlying identification necessary for any literary influence. Like Virginia Woolf's belief that women writing look back through their literary foremothers, Rich's approach to the female literary tradition operates on a family model of influence in which mothers and daughters seek to transcend the divisive attitudes of patriarchy. This desire to recreate a strong mother–daughter bond through her reading reverses Harold Bloom's theory of the oedipal rivalry between literary fathers and sons.[2] Different women writers have come to represent for Rich the variety of strategies by which women have confronted, subverted, transformed, or been silenced by patriarchy. The result has been essays of critical brilliance, which have not only opened up new perspectives on various women writers but also identified the issues undergoing exploration in Rich's own poetic development. Her early essay on Anne Bradstreet, for example, discusses the movement in Bradstreet's poetry from ordinary "public" poems to extraordinary poems "written in response to the simple events in a woman's life." In her own poetry of the sixties, Rich was herself gradually changing from a poet who had erased all traces of gender to one who explored the dailiness of women's lives, who was beginning to see the links between the personal and the political. Rich's subsequent essays on writers like Emily Dickinson, Woolf, and Judy Grahn mirror her own development and consequently help to demonstrate their areas of influence.[3]

The powerful presence of H.D. in *The Dream of a Common Language* and the brilliant reading that stands behind it are a case in point. Rich has written relatively little about H.D.; her occasional discussions do not seem to explain the central position she gave H.D. by opening a major poetic statement of her lesbian-feminist vision with lines from *Trilogy*. However, a closer look demonstrates that Rich connected H.D. particularly with her own lesbian feminism. Rich has seen in H.D.'s work a comprehensive critique of the violence at the core of patriarchy, a quest for the personal and mythic maternal principle to counter the patriarchy, and a desire to strengthen those bonds between women as friends and lovers that support their emotional, intellectual, and erotic lives. These ideas go to the very heart of Rich's feminist theory as it evolved after the publication of *Diving into the Wreck* (1973); they also constitute the recurring themes of *The Dream of a Common Language*. Her interaction with H.D. consequently reveals the larger process of change in Rich's theoretical and poetic formulations of feminism.[4]

Rich's analysis of patriarchal violence and the symbolic primacy of the mother is encoded in H.D.'s epics more fundamentally than in any other poetic foremother. In her essays Rich explains that she had read H.D.'s Imagist poems when she was a young woman, but that in college, "we did not read, and courses in modern poetry still do not teach, H.D.'s epic poem, 'Trilogy,' in which she confronted war, nationalist

insanity, the ruin of the great cities, not mourning the collapse of West-
ern civilization but turning back for her inspiration to prehistory, to a
gynocentric tradition" (LSS, pp. 208–9). When Rich began reading
Trilogy, she was at work on an essay entitled "The Anti-feminist
Woman," by her own account the seed for Of Woman Born. In this
essay, she identified patriarchy as an institution not only unjust to
women but dangerous to all forms of life. "I am a feminist," she
wrote, "because I feel endangered, psychically and physically, by this
society, and because I believe that the women's movement is saying . .
. that we can no longer afford to keep the female principle enclosed
within the confines of the tight little postindustrial family" (LSS, pp.
83–84).[5] Motherhood, as both institution and experience, is at the sym-
bolic center of this "female principle" as Rich identified it. Understand-
ing why feminist theory had to begin by "exploring whatever else
woman is and might be besides a body with uterus and breasts," Rich
nonetheless stated: "I believe that a radical reinterpretation of the con-
cept of motherhood is required which would tell us, among many
other things, more about the physical capacity for gestation and nurture
as an intellectual and creative force" (LSS, p. 77). Rich called for the
use of woman's procreative potential as the symbolic paradigm of the
life force that must counter the "deathspiral" of patriarchy. Seeking
images to describe that force led Rich into a revisionist mythmaking;
she used traditions of matriarchy, mother-right, and worship of the
great goddesses of gynocentric "periods of human culture which have
shared certain kinds of woman-centered beliefs."[6] In this feminist en-
terprise H.D. served as her model: "H.D. insisted that the poet-as-
woman should stop pouring her energies into a ground left sterile by
the power-mongers and death-cultists: 'Let us leave / the place-of-a-
skull / to them that have made it.' . . . What the male poets were
mourning and despairing over had never been ours, and, as H.D. saw,
what we have yet to create does not depend on their institutions; would
in fact rather be free of them" (LSS, pp. 256–57).

It was not in H.D.'s epic works that Rich first discovered a theory
of the interconnections between sexual polarity and war, and the heal-
ing potential of a countering female principle. Rather, Rich's own ideas
provided the feminist lens through which she could accurately see the
presence of these themes in H.D.'s work. The exploration of violence
and the vision of love embodied in the avatars of female divinity form

the motivating purpose and symbolic center of both H.D.'s modernist epics of war, *Trilogy* and *Helen in Egypt*. Refusing to escape to the relative safety of the United States, H.D. lived through two world wars in London. She regarded war as the epitome of the forces that shattered the intersecting personal and public domains of history. Like her friends T. S. Eliot, Ezra Pound, and William Carlos Williams, H.D. expressed the despair for the fragmentation of symbolic systems that characterized modernist poetry. For H.D., as for these other modernists, the experience of modern wastelands initiated a quest poetry of epic proportions whose task was to create new meanings that could replace the inadequacies of the old. But in stark contrast to the male modernists, H.D. directly identified violence as the central force motivating and expressing the disintegration of Western civilization. She brought a woman's perspective both to her analysis of modern fragmentation and to her quest for a vision of regeneration.

Trilogy argues fundamentally that a world at war has lost touch with the female forms of divinity and that the search for life amid death is inextricably linked with the recovery of the Goddess. The poet's alchemical purification of language initiates the necessary re-vision of culture that restores to Venus, whose name has come to stand for "venery," her original and ancient power. "Now polish the crucible," the poet says, "and in the bowl distill" the bitter words. "Set the jet of flame," she continues, "till *marah-mar* / are melted." The poet's alchemy transforms the words into the living jewel: "Star of the Sea, / Mother" (*T*, p. 77). Once restored, the Goddess appears in the poet's dream as the central vision of the epic. Garbed in the shining robes of the Lamb in *Revelation*, H.D.'s "Lady" embodies salvation and rebirth. She resembles the madonna of Christian tradition, the even more powerful Isis of Egyptian religion. But she appears without the Child, the male symbol of salvation. Instead, she carries a "book of life," whose pages are blank, waiting to be inscribed anew by the poet. She is "not-fear, she is not-war," and "she carries over the cult / of the *Bona Dea*" (*T*, pp. 103–4). In H.D.'s poetry of survival, the Lady is indeed the embodiment of the "woman-centered beliefs" that Rich would restore to an endangered planet.

Trilogy does not explicitly link war with patriarchy. But in her profoundly antifascist epic *Helen in Egypt*—written between 1952 and 1954 partially in answer to the fascism in Pound's *Cantos*—H.D. returned to the subject of war and directly connected violence with patriarchy.[7] The narrative retells the story of Helen—the Greek Eve, "Helena, hated of all Greece"—from Helen's perspective. At its beginning, Helen has repressed all memory of her escape from a dull marriage for the springtime love of Paris. But in the course of the meditative "Pallinode" (the first of three sections in the epic), she learns to redefine her own and all women's innocence by understanding the sterility and violence at the core of the masculine ethos. The Trojan War, and by mythological extension war itself, represents the forces of Death in confrontation with the forces of Love. Forms of the Goddess—Thetis, Aphrodite, Isis, and ultimately Helen—are regenerating Love, "a fountain of water / in that desert" where the "purely masculine iron ring" of war "died of thirst" (*HE*, pp. 48, 51, 55). The "Pallinode" presents H.D.'s view of polarized male and female worlds wherein women express the inner, spiritual powers of Eros, while men command state power and weaponry in a cycle of death from father to son.

Both *Trilogy* and *Helen In Egypt* deeply reinforced the direction of Rich's thought and the urgency of finding poetic expression for her feminist vision. In particular, *Trilogy* and *The Dream of a Common Language* are companion volumes whose echoing ideas and language establish reverberating intertextualities. Experimental polarities, particularly the opposition between love and violence, provide the underlying dualistic structure of both volumes. H.D. contrasts the poet's inner visions of a mystical love with the cataclysmic war whose bombs have destroyed the London neighborhoods through which the poet walks. Rich broadened the "death-spiral" of patriarchy to include the institutions producing the postmodernist wasteland of hunger, atomization, and alienation. The city, especially Manhattan, frequently serves as her objective correlative for the spiritual state of mind engendered by a world that devalues the "female principle." "Twenty-One Love Poems," the structural center of the volume, counters the hostile world of the city with the transformative private world of the poet and her lover.[8]

Both H.D. and Rich insist on confronting the worst representations of societal disease. Neither seeks escape to a peaceful countryside that obscures the violence dominating Western culture; both are determined to create an alternative in the very heart of destruction. Their tasks take somewhat different forms, but the dynamic of transformation and the polarity out of which it emerges are similar. H.D., much more the traditional mystic, has apocalyptic visions of the forces of life amid death. As she "crossed the charred portico, / passed through a frame—doorless" after a bombing raid, she saw the "sign" of Astoroth, "sealed with the seal of death": "She set a charred tree before us," the may-apple tree still blooming, though "burnt and stricken" (*T*, pp. 82–87). Rich, not interested in the esoteric traditions so central to H.D.'s mythos, nonetheless searches for life in the rubble of destruction: "We want to live like trees, / sycamores blazing through the sulfuric air / . . . / still exuberantly budding, / our animal passion rooted in the city" (*DCL*, p. 25).

Rooted in the city, scarred by war, H.D. and Rich both found evidence of a regenerating life force within a desecrated "female principle." The structural center of both volumes is love, an Eros whose intangible power is the only force strong enough to confront the tangible power of society. Rich's choice of a quotation from *Trilogy*—"I go where I love and where I am loved"—highlights the centrality of a newly defined Eros in both poets' mythmaking. In philosophical and structural function, Rich's "Twenty-One Love Poems" parallels H.D.'s vision of the "Lady."

Both the *Trilogy* and *The Dream of a Common Language* associate the principle of life with images of matriarchal prehistory, in which, as Rich wrote, the mother's "capacity for gestation and nurture" served as an "intellectual and creative force." H.D.'s presentation of her own Atlantis myth in the final volume of the *Trilogy* has its companion in Rich's revision of the matriarchy myth in *The Dream of a Common Language*. Rich's epigraph from *Trilogy* comes from a section in which H.D. images her quest as the flight of the wild geese "who still (they say) hover / over the lost island, Atlantis; / seeking what we once knew." These birds abandon the "foolish circling" of the "steel sharpened on the stone." They know "only love is holy and love's ecstasy" (*T*, pp. 117–22). What follows is "the tale of jars," H.D.'s own parable of the dramatic confrontation between an Arab merchant named Kaspar and Mary Magdalene. Kaspar, suddenly interrupted by Mary's "unseemly" appearance in his shop, is offended by the indecency of her unveiled hair, by her refusal to contain this symbol of woman's power. Annoyed when she ignores his repeated rebuffs, Kaspar represents the patriarchal world that tolerates the presence of women only when their power, especially their sexual power, is controlled by men. Suddenly, however, he sees a grain of light in her hair that reveals a vision of Paradise, the Atlantis lost through man's desecration of woman. This revelation converts Kaspar to a worship of Mary, which in turn makes him worthy to bring a gift to the Child in later years. The epic ends with his journey to Bethlehem, where he kneels not before the Child but before Mary, the primal mother who embodies the related principles of love and life. In the iconography of the *Trilogy,* Atlantis regained is not an actual historical era but rather a state of mind symbolized by the matriarchal woman.[9]

Rich's short poem "Mother-Right" evokes the matriarchal concept as one with symbolic importance whether or not it reflects a historical reality. Echoing J. J. Bachofen's *Mother-Right,* the title identifies the tradition of matriarchy as the intellectual subject underlying the poem's flashing succession of condensed images. The man in the poem stands firmly "planted / on the horizon," regarding the earth as property to be measured out in boundaries (*DCL,* p, 59). The woman, in contrast, is a figure of motion, running with her child in a field, "making for the open." She is attuned to the earth—"The grass   the waters underneath   the air"—rather than possessive of it. The poem, however, represents a critical re-vision of the matriarchal myth. Bachofen envisioned the mothers of matriarchy as soft, fecund, and inert. Progress, he believed, was achieved by the aggressive thrust of men, whose creativity is centered in the brain rather than the womb.[10] Rich's poem, in contrast, creates a matriarchal image of freedom, strength, and motion. Evoking prehistory, revised from a feminist perspective, the poem nonetheless ends with a prevision of the future. At the end, the woman has been trapped within man's boundaries and must recapture her freedom: "the woman   eyes sharpened in the light / heart stumbling   making for the open" (*DCL,* p. 59). Just as H.D.'s "tale of jars" bore a message for a modern world consumed in violence, Rich's poem about an imaginary prehistory ends with an omen for the present. The image of the matriarchal mother stand symbolically at the center of both poets' re-vision of culture.

The emphasis on the mother in the poetry of H.D. and Rich led both women to explore the mother–daughter relationship as an essential element in their reconstitution of an authentic female principle. In *Of Woman Born,* Rich outlined the causes of conflict between mothers and daughters in a phallocentric world and insisted that women must find ways to heal these divisions. Her theoretical argument serves admirably as a description of the mother–daughter dynamic in the life and poetry of H.D., as well as in Rich's own. Striking biographical parallels highlight the pattern they share: in each some failure or flaw in the early relationship between mother and daughter creates a strong desire for reunion with the mother, which in turn motivates the poetic creation of potent mother symbols. Both women were the favorites of professor-fathers who encouraged their intellectual development. Both had mothers named Helen, whom they associated with Helen of Troy, particularly as she is described in Poe's famous poem. Both believed that their mothers' own victimization served as barrier between the mother's frustrated nurturance and the gifted daughter's unsatisfied need. Both ultimately broke away from a life built on pleasing their fathers and turned instead to their mothers to create the major symbols of their mythos. As poets, both engaged in a process whereby the daughter-poet gives birth to the potent mother symbol who then nourishes her art. So H.D. writes about the motivating force behind *Helen In Egypt:* "My older brother was my mother's favorite; I, my father's. But the Mother is the Muse, the Creator, and in my case especially, as my mother's name was Helen." So Rich writes in *Of Woman Born:* "There was, is, in most of us, a girl-child still longing for a woman's nurture, tenderness, and approval, a woman's power exerted in our defense . . . ; it is the germ of our desire to create a world in which strong mothers and daughters will be a matter of course."[11]

From her analysis with Sigmund Freud (1933–34), H.D. learned to link the mother of her desire with the mother symbols of mythological and mystical traditions. Helen Doolittle's favoritism toward her son and subservience to her husband had divided mother from daughter. In her epics, H.D. reconstituted the Goddess to represent the potent mother denied her by patriarchy. H.D.'s Goddess contains a strongly religious component based on a hermetic mysticism largely absent from Rich's poetry,[12] but Rich's feminist reconstitution of a matriarchal mother-daughter bond—especially in poems like "Sibling Mysteries" and "Transcendental Etude"—has striking parallels with H.D.'s mythos. "Sibling Mysteries," whose title evokes the potent mother of the Eleusinian mysteries as well as the prophet-poet of *Trilogy,* begins with a family constellation in which the poet, her sister, and her mother live within and without "the kingdom of the sons." Their relationships to their fathers and later to their husbands have divided the sisters; the poet asks for her sister's help in establishing a reunion of all three women.

Like H.D., Rich uses the personal dynamics of her own family to represent the structure of woman's oppression in patriarchy. The attempt to communicate with her sister is the prototypical task of sisterhood, and the role of the mother in this search suggests the primacy of a reinstated maternal principle. Like H.D., Rich creates overlapping palimpsests of the personal, political, and mythic: "Remind me how we loved our mother's body":

> and how she sent us weeping
> into that law
> how we remet her in our childbirth visions
>
> erect, enthroned, above
> a spiral stair.
>
> (DCL, p. 48)

As in so much of H.D.'s work, memory is a potent, transformative force that the poet uses to reconstitute the family. The poem's hypnotic structure—"Remind me" at the beginning of each section—conjures up memories of disparate shared experiences: hikes, pregnancies, and camping trips. The recollections resonate with imagery of nature as symbol and occasion of ritual. Fire, food, clay, water, art, childbirth, and child rearing evoke both the ritual of women's everyday life and their contributions to civilization in the prehistorical period. While rooted in memories of the everyday, the poet superimposes mythic prehistory onto the common life of women. The "spiral stair" of the enthroned mother echoes *Trilogy*'s Mary Magdalene and her "message / through spiral upon spiral of the shell / of memory that yet connects us / with the drowned cities of pre-history" (*T*, p. 156).[13] In the "kingdom of the fathers," the power of the mother, of women, has been contained, defiled, or ignored. Both poets seek to unveil that power by returning to the mother as symbol of creative regeneration.

"Sibling Mysteries" contains a lesbian-feminist dimension in its family constellation that appears to separate Rich from H.D. The poem serves as antitext to the anthropological fantasy of Freud's *Totem and Taboo*, in which he posits oedipal male rivalry as the origin of social organization. Transforming Freud, Rich's poem argues implicitly that the institution of heterosexuality results from the patriarchy's success in separating women from their mothers—in making the mother's flesh "taboo to us." Reunion with the mother, the sensuous mother, accomplished symbolically, fuses what has been sundered and allows women to escape "the kingdom of the fathers." Women have never been "true brides" of the father, and in recovering their love of the mother, they become "brides of each other / under a different law."

For Rich, reconstitution of a mother-centered world is inseparable from lesbianism. In "Transcendental Etude," she calls this desire for the mother "homesickness" and connects it to the "homesickness for a woman, for ourselves." Love of the mother, of the woman-lover, of the woman-self represent different forms of the same woman-identified act. A total love of woman—of body, soul, and intellect—brings wholeness as a woman: "A whole new poetry beginning here" (*DCL*, p. 76). The structure of *The Dream of a Common Language,* a volume of separate poems that nonetheless constitute a whole, embodies Rich's theory that authentic women's relationships in a patriarchy are essentially lesbian.

"Twenty-One Love Poems," first published as a separate work, occupies the center of Rich's three-part volume and explores how "two lovers of one gender" attempt to live, love, and work together, an accomplishment "nothing in civilization has made simple" (*DCL*, p. 31). Rich avoids the reduction of lesbianism to sexuality (as suggested in words like "sexual preference" or "sexual orientation") by portraying a range of concerns about life, work, and relationship in a hostile world. But "(The Floating Poem, Unnumbered)" in its celebration of two women's lovemaking shows how essential the erotic component of lesbian love is to Rich. *The Dream of a Common Language* argues throughout that woman-identified love, ultimately lesbian in its defiance of the laws of the fathers, makes the poet's work possible.[14]

At first glance, it seems as if Rich's identification of mother love with lesbianism separates her from H.D. While the goddesses in H.D.'s epics represent her mother and symbolize the female principle, they coexist with the poet's search for male forms of divinity as well. As a deeply religious poet, H.D. accepted the fundamental premise of hermetic tradition: the existence of an androgynous Divine One transcending all dualisms but manifest sometimes in female, sometimes in male iconography. The narratives of *Helen in Egypt* and *Hermetic Definition* are profoundly heterosexual, and the only relationships between women that H.D. explores are the bonds between Helen and her twin Clytaemnestra, between Helen and the mother goddesses.

However, a close look at H.D.'s life, her analysis with Freud, and her unpublished texts reveals not only her underlying common bond with Rich but also the light which Rich's probing perspective sheds on

H.D.'s texts. According to H.D.'s account, Freud said that she "had
not made the conventional transference from mother to father," that
her dreams and visions represented her desire for reunion with her
mother, the "phallic mother" of the preoedipal stage. Freud believed
that the lesbian remains fixated in her early love for her mother, which
she projects onto the lovers who serve as mother substitutes. Freud's
diagnosis of H.D.'s "mother-fixation" connects her desire for her
mother (about which H.D. openly wrote) with lesbianism (about
which she did not openly write).[15]

H.D. privately ignored the prescriptive norms that pervaded
Freud's concepts of sexuality and his judgment that she could never
have been "biologically happy" with a woman. But she fully accepted
the theory that her unconscious desire for her mother was projected
onto her love for women—predominantly upon Frances Josepha
Gregg, the woman with whom she first came to London, and later
upon Bryher (Winifred Ellerman), with whom she lived on and off for
most of her adult life. *HERmione,* a roman à clef by H.D. only recently
published, portrays the conflict she felt between her love for Pound, to
whom she was engaged in 1910, and her love for Gregg, about whom
she wrote three novels that she left unpublished. Her relationship with
Bryher, who "seemed to take the place of Frances," began some ten
years later after her initially happy marriage to the poet Richard Al-
dington had dissolved in betrayal and bitterness.[16] By 1918, Alding-
ton's affairs during his wartime leaves led to H.D.'s decision to go to
Cornwall with Cecil Gray, where she became pregnant just about the
time she met Bryher. Aldington wrote to her that he did not mind
lovers, even "girl-lovers," but her pregnancy meant that she now be-
longed to Gray. H.D. refused to marry Gray, and her steadily growing
relationship with Bryher helped to sustain her as she faced a series of
traumatic events: the war-related deaths of her father and brother; her
near-fatal illness from the influenza of 1919; the birth of Perdita in
March; and Aldington's final, brutal rejection in April.[17] Bryher's love
and promise of a trip to Greece saved H.D.'s life. Associated with her
love for Bryher, H.D.'s occult visions began on the Scilly Isles, where
they spent an idyllic month together in July 1919. During their voyage
to Greece in 1920, the transcendental experiences continued and finally
culminated in a series of light-pictures projected onto the hotel wall in
Corfu. H.D. believed that this "writing-on-the-wall" contained the se-
crets of her artistic destiny. Unsatisfied with her own efforts to trans-

late these omens of creativity, H.D. described the light-pictures to
Freud some thirteen years later. *Tribute to Freud* presents a portion of
their collaborative interpretation, emphasizing the vision's representa-
tion of her desire to be a priestess and her wish to be Moses, the found-
er of a new religion. But only her private letters to Bryher reveal that
Freud regarded her occult experiences, her love for Bryher, and her
desire for her mother as interconnected symptoms of "mother-fixa-
tion," the motivating impulse of her lesbianism.[18]

The "Lady" of *Trilogy,* Mary Magdalene, and the other forms of
the Goddess in H.D.'s poetry have their roots in her discussions with
Freud about "mother-fixation," lesbian desire, and visionary experi-
ence. To Bryher only she reported on one dream she analyzed with
Freud whose symbols were a major source for *Trilogy.* In the dream,
she, Bryher, and a young girl went out to the country at night and saw
a "giant moon, bigger than the sun." The moon was rainbow colored,
gradually projecting the image of a "mystic" woman "draped in flow-
ing rainbow coloured robes, seated like a madonna in a curved frame.
But she was not Madonna in that sense, she was Greek, she was Ar-
temis, yet she was pregnant." The dream, which revealed a "band of
sisters" worshiping the "mother in heaven," demonstrated that "I had,
in the uc-n [unconscious] completely turned about to a homo layer."[19]
In a poem she wrote during this period but refused to publish, H.D.
further makes the connection between lesbianism and a woman-cen-
tered religion necessary for the world's survival. "The Master" begins
in worship of Freud, but while she never denies this reverence, the poet
explores the dimensions of her "anger with the old man," with his
"man-strength" and "mysteries." *"Woman is perfect,"* she announces,
not the castrated male of psychoanalytic theory. That perfection, suffi-
cient unto itself, is erotically based and, by extension, serves as the
center of a new religion in which a woman named Rhodocleia is "that
Lord become woman"—that is, the Divine taking female form. Section
5 of "The Master" parallels Rich's "Floating Poem" in function.

> She is a woman,
> yet beyond woman,
> yet in woman
> her feet are the delicate pulse of the narcissus bud,
>
> . . . .
> there is purple flower
> between her marble, her birch-tree white
> thighs,

or there is a red flower,
there is a rose flower
parted wide
as her limbs fling wide in dance
. . . .
for she needs no man,
herself
is that dart and pulse of the male,
hands, feet, thighs,
herself perfect.[20]

H.D.'s epics are not explicitly lesbian in the way that the poem she suppressed defiantly is. But the goddesses in *Trilogy* and *Helen in Egypt* are encoded versions of H.D.'s exploration of her love for women and her belief that women embody a principle of life which the violent world of patriarchy must learn to absorb and revere. Rich, familiar only with the coded epics, was nonetheless attuned to aspects of H.D.'s work that have become definitively known only after the publication of *The Dream of a Common Language*. It was this sensitivity, I believe, that led Rich to highlight H.D.'s visions of Corfu with Bryher at her side as a model of how women working together empower each other and "give courage at the birth throes of one another's insight."[21]

The aspects of H.D.'s life and work that Rich has rejected reveal as much about Rich's development as the issues to which she was so acutely attuned. Rich concluded her discussion of H.D.'s and Bryher's empowering bond at Corfu with a warning against the trap male mentors pose for women. Such a mentor can give only the "illusion of power," possible success "in the common world of men. But he has no key to the powers she might share with other women" (*LSS*, pp. 209–10). Rich did not explicitly direct her comments to H.D., but given the significance of male mentors and lovers for H.D., Rich certainly might have had her in mind. "The Master," which substitutes H.D.'s own gynocentrism for Freud's androcentrism, nonetheless remains a poem that testifies to his genius and to his continuing importance to her. Other men served as her mentors and companions as well, among them Pound, Aldington, D. H. Lawrence, Gray, and Kenneth Macpherson. Her love for these men often entangled her in an artistic, erotic, and religious intensity that equalled her involvements with women.

She wrote to Bryher that she "was that all-but extinct phenomena [*sic*], the perfect bi-[sexual]," and she was grateful to Freud for teaching her to accept that she "had two loves separate."[22] Rachel Blau Du-

Plessis has argued convincingly that H.D.'s conflicted relationships with her male lovers and companions vitalized her art, particularly as it was expressed in the long poems of the fifties. Entrapped by "romantic thralldom," the "scripts" of conventional heterosexual romance, H.D. repeatedly experienced her involvements with men as a pattern that began with attraction, moved to a companionship with love and work entwined, and ended with male rejection and betrayal. In her poetry, DuPlessis concludes, H.D. transformed the actual male suitor, whose love had been experienced as an attack, into a spirit twin to her own soul with whom she transcends the patriarchal divisions of male and female, victim and victimizer.[23] Within this context, the poet invokes the protection of the Goddess to fortify herself as she makes her forays into the dangerous territory of heterosexuality.

H.D. never gave up the hope of finding in her life or creating in her art the ideal male companion, converted by her influence to a humanism based in a reverence for life symbolized by the Goddess. In *Helen in Egypt,* the pervasive imagery of twins expresses that desire, as does the transformation of Achilles from a warlord into a worshiper of Eros. The myth of Isis, the goddess with whom Helen most deeply identifies, infuses the human quests of Helen and Achilles. In Egyptian religion, Isis is the twin, lover, and savior of Osiris. After Set dismembers Osiris, Isis travels the world over in search of her lost twin-husband. Her magic revives the scattered limbs of Osiris; her reunion with him results in the birth of Horus and the rule of Isis and Osiris as a single regenerative power. In H.D.'s poetic recapitulation of the myth, Achilles' love for Helen leads to the death of the warlord and the birth of the "new mortal," her Osiris. They come to realize that "it was God's plan / to melt the icy fortress of the soul, / and free the man" (*HE,* pp. 51–52). Reflecting concepts of androgyny H.D. adapted from both esoteric tradition and psychoanalysis, this liberation of Achilles from the masculine ethos and Helen's concurrent quest for wholeness represent H.D.'s desire to transcend all dualisms, especially the polarity of male and female. The birth of their child Euphorian, whose gender is not specified, symbolizes that desire for transcendence. Taken as a whole, the complex epic begins by demonstrating the separation of male and female worlds, moves to an eloquent revaluation of woman as Eros, explores the oppositions of Eros and Thanatos within all individuals, and concludes with symbolic affirmations of transcendence.[24]

Rich has never commented directly on H.D.'s search for an androgynous male lover-companion or her belief in men's potential for transformation. But evidence suggests that Rich carried on a silent debate with H.D. that helped to widen the gap between the feminist humanism of *Diving into the Wreck* and the lesbian feminism of *The Dream of a Common Language*. In the early seventies, Rich used the concept of a feminist androgyny to demonstrate the failure of patriarchy and to envision the transcendence of patriarchal values open to women and men. "The Stranger" presented the gender-free poet as the "androgyne," "the living mind you fail to describe / in your dead language." The sex of the diver in "Diving into the Wreck" is carefully left unspecified, so that both women and men could identify with the search for the "she-he," the potentially androgynous self wrecked by a sexually polarized world. In "When We Dead Awaken," Rich called eloquently for the birth of woman, but she also envisioned the necessity and the potential for men's transformation: "One thing I am sure of: just as woman is becoming her own midwife, creating herself anew, so man will have to learn to gestate and give birth to his own subjectivity."[25]

By the time *The Dream of a Common Language* took shape, Rich no longer envisioned the transformation of men, much less associated childbirth imagery with their potential changes. In reprinting "When We Dead Awaken" in *On Lies, Secrets and Silence,* she left out her earlier call for man's rebirth and rewrote her concluding paragraphs to emphasize the continuing sterility of men. Paralleling this change is her repudiation of the concept of androgyny; section 13 of "Natural Resources" opens with the declaration: "There are words I cannot choose again: *humanism   androgyny*" (*DCL,* p. 66). This poem, whose fourteen sections create a symbolic mythos of feminist quest, explores at length her rejection of androgyny and her advocacy of a separatist lesbian feminism. The separatism of *The Dream of a Common Language* is not a simplistic separatism that involves withdrawing "from the immense, burgeoning diversity of the global women's movement," which Rich describes as tempting but ultimately too narrow to accomplish the broader goals of lesbian feminism (*LSS,* p. 227). Rather, it emerges out of Rich's belief that women must devote all their creative energies to one another.[26] Man's all-consuming need, the poem argues, has required "women's blood for life / a woman's breast to lay its nightmare on" and has resulted in "women stooping to half our height" (*DCL,* pp. 63–64). Women must develop the "impatience" of the spider's rebuilding, as they "make and make again" a new way of being. Such impatience characterizes the poet's ironic interchange in section 4 of "Natural Resources" with the insensitive male interviewer (*DCL,* p. 61), and contrasts with the curiosity about masculine consciousness expressed in the early version of "When We Dead Awaken."

The poet's exchange with the interviewer leads her to reflect in the following four sections of the poem on the experiences that have led to her present stance. The argument and imagery of these sections directly echo *Helen in Egypt* and strongly suggest that Rich's silent debate with H.D. was of central importance to her change in perspective. The poet reflects that the main diversion of women's energies from themselves has been their search for the "man-who-would-understand, / the lost brother, the twin." Echoing the image of the twin so central to H.D.'s epic, the poet remembers that "It was never the rapist: / it was the brother, lost, / the comrade / twin whose palm / would bear a lifeline like our own" (*DCL,* p. 62).[27] In other ways as well Rich's imagery carries recollections of Helen's soldier-lover, Achilles, whose motif is the lightning, whose dangerous "flash" Helen must transform to love (*HE,* p. 100). Rich's "comrade / twin" is "decisive, arrowy, / forked-lightning of insatiate desire," the "fellow-creature / with natural resources like our own" (*DCL,* p. 62). "For him did we leave our mothers, / deny our sisters, over and over?" she asks. "Did we invent him, conjure him?" Rich's question hovers over H.D.'s troubled relationships with men like Pound and Aldington and the brilliant poems she constructed out of those experiences.

The exchange between Rich and H.D. is a literary dialogue of resonance and dissonance that highlights essential elements of each poet's work. In H.D.'s poetic critique of culture, Rich found confirmation for her own growing analysis of the connections between worldwide violence and the oppression of women. H.D.'s matriarchal mythos and her celebration of woman in the form of mother symbols charted for Rich a pathway that connected the female iconographies of tradition and the personal dimensions of women's love for other women. For both poets, the mother as symbol and living presence is central for woman's rebirth and for the regeneration of civilization. Whether highly coded or directly affirmed, love for the mother in both poets is part of a healing self-love and a sustaining lesbian love of other women. Here, however, in the very center of similarity, the two poets part ways.

H.D.'s regeneration of woman as symbol and self took place within a context that included men as mentors, lovers, and companions. She never gave up her search for "the-man-who-would-understand" (*DCL*, p. 62), for the masculine forms of divinity that she balanced with the woman symbols he had resurrected. In contrast, the growth of Rich's lesbian feminism coincided with her abandonment of the radical humanism that pervaded her poetry during the sixties and culminated in the androgyny of *Diving into the Wreck*. Unlike the Lady's rainbow that affirms the Divine One in H.D.'s *Trilogy*, the rainbow at the conclusion of "Natural Resources" holds out the promise of transformation only in the bonding of women through history: "I have to cast my lot with those / who age after age, perversely, / with no extraordinary power, / reconstitute the world."

NOTES

This essay first appeared in *Signs* 9, no. 2 (Winter 1983): 228–45; a longer version came out in *Reading Adrienne Rich: Reviews and Re-Visions, 1951–81*, edited by Jane Roberta Cooper (Ann Arbor: University of Michigan Press, 1984). For their insightful criticism of drafts, I would like to thank Gertrude Hughes, Rachel Blau DuPlessis, Marilyn Arthur, and Jane Roberta Cooper. For Rich's response to the essay and my reply, see *Signs* 9, no. 4 (Summer 1984): 733–40.

1. H.D., *Trilogy* (New York: New Directions, 1973), p. 115, hereafter cited as *T*. Hilda Doolittle (1886–1961), pen name H.D., first published the *Trilogy* in three separate volumes, 1944–46. Adrienne Rich, epigraph in *The Dream of a Common Language: Poems, 1974–1977* (New York: W. W. Norton and Co., 1978), hereafter cited as *DCL*.

2. See Virginia Woolf, *A Room of One's Own* (New York: Harcourt, Brace and World, 1957), p. 101; Harold Bloom, *The Anxiety of Influence* (New York: Oxford University Press, 1973); Betsy Erkkila, "Emily Dickinson and Adrienne Rich: Dreaming of a Common Language" (paper delivered at the Modern Language Association Convention, Los Angeles, December 1982). In "When We Dead Awaken: Writing as Re-Vision" (1971), Rich discussed her introduction to the female literary tradition, inspiring a decade of feminist critics; reprinted in Rich, *On Lies, Secrets and Silence: Selected Prose, 1966–1978* (New York; W. W. Norton and Co., 1979), hereafter cited as *LSS*.

3. See Rich, "The Tensions of Anne Bradstreet" (1966), in *LSS*, "When We Dead Awaken," pp. 44–47, *Snapshots of a Daughter-in-Law* (New York: Harper and Row, 1963), and *Necessities of Life* (New York: W. W. Norton and Co., 1966). All Rich's essays on women writers have their companion poems.

4. Rich's discussions of H.D. are in "When We Dead Awaken," pp. 39, 40, "Conditions for Work: The Common World of Women" (1976), in *LSS*, pp. 208–9, "Power and Danger: Works of a Common Woman," in *LSS*, pp.

247, 256–57. I have stressed the change in Rich's thought, highlighted by her reading of H.D., but for excellent discussions of important continuities in Rich's poetry, see Albert Gelpi, "Adrienne Rich: The Poetics of Change," in *Adrienne Rich's Poetry,* edited by Barbara Charlesworth Gelpi and Albert Gelpi (New York: W. W. Norton and Co., 1975), pp. 130–47; Judith McDaniel, *Reconstituting the World: The Poetry and Vision of Adrienne Rich* (Argyle, N.Y.: Spinsters, Ink, 1978).

5. Rich, *Of Woman Born: Motherhood as Experience and Institution* (New York: Bantam Books, 1977), p. 257. See also Rich, "The Anti-feminist Woman" (1972), "Motherhood in Bondage" (1976), "Husband-Right and Father-Right" (1977), and "Motherhood: The Contemporary Emergency and the Quantum Leap" (1978), all in *LSS;* Wendy Martin, "From Patriarchy to the Female Principle: A Chronological Reading of Adrienne Rich's Poems," in Gelpi and Gelpi, *Adrienne Rich's Poetry,* pp. 175–88.

6. Rich, *Of Woman Born,* p. 93; see also pp. 84–109, and *LSS,* pp. 75–77, 80. Rich's poetry of the sixties had attacked the atomic bomb, the Cold War, racist violence, and the Vietnam War. By the early seventies, Rich made the theoretical connection between the culture of violence and patriarchy.

7. H.D., *Helen in Egypt* (1961; reprint, New York: New Directions, 1974), hereafter cited as *HE.* For extended discussions of H.D.'s epics and their roots in psychoanalysis and hermetic tradition, see Susan Stanford Friedman, *Psyche Reborn: The Emergence of H.D.* (Bloomington: Indiana University Press, 1981). See also Susan Gubar, "The Echoing Spells in H.D.'s *Trilogy,*" *Contemporary Literature* 19, no. 2 (Spring 1978): 196–218.

8. See Rich, "Not Somewhere Else, But Here," "Upper Broadway," and "Nights and Days" in *DCL,* pp. 39–46, "Teaching Language in Open Admissions," in *LSS,* p. 54, and "The Stranger," in *Diving into the Wreck* (New York: W. W. Norton and Co., 1973), with its echoes of T. S. Eliot's "The Love Song of J. Alfred Prufrock."

9. In her unpublished "Autobiographical Notes," H.D. jotted down from her reading that "Schleimann said Atlantis is Crete," that "women [are] equal in Crete," and that Cretan religion was "strangely wild, strangely civilized— mother-nature—lady of wild-wood . . . supreme God herself" (p. 46). The manuscript, along with most of H.D.'s unpublished writings, is at the Beinecke Rare Book and Manuscript Library, Yale University, New Haven, Conn. H.D. fused the three Marys of the New Testament to create her own Atlantis myth. See Friedman, *Psyche Reborn,* pp. 78, 113–15, 306–7. Rich brought this passage vividly to life in her reading of and commentary on *Trilogy* at an evening "Tribute to H.D." at the Manhattan Theatre Club (May 16, 1978).

10. See Rich's discussion of Bachofen, Robert Briffault, and Erich Neumann in *Of Woman Born,* pp. 70–97. Both Rich and H.D. bracketed questions about the historicity of matriarchy and worked with it as a symbolically necessary concept. H.D., like Rich, revised the androcentric myths of matriarchy; see Friedman, *Psyche Reborn,* pp. 269–72.

11. H.D., *Tribute to Freud* (1956: reprint, Boston: David R. Godine,

1974), pp. 43–44, and *End to Torment* (New York: New Directions, 1979), p. 41; Rich, *Of Woman Born,* pp. 219–20.

12. For extended discussions of the mother symbol in H.D.'s analysis, hermetic researches, and poetry, see Friedman, *Psyche Reborn;* Susan Friedman and Rachel Blau DuPlessis, "'I Had Two Loves Separate': The Sexualities of H.D.'s *Her,*" *Montemora* 8 (1981): 7–30; Susan Gubar, "H.D.'s Revisionary Theology" (paper delivered at the Modern Language Association Convention, Houston, December 1980).

13. The spiral is a frequent image in *Trilogy* and *Helen in Egypt,* as well as in H.D., *Hermetic Definition* (New York: New Directions, 1972), and *Vale Ave, New Directions* 44 (1982): 18–166. See Gubar's superb discussion of the image in "The Echoing Spells of H.D.'s *Trilogy.*" Rich's echoing of H.D.'s spiral imagery is a small part of the much larger influence H.D.'s lucid, concise language, stanza structure, and imagist craft had on Rich. In "'Cartographies of Silence': Rich's *Common Language* and the Woman Writer," *Feminist Studies* 6, no. 3 (Fall 1980): 530–46, Joanne Feit Diehl rightly connected the "conversational" language of *The Dream of a Common Language* with the evolution of Rich's feminist perspective. But see the longer version of this essay for a discussion of H.D.'s formalist influence on Rich. For an analysis of how Rich's ongoing dialogue with the male literary tradition pervades even "Twenty-One Love Poems," see Barbara Gelpi, "Is a Common Language Really a Dream?" (paper delivered at the Modern Language Association Convention, Los Angeles, December 1982).

14. Rich's related prose discussions of a broadly defined lesbianism include "It Is the Lesbian in Us . . ." (1976), in *LSS,* pp. 199–202; "The Memory of Our Love for Women Is What We Have Constantly to Expand" (1977), in *LSS,* pp. 277–80; Preface, *LSS,* p. 17; "Compulsory Heterosexuality and Lesbian Existence," *Signs* 5, no. 4 (Summer 1980): 631–60.

15. See H.D., *Tribute to Freud,* p. 136; Sigmund Freud, "The Psychogenesis of a Case of Homosexuality in a Woman" (1920), in *The Standard Edition of the Complete Psychological Works of Sigmund Freud* (London: Hogarth Press, 1950), 2:202–31, and Freud, "Femininity" (1933), in his *New Introductory Lectures,* translated by James Strachey (New York: W. W. Norton and Co., 1965), pp. 112–35. For extended discussion, see Friedman and DuPlessis, "'I Had Two Loves Separate.'"

16. H.D., *HERmione* (New York: New Directions, 1981), and *Tribute to Freud,* p. 152. H.D.'s other unpublished novels about Gregg are *Paint It Today* (1921) and *Asphodel* (1922) at the Beinecke Rare Book and Manuscript Library.

17. H.D. named Gray as Perdita's father in her 1937 divorce papers. See letters from Richard Aldington to H.D., summer 1918, at the Beinecke Rare Book and Manuscript Library. For a detailed account of these events, see H,D., *Bid Me to Live (a Madrigal)* (Redding Ridge, Conn.: Black Swann Books, 1983); and Susan Friedman, "'Remembering Shakespeare always, but remembering him differently': H.D.'s *By Avon River,*" *Sagetrieb* 2, no. 2 (1983).

18. See H.D.'s letters to Bryher written while she was in analysis with

Freud, March 1–June 2, 1933, and October 30–December 2, 1934, at the Beinecke Rare Book and Manuscript Library.

19. H.D. to Bryher, May 26, 1933, at the Beinecke Rare Book and Manuscript Library.

20. H.D., "The Master," *Feminist Studies* 7, no. 3 (Fall 1981): 407–16, esp. 411–12. For extended discussion, see Rachel Blau DuPlessis and Susan Friedman, "'Woman Is Perfect': H.D.'s Debate with Freud," *Feminist Studies* 7, no. 3 (Fall 1981): 417–30.

21. Rich, *LSS*, pp. 208–9. Among the many critics who have written about H.D.'s Corfu visions, Rich is the only person who has stressed the importance of Bryher's presence.

22. H.D. to Bryher, November 24, 1934, at the Beinecke Rare Book and Manuscript Library; H.D., "The Master," p. 409.

23. Rachel Blau DuPlessis, "Romantic Thralldom in H.D.'s *Helen in Egypt*," *Contemporary Literature* 20, no. 2 (Summer 1979): 178–203, and "Family, Sexes, Psyche: An Essay on H.D. and the Muse of the Woman Writer," *Montemora* 6 (1979): 137–56; Friedman and DuPlessis, "'I Had Two Loves Separate.'" Janice Robinson's theory that H.D. remained obsessed with Lawrence for forty years is not supported by the manuscripts that testify to the importance of many other men in her life (see *H.D.: The Life and Work of an American Poet* [Boston: Houghton Mifflin Co., 1982]). For an excellent discussion of the presence of these men in her poetry, see Albert Gelpi, "Hilda in Egypt," *Southern Review* 18, no. 2 (April 1982): 233–50.

24. See Friedman, *Psyche Reborn,* pp. 273–96.

25. Rich, *Diving into the Wreck*, pp. 19, 22–24, "When We Dead Awaken," in Gelpi and Gelpi, *Adrienne Rich's Poetry*, p. 98, and "Toward a Woman-centered University" (1973–74), in *LSS*, p. 141.

26. Rich's repudiation of the term *androgyny* is not an isolated event. For other feminist critiques, see for example the articles by Barbara Charlesworth Gelpi, Cynthia Secor, and Daniel Harris in the special issue on androgyny of *Women's Studies: An Interdisciplinary Journal* 2, no. 2 (Fall 1974); Mary Daly, "The Qualitative Leap Beyond Patriarchal Religion," *Quest* 1, no. 4 (Spring 1975): 20–40, and *Gyn/Ecology* (Boston: Beacon Press, 1978); Janice Raymond, "The Illusion of Androgyny," *Quest* 2, no. 1 (Summer 1975): 57–66, and *The Transsexual Empire: The Making of the She-Male* (Boston: Beacon Press, 1979). For an overview of feminist debate about androgyny, see Susan Stanford Friedman, "Androgyny: An Overview of Feminist Definition and Debate," paper delivered at the Working Conference on Androgyny and Sex Role Transcendence, Ann Arbor, 1978.

"True separatism," Rich wrote, "has yet to be defined" (*LSS*, p. 229). For her other discussions of separatism, see *LSS*, pp. 223–30; "Compulsory Heterosexuality"; *Of Woman Born*, pp. 183–217; and her important meditations on the connections between lesbian feminism and the global struggle against all forms of oppression in "Notes for a Magazine: What Does Separatism Mean?" *Sinister Wisdom* 18 (1981): 83–91. This last essay indicates a shift in Rich's thinking since the publication of "Natural Resources"; see the critiques of Rich's more recent stance toward separatism in "Responses," *Sinister Wisdom* 20 (1982): 100–105.

27. Rich may also have had in mind Sylvia Plath's lines in "Daddy": "Every woman adores a Fascist, / The boot in the face," *Ariel* (New York: Harper and Row, 1965), p. 50.

Epilogue: Philomela's Loom

Patricia Klindienst Joplin

> Why do you trouble me, Pandion's
> daughter, swallow out of heaven?
>
> —Sappho[1]

> Aristotle, in the *Poetics* (16.4), records a striking phrase from a play
> by Sophocles, since lost, on the theme of Tereus and Philomela. As
> you know, Tereus, having raped Philomela, cut out her tongue to
> prevent discovery. But she weaves a telltale account of her violation
> into a tapestry (or robe) which Sophocles calls "the voice of the shut-
> tle." If metaphors as well as plots or myths could be archetypal, I
> would nominate Sophocles' voice of the shuttle for that distinction.
>
> —Geoffrey Hartman, "The Voice of the Shuttle:
> Language from the Point of View of Literature"[2]

In returning to the ancient myths and breaking them open from within
to the woman's body, the woman's mind, and the woman's voice, con-
temporary women—thieves of language[3]—stage a raid on the treasured
icons of a tradition that has required women's silence for centuries.
When Geoffrey Hartman asks of Sophocles' metaphor, "the voice of
the shuttle," "What gives these words the power to speak to us even
without the play?",[4] he celebrates language and not the violated wom-
an's emergence from silence. He celebrates the male poet's trope for
archetypal violence and not the woman's elevation of her safe, femi-
nine, domestic craft—weaving—into art, her new means of resistance.
If the feminist critic coming to the story of Philomela and to Sophocles'
metaphor preserved for us by Aristotle asks the same question, she does
not arrive at the same answer. We would begin further back: with Sap-
pho, nearly lost to us, for whom Philomela transformed into a word-
less swallow is an ominous sign of what threatens the woman's voiced
existence in culture.[5]

When Hartman exuberantly analyzes the structure of the trope for
voice, he makes a by now fully visible and all too familiar elision of

gender. When he addresses himself to the story or context that makes
the metaphor for regained speech a powerful text, the story is no longer
about the woman's silence or the male violence (rape and mutilation)
behind it. Hartman assumes the posture of a privileged "I" addressing a
known "you" who shares his point of view: "You and I, who know
the story, appreciate the cause winning through, and Philomela's
'voice' being restored; but by itself the phrase simply disturbs our sense
of causality and guides us, if it guides us at all, to a hint of supernatural
rather than human agency."[6] In the moment she reclaims a voice, Phi-
lomela is said to partake of the divine; her utterance "skirts the or-
acular."[7] Noting how Philomela's woven text becomes a link in the
chain of violence, Hartman locates behind the woman weaver the my-
thic figure of Fate who "looms" like the traditional dark woman of
myth, spinning the threads from which the fabric of our lives is woven
in intricate design.

How curiously the critic remains unconscious of the implications
of his leap to distant Fate—the dangerous, mysterious spinning woman
with enormous power—away from Philomela—a virgin overpowered,
raped, mutilated, and imprisoned by Tereus, who refused to listen to
her. Why is the figure of depersonalized and distant Fate so preferable
for this critic? Perhaps because he cannot see that in her human form
she is a violated woman musing over her loom until she discovers its
power to avenge her wrongs. With the appeal to Fate, the critic shifts
the burden of responsibility for violence from the male, Tereus, to a
notorious "female," meanwhile preserving in anxious wordplay evi-
dence of his own resistance to recognition. Perhaps because he will not
see the shape of male violence, the critic cannot see the active, the em-
powered, the resistant in Philomela. He cannot see that the *woman,* by
an act of will and courage born of acute suffering, makes her loom do
what she once hoped her voice could do. In the most famous version of
the myth, after Tereus rapes her, Philomela vows to overcome her
training to submission and to tell her story to anyone who will listen:

> What punishment you will pay me, late or soon!
> Now that I have no shame, I will proclaim it.
> Given the chance, I will go where people are
> Tell everybody; if you shut me here,
> I will move the very woods and rocks to pity.
> The air of Heaven will hear, and any god,
> If there is any god in Heaven, will hear me.[8]

As Hartman suggests, the tension of the linguistic figure—"the voice of the shuttle"—is like the "tension of poetics."[9] But for the feminist who attends to the less obvious details of the text and context, the story of a woman's emergence from imposed silence is filled with the tension of *feminist* poetics. For the feminist reader finds in the image of the woman weaver a link to the ancient tradition of women's work and feminine community—a tradition identified, in this myth, as the locus of a hidden power.

In *A Room of One's Own,* Virginia Woolf provides us with a comic metaphor for feminist poetics in the tailless Manx cat, unfortunate inhabitant of the Isle of Man. Woolf's narrator notes the Manx cat's apparent "lack" as its most obvious "difference" from cats with tails and wonders at the loss of this crucial member.[10] Is the cat with no tail a freak of nature, a mutation? Or is it a product of culture, a survivor, then, of amputation, mutilation? The cat, lacking a tail, of course cannot tell her. The figure is mute but pregnant with meaning. The lost tail as *tale* craftily resists the violence inherent in Freud's reductive theory of women's castration as the explanation for our silence in culture while simultaneously testifying to a real sense of loss and a gender-specific one at that. The narrator perceives a difference so radical that the tailless cat seems to "question the universe" and its Author simply by being there. This question echoes Woolf's similar rejection of Milton's vitiating fiction, his particular version of our original fall in "Eve . . . evil."[11] Freud's and Milton's fictions, like the story of Philomela, conceal and reveal at once. For Woolf, the lost tail signifies a present absence: our broken tradition, the buried or stolen tales of women who lie behind us in history. The lost tail—made known by its stumpy remnant—is not only the loss of a continuous historical tradition (the voice of the "mothers" we try to look back through) but it is also our own tales, or voices, by extension suggesting the legacy of the cut-off voice or amputated tongue in all we still find it hard to say. We are not castrated. We are not less, lack, loss. If we at times feel like thieves and criminals when we speak, it is because we know that something originally ours has been stolen from us, and that the force used to take it away still threatens us as we struggle to win it back.

In the legend of Philomela we can recover the prior violence Woolf ironized in the punning metaphor of the tailless cat. Our muteness is our mutilation, not a natural loss but a cultural one, resisted as we move into language. Woolf taught us to see the obstacles. Any writer's desire to come into language is a burden, and those women who have carried the burden before us have not always been heard. To the keen anxiety of the writer's approach to the further reach of language, the limit or boundary where expression fails and death alone speaks, is added, for women, a hidden but felt sexual anxiety, a premonition of violence.[12] When Hartman ends his essay by noting that "There is always *something* that violates us, deprives our voice, and compels [*sic*] art toward an aesthetics of silence,"[13] the specific nature of the woman's double violation disappears behind the apparently genderless (but actually male) language of "us," the "I" and the "you" who agree to attest to that which violates, deprives, or silences only as a mysterious, unnamed "something." For the feminist unwilling to let Philomela become universal before she has been met as female, this is the primary evasion. Our history teaches us that it is naive to trust that the "truth will out" without a struggle—including a struggle with those who claim to be telling us the truth. It may be that great art is always very close to violence in the artist's decisive moment of rupturing the boundaries of the known; but the woman writer and with her the feminist critic must also ask why culture has been so particularly violent toward women who strove to cross that threshold themselves.

What in the text, "the voice of the shuttle," feels archetypal for the feminist? The image of the woman artist as a weaver. And what in the context? That behind the woman's silence is an act of violence, not castration but rape. When Philomela imagines herself free to tell her own tale to anyone who will listen, Tereus realizes for the first time the power of the woman's voice should it become public. In private, his superior physical force is enough. In public, however, Philomela's voice, if heard, might make them equal. Philomela must be silenced and imprisoned to protect Tereus from discovery.

But Tereus's plot is mysterious in its beginning and in its end. For why should Tereus choose to violate Philomela to begin with? And why, having raped and silenced her, does he preserve the evidence against himself by only locking her away rather than killing her? And why is Philomela's moment of triumph over silence and mutilation overcome by an act of revenge that only silences her more completely? In most versions of the myth, especially Ovid's, Tereus is said to be smitten with an immediate passion for the beautiful virgin, the younger daughter of Athens's aging King Pandion. What commentators on the story do not observe is that both Philomela and her sister, Procne, serve as objects of exchange between these two kings: Pandion of Athens and Tereus of Thrace, one old, one young. The old king gave his elder daughter, Procne, to Tereus to bind a military alliance with the young king said to descend from Ares, god of war. The younger daughter, Philomela, is the marriageable female Tereus seizes to challenge the primacy of the Father King. Tereus's mythic passion deflects attention from the myth's underlying structure: the rivalry between two kings and two cultures, Greek and barbarian.[14] Tereus's desire is said to emerge only when Procne, after five years of married life in Thrace, becomes lonely for her sister and asks Tereus to go to Pandion to ask that Philomela be allowed to visit her. When Tereus sees Philomela with Pandion, he feels uncontrollable desire, and he will brook no frustration of his plan to take her for himself.[15]

The cover story for Philomela's violation displaces responsibility for Tereus's lust onto the woman herself: as Ovid would have it, the chaste woman's body is fatally seductive. Not only are we asked to believe that Procne sets the fateful chain of events into motion with *her* desire for her sister, but that Philomela unwittingly and passively elicits Tereus's desire by being what she is: pure. But if it is Philomela's purity that makes her so desirable, it is not because virginity is beautiful. Tereus's passion is aroused not by purity but by power: her unruptured hymen is a token of her father's intact power, for Pandion holds the right to offer Philomela to another man in a political bargain because Philomela is still a virgin and therefore unexchanged. If the sexual violence implicit in the exchange of women is what the myth conceals incompletely, what it reveals is how this expression of male dominance requires the violent appropriation of the woman's power to speak.

When Philomela transforms her suffering, captivity, and silence into the occasion for art, the text she weaves is overburdened with a desire to tell. Her tapestry not only redresses a private wrong, but should it become public (and it was because she had begun to connect the private to the political that her tongue was cut out) it threatens to retrieve from obscurity all that her culture defines as outside the bounds of allowable discourse, whether sexual, spiritual, or literary.

Let Philomela and Procne as sisters suggest to us the relation of woman writer to feminist critic in the last decades, and let us consider the myth's two recognition scenes and their implications for us. The texts women artists weave have often been, like Philomela's, born of necessity, of closeted wrongs. We have often spoken in clotted words when we first tried the power of our voices. But the beauty of this myth springs from the image of the single weaver and her loom—an invitation to see how necessary and powerful the woman's audience can be to the motive, shape, and outcome of her art. Consider the moment when Philomela, utterly cut off from the larger world, was seized with a new idea. Like women writing at home, in the domestic sphere, Philomela, who must have spun and woven all her life, decides to use her decorative craft to a new end. Using the only work allowed her, armed with patience and discipline, Philomela's new motive—her hope of being heard by another woman, her sister—alters her vision. Philomela's rescue from a year's captivity and muteness requires not only the domestic feminine craft (weaving) and its instruments (the loom, the shuttle) to produce the fabric/text. Philomela's release from violation and silence requires other women: a servant to carry the text; and a sister to receive, to interpret, and then to act upon it.

We should remember how carefully Philomela must have worked to weave her tale: the possibility of discovery, the threat of renewed violence against her. Only because her activity was apparently harmless, the same weaving, the same safely enclosed feminine activity, was it allowed to happen at all. (What a model prisoner she must have seemed: so intent on her proper task.) We think of the ambiguous domestic arrangements of our great women writers: Jane Austen writing in the family sitting room. We think of Emily Dickinson's sly domestic economy: all those poems written on scraps of paper, sent as gifts in letters, or hidden away. Few suspected, but no one really knew how immense a domain she had created for herself in the well-regulated family house; no one was prepared for the number or greatness of the poems she left behind. We think of Dickinson's cherished Elizabeth Barrett Browning, who took to her sickbed (that was allowed) in order to cultivate her gifts. And we think of the isolated Brontës; and, in twentieth-century America, of the stunning resilience of women of color whose voices have reached us against enormous odds. We think, in short, of how many women have found in captivity and constraint the power of imagination, the suppleness of spirit to turn captivity into release, constraint into creativity.

Next, we have the vital link in the mythic texts, the small detail: Philomela entrusted her rolled fabric to an old servant woman and asked her (somehow) to deliver it to the Queen, Procne. Let her be like Mrs. McNab, the charwoman in the "Time Passes" section of Woolf's

To the Lighthouse, who proved such a humble but resolute stay against nature, time, and war. Let the unlettered woman be all those—humble, strong, or stooped; faithful if unknowing, cunning if knowing—who helped pass from hand to hand the legacy: our discarded, neglected, or broken tales. Without these obscure women, the tale would have been lost. We would still be impoverished. And let Procne be us.

When the tale comes to light—when the old, loyal servant puts into our hands the rolled fabric and we unroll it in our familiar domestic routine—the myth records that the woman reader suffers her own moment of shocked silence. ("So *this* is why you have been silent? So *these* were the conditions of your life?"). For Procne, the Queen— daughter, wife, and mother to kings—reading Philomela's text immediately ruptures her understanding of her place in all these relationships. When Tereus returned from Athens and told her that her sister was dead, Procne had rent her garments and put on mourning. She had built a tomb and performed the sacred rites of burial, mourning her terrible loss. But once she reads Philomela's text, learning that her sister is alive, and her own husband the violator, Procne puts off her mourning. She finds in the text instructions for reaching the castle/prison where Tereus has hidden Philomela. And she brings her home.

We have had in common with Procne the need to recover what it means to be and to have a sister. Before Procne finds her, Philomela has in common with her counterparts in Roman legend and literature, Lucrece and Virginia, her isolation from other women as she is violated by men. The attempt to suppress any evidence of an articulated women's community is a crucial, but usually invisible, aspect of these myths.[16] And even when we find a daughter whose mother seeks to protect her in the crisis, neither woman's voice is heard. Procne is like many a violated and then violent woman in Greek myth. She is like Clytemnestra enraged at Agamemnon's willful sacrifice of their daughter, Iphigenia, to the Trojan War. Clytemnestra, queen and wife, moves from grief and rage to bloody revenge when neither her status as the king's spouse nor her power or voice as mother can save her daughter.

We, like Procne, have received discarded, dismembered stories from lost sisters long believed dead; sisters we have looked for and desired, sisters we have missed and grieved for. When we first unfolded the tales feminist artists, historians, and scholars retrieved for us we, too, suffered an extended moment of shocked silence. Philomela did not die: she was hidden from us. We are not engaged in a long funeral, we have a rescue to perform. Those who gave us the sad news that we had no sister lied to us. Now we, too, have faced a moment of recognition of our place in culture. And we, too, have felt a momentary impulse to leap, as myths have people immediately leap, from having endured violence to exacting revenge. But in the collapsed space between Procne's moment of recognition and her revenge, the myth tells us what is lost when we choose to return violence for violence: her sister's moment at the loom; the craft's elevation to an art. For the loom and its shuttle bind and connect what had been broken. The tapestry at once testifies to and heals the rupture within Philomela, between the separated sisters. Art came out of the violence, but just as paradoxically it may be swallowed up in it again.

Let us consider the sister's mode of revenge before returning to the loom. When Philomela at long last reaches Procne (the original end of her interrupted journey), her desire to live with her sister in peace is overcome by Procne's rage to avenge the sexual assault that separated them, that polluted their blood bond as sisters and turned it into a source of mutual shame. The myth suggests that the man who was violent first is too powerful to be the direct target of revenge. As Procne imagines finding a knife to stab or finally to castrate Tereus with, their son, Itys, enters. As Ovid has it, the speaking child enrages Procne: "If this boy may speak, why has my sister been silenced?" This is Procne's moment of deeper recognition: who has a voice in her culture? Neither she nor her sister, but her son, because he will one day be king. The child is taken away and killed. Sacrificed to his father's violence, Itys is dismembered, his flesh skewered over the hearth, his bones boiled in a cauldron. Then Tereus is called in for a royal feast. Procne serves him the flesh of his son, and only as he finishes eating and calls for Itys, does Tereus learn that he has devoured him.

Here, Philomela comes forward and thrusts Itys's head at Tereus. In this recognition scene, Tereus sees his own plot uncovered, but the substitution of an innocent victim (the child) for the guilty man (the father) only initiates the cycle of violence and revenge anew. The sisters' violence not only leaves unchanged the rigid division between men and women, but it makes the women so much like the man who first moved against them that the reader can share no satisfaction in their attempt at justice.[17] The escalating bloodshed is cut off as Tereus rises up to kill the sisters and the gods transform them all into birds: Tereus into the hoopoe or hawk, Procne into the nightingale, Philomela into the swallow. It is by way of later Roman tradition that the sisters are reversed,[18] Philomela becoming the nightingale, taken up by the English tradition as the pathetic bird eternally pressing her breast to a thorn to make herself sing.

Because later tradition makes Philomela an attractive but dangerous singer of a wordless song of pain that male poets then translate into art, we learn more in drawing near to the loom of Greek legend. As long as the woman cannot speak and be heard, as long as culture enforces submission and silence (making explicit what is implicit: the rule of sexual dominance, the articulation of only one body, one being, and one voice—the male's), it would seem the sisters are more likely to reproduce an inverted form of the violence used against Philomela: the sisters trade dismemberment and decapitation of the boy for rape and mutilation of the woman.

Like Procne, some women have wished to repay silence with silence: "Now I, alone, may speak, and you must learn what it means to be mute." But here, the feminist ignores the implications of imitating male violence. Any claim to a privileged possession of the truth, any appropriation of sole power to speak carries with it the potential to violate another. What the stories of violated and then violent women in myth teach us in common, whether we speak of Medusa, Philomela, Clytemnestra, or Medea, is how an initial moment of powerlessness, when avenged, can lead to a purely destructive assertion of a woman's power. As Alicia Ostriker observes of the revisionist myths of modern American women poets, the woman's will to be destructive (or to be destroyed) is often the product of her powerlessness to be or to do anything else.

Access to language, access to an audience are crucial. After all, had there been any hope that Tereus would hear Philomela's voice and be moved to remorse, it might have been enough for her to display not Itys's bloody head but her own beautifully crafted tapestry. Because they have been so isolated and because the whole story unfolds against the dimly visible backdrop of war and the exchange of women, the sisters cannot envision the possibility of removing the confrontation from the domestic hearth. They do not try the peaceful force of the weaving itself on the man who thought his power was sufficient to break a woman's spirit, the man who thought physical brutality would go undiscovered and unpunished. We do not see the sisters call for

justice in the public domain because it was the king himself, as head of
state, who drew the patriarchal appropriation of language, sexuality,
and power to its logical extreme in raping and silencing his rival's vir-
gin daughter, Philomela.

Can women now weave texts and interpret them without re-
producing another sacrificial crisis? Can women now tell their tales and
be heard without marking a new, more innocent victim? without vic-
timizing ourselves? The work of modern women writers makes it clear
that we can.[19]

> What we have in common are the words at our backs. The idioms
> for revenge are "report a crime" and "report to five families." The
> reporting is the vengeance—not the beheading, not the gutting,
> but the words. And I have so many words—"chink" words and
> "gook" words too—that they do not fit on my skin.[20]

But the writer's act of renunciation, and writing as the healing of what
is torn in herself and in her community, requires that she be *heard*. Why
does "the voice of the shuttle" have the power to speak to us even
without the original woman's story? Because, like Maxine Hong King-
ston's novel, *The Woman Warrior: Memoirs of a Girlhood Among Ghosts,*
women's writing now helps us to remember against all odds what we
have been required and trained to forget. Philomela and her loom speak
to us because together they are an assertion of our will to survive over
everything that threatens to silence us, including the male literary tradi-
tion and its critics who have preserved Philomela's "voice" without
knowing what it says. Philomela speaks to us, speaks *in* us, because, as
Kingston's woman warrior knows in becoming a woman writer, the
woman's body is the original page on which her story is written in
blood.

The work of modern women writers speaks of the need for a com-
munal, collective act of re-membering. For us, both the female sexual
body and the woman's text must be rescued from oblivion—from cul-
turally induced amnesia or the quiet but steady dismemberment of our
tales by misogynist criticism. We must remember in order to forget;
otherwise, we will be haunted by and continually relive the pain and
rage of each moment we have yielded to the pressure on us to not-see
and to not-say what we know is true. Women have served as a sacri-
ficial offering to the male artistic imagination (the nightingale leaning

on her thorn—*choosing it*—to inspire the male poet), but the woman writer and the feminist critic can remember the embodied, resisting woman.[21] Each time we do, we resist our status as victim, we interrupt the structure of reciprocal violence.

Women's writing is rich with the hope of community/communion, a movement into language acknowledging loss and violation but refusing to reproduce it. Anamnesis—remembering—is a sacred activity in women's writing (which *is* the sign of women's community), and our words have become food for other women.[22] The human community, if it is to continue, requires this in us. For in our confrontation with the ethical problem inherent in the urge toward violent revenge, in our recognition of the victim's temptation to speak the language of revenge, we face our potential either to perpetuate or to radically subvert the dialectics of dominance and submission.[23]

Why does Philomela's silence speak to us? Because it addresses our deepest questions and fears about our place in history. The woven tapestry is a tale seeking its audience, a story preserved and frequently misinterpreted until it reaches the right listeners: other women, sisters. Before we can help, or in order to help teach men who are willing how to hear such a voice, we have had to learn to hear it ourselves.

In envisioning the future of women's writing, let us include a moment of return to celebrate Philomela and her loom. In our choices we can revise the myth as it lives in us by recognizing bloody revenge as intrinsic to historical moments when women are isolated and dominated by men. The myth leaves unrealized and perhaps we must leave unwritten the scene in which Philomela, rescued by Procne, might go on weaving new and different tales on her loom—after Tereus has heard her voice and been moved to self-recognition and change.

If the voice of the shuttle is oracular it tells us Fate never was a woman looming darkly over frightened men; she was a male fantasy of female reprisal. In celebrating the voice of the shuttle as ours, we celebrate neither Philomela the victim nor Philomela the avenger waving Itys's bloody head. Rather we celebrate Philomela weaving. We can return to the woman who, in recovering her own voice, uncovers not only her own power, but discovers its potential for peace. Armed with the vision of art as a means of resistance to all that would destroy us, we need no longer be trapped in the structure of violence. We can refuse to let revenge overtake the loom again. We have that power. We have that choice.

NOTES

For a discussion of the myth's place in fifth-century Greek culture and its implications for literary theory and feminist thought, see the longer version of this essay, "The Voice of the Shuttle is Ours," *Stanford Literature Review* 1, no. 1 (Spring 1984).

1. *LP* 135. See also Fragment no. 197 in *Greek Lyric Poetry, Including the Complete Poetry of Sappho*, translated by Willis Barnstone (New York: Schocken Books, 1972), p. 83.

2. Geoffrey Hartman, *Beyond Formalism, Literary Essays 1958–1970* (New Haven: Yale University Press, 1970), p. 337.

3. The phrase is taken from the title of Claudine Herrmann's *Les Voleuses de langue* (Paris: Des Femmes, 1979). See Alicia Ostriker's essay, "The Thieves of Language: Women Poets and Revisionist Mythmaking," in this volume.

4. Hartman, *Beyond Formalism*, p. 337.

5. About 95 percent of Sappho's estimated nine thousand lines of poetry were destroyed between the first and fifteenth centuries A.D. As Paul Friedrich notes, "Of her five-hundred-odd poems, there survive to this day between six and seven hundred lines. Her work was extirpated from the Greek-speaking world just as ruthlessly and almost as successfully as the image of her persona, Aphrodite." See *The Meaning of Aphrodite* (Chicago: University of Chicago Press, 1978), p. 127.

6. Hartman, *Beyond Formalism*, p. 338.

7. Ibid., p. 347.

8. Ovid, *Metamorphoses*, translated by Rolfe Humphries (Bloomington: Indiana University Press, 1955), p. 147.

9. Hartman, *Beyond Formalism*, p. 338.

10. For Woolf's use of the Manx cat as a way of introducing the feminist question of how difference became hierarchy see *A Room of One's Own* (New York: Harcourt, Brace and World, 1929, reprinted 1957), pp. 11ff.

11. Hartman discusses the line "O Eve in evil hour . . . " (*Paradise Lost*, IX. 1067) but does not play out the implications of the "reader insult" and "language injury" Milton works there. The punning on Eve/evil is, of course, part of what Woolf rejects as Milton's bogey in *A Room of One's Own*.

For Freud, the mother's genitals, because they represent the fait accompli of castration, are terrifying. (To whom and why are, of course, the obvious questions.) See his "Medusa's Head," in *Sexuality and the Psychology of Love*, edited by Philip Rieff (New York: Collier, 1963), pp. 212–13. What Freud leaves out of his discussion of Medusa's snakey head as the mother's monstrous genitals is the original violence against Medusa. She was not castrated—but raped—by Poseidon. By a process of reversal, Freud projects onto the woman victim the punishment (castration) for the crime against her (rape).

12. For Woolf's own account of her struggle not to be silenced see "Professions for Women," in *The Death of the Moth and Other Essays* (New York: Harcourt Brace Jovanovich, 1942, reprinted 1970), pp. 235–42, and the earlier, angrier version of the same essay in which she appeals to "the sacred name of

Sappho" published as "Speech of January 21, 1931," in *The Pargiters: The Novel-Essay Portion of THE YEARS,* edited by Mitchell A. Leaska (New York: Harcourt Brace Jovanovich, 1977), pp. xxvii–xliv.

13. Hartman, *Beyond Formalism,* p. 353, emphasis added.

14. For a relevant discussion of the distinction between "Hellenes, Greek speakers, and *barbaroi,* babblers" in which this myth is grounded, see Page du-Bois, *Centaurs and Amazons, Women and the Pre-History of the Great Chain of Being* (Ann Arbor: University of Michigan Press, 1982), p. 78.

15.   . . . And Tereus, watching,
      Sees beyond what he sees: she is in his arms,
      That is not her father whom her arms go around,
      Not her father she is kissing. Everything
      Is fuel to his fire. He would like to be
      Her father at that moment; and if he were
      He would be as wicked a father as he is husband.

                                        (ll. 478–84)

Ovid's choice to elaborate on the erotic theme of incest is not merely an element of his voyeurism; it is the sign of mimetic desire/rivalry. Tereus wants to become Pandion finally not to have full control over Philomela, but rather to control Athens.

16. In Livy, Ovid, Chaucer, Shakespeare, and Macaulay, Lucrece and Virginia have neither mother, sister, nor daughter. The women who serve them (Lucrece's servants, Virginia's nurse) are depicted as being as voiceless and powerless as they are.

17. In fact, this myth was incorporated into later Greek literature as a warning against women's proverbial capacity for revenge. See, for example, Achilles Tatius's novel *Leukippe and Kleitophon:* "Only passionate women making a man pay for a sexual affront, even if they must endure as much harm as they impose, count the pain of their infliction." I thank John Winkler for bringing this text to my attention and for providing me with his translation of this passage forthcoming in *The Ancient Greek Novels in Translation,* edited by Bryan P. Reardon (Berkeley: University of California Press).

In returning to the problem of revenge and the desire for justice I do not mean to lend any support to the misogynist readings of the past, or to ignore the fact that in Greek culture women could not speak in public without incurring shame (thus Philomela's initial vow to overcome all shame and *tell* her story). Rather I wish to use the myth to raise the question for us.

18. See Apollodorus, *The Library,* translated by Sir James George Frazer (New York: G. P. Putnam's Sons, 1921), 2:98.

19. I wish to remind my readers that I am intentionally reading double here, taking the myth as a possible lesson even while uncovering its complex violence. While the myth seems thematically dedicated to revealing the circular or self-destructive nature of reciprocal violence (revenge), it is structurally dedicated to the preservation of a threatened social order *which is served by the myth of passion and acts of revenge.* An outsider and marginal insiders are pitted against each other for a conflict to the death which leaves the central power of the

father/king unchallenged. Procne and Philomela as reunited sisters must "inevitably" imitate and then outdo Tereus's violence so that it is *women's* fault that the alternative—Philomela's art and women's community—*will turn out to make no difference after all.*

20. This is the close of the "White Tigers" section of Maxine Hong Kingston's *The Woman Warrior: Memoirs of a Girlhood Among Ghosts* (New York: Vintage Books, 1977), pp. 62–63. To emphasize the feminist aspect of Kingston's work here is not to ignore her struggle to remember and to affirm her complex heritage as a Chinese-American *and* as a woman.

21. Sometimes the resisting woman writer separates herself from the invitation to become a victim by writing a fiction. Philomela is evoked several times in the work of Virginia Woolf, but most pointedly in the sickroom when her first woman hero, Rachel Vinrace, lies dying. The narrator tells us that the young woman "pushed her voice out as far as possible until sometimes it became a bird and flew away, she thought it doubtful whether it ever reached the person she was talking to." See *The Voyage Out* (New York: Harcourt, Brace and World, 1920), p. 347.

22. The Chilean poet and Nobel Laureate Gabriela Mistral offered her text and her body for those who need it.

> If I am put beside
> the born blind,
> I will tell her softly, so softly,
> with my voice of dust,
> "Sister, take my eyes."

See "El Reparto" ("Distribution") in *Selected Poems of Gabriela Mistral,* translated and edited by Doris Dana (Baltimore: Johns Hopkins University Press, 1961).

23. Maya Angelou, for example, survived to write *I Know Why the Caged Bird Sings.* And Alice Walker knew that women could turn violence back on themselves when she envisioned the women in *Meridian* cutting down their own singing tree—the tree planted for a black Philomela whose power to tell tales was so powerful that the master cut out her tongue after his son died of a heart attack listening to her. In Walker's latest fiction, *The Color Purple,* the writer offers us one of the most powerful meditations on the refusal to return violence for violence that we have had for a long time.

Contributors

PAULA GUNN ALLEN has taught at several California universities including San Francisco State, San Diego State, the University of California at Los Angeles and the University of California at Berkeley. She has published four poetry chapbooks; two other books: *Shadow Country* (poetry) and *The Woman Who Owned the Shadows* (novel); as well as several articles on Native American literature, and edited a volume titled *Studies in American Indian Literature, Critical Essays and Course Designs*.

CAROLYN BURKE is a research associate and lecturer in humanities at the University of California, Santa Cruz. She has written on women's literature and feminist theory in France and the United States and is currently completing a book on Mina Loy.

MARY DeSHAZER is an assistant professor of English and Women's Studies at Xavier University in Cincinnati, Ohio. She has published articles on May Sarton and other contemporary women poets, feminist educational reform, and sexism and language. She is currently completing a book on women poets and creative inspiration.

JOANNE FEIT DIEHL is an associate professor of English at the University of California at Davis. She is the author of *Dickinson and the Romantic Imagination* and several articles on feminist literary theory and nineteenth-century American literature.

ULLA E. DYDO has taught English at Vassar College and Brooklyn College and now teaches at Bronx Community College, C.U.N.Y. She is currently writing a book on Gertrude Stein's *Stanzas in Meditation* and her work from 1925 to 1932.

JOHN FELSTINER is a professor of English at Stanford University. His publications include *The Lies of Art: Max Beerbohm's Parody and Caricature, Translating Neruda: The Way to Macchu Pichu* and numerous articles on contemporary poetry.

SUSAN STANFORD FRIEDMAN is an associate professor of English and Women's Studies at the University of Wisconsin at Madison. Author of *Psyche Reborn: The Emergence of H.D.* and co-author of *A Women's Guide to Therapy,* she is currently at work on a book about H.D.'s prose and a study of childbirth and women's creativity in literature.

ALBERT GELPI is the Coe Professor of American Literature at Stanford University. His publications include *Emily Dickinson: The Mind of the Poet; The Poet in America: 1650 to the Present; Adrienne Rich's Poetry* (co-edited with Barbara Charlesworth Gelpi); and *The Tenth Muse: The Psyche of the American Poet.*

SANDRA GILBERT is a professor of English at the University of California, Davis. She is the author of *Acts of Attention: The Poems of D. H. Lawrence; The Madwoman in the Attic: The Woman Writer and the Nineteenth Century Literary Imagination* (co-authored with Susan Gubar); and *The Summer Kitchen: Poems.* She has written extensively on women writers and feminist criticism and has published both poetry and fiction in numerous literary journals.

PATRICIA KLINDIENST JOPLIN is an assistant professor of English and the Humanities at Yale University. She was a graduate student in the Modern Thought and Literature program at Stanford University at the time of the women's poetry conference for which her essay was originally prepared. She is currently completing a book on Virginia Woolf.

DAVID KALSTONE is a professor of English at Rutgers University. He is the author of two books on contemporary poetry—*Five Temperaments* and *Becoming A Poet: Elizabeth Bishop, Robert Lowell, and Marianne Moore.*

DIANE WOOD MIDDLEBROOK is a professor of English at Stanford University. Her publications include *Walt Whitman and Wallace Stevens; Worlds into Words: Understanding Modern Poems; Gin Considered as a Demon* (poems). She is currently at work on a biography of Anne Sexton.

BARBARA ANTONINA CLARKE MOSSBERG is an associate professor of English at the University of Oregon. She has written *Emily Dickinson: When a Writer Is a Daughter,* and the forthcoming *Sylvia Plath,* as well as several articles on American women poets.

ALICIA OSTRIKER is a professor of English at Rutgers University. She is the author of five books of poems, most recently *The Mother/Child Papers* and *A Woman Under the Surface,* and a volume of critical essays, *Writing Like a Woman.*

ANDREA BENTON RUSHING is an associate professor of English at Amherst College. She is a specialist in Black American Literature.

MARILYN YALOM is deputy director of the Center for Research on Women (CROW), Stanford University, and lecturer in the Modern Thought and Literature program. She was for many years professor of foreign languages and literature at California State University, Hayward. She is the editor of *Women Writers of the West Coast* and the author of *Maternity, Mortality and the Literature of Madness.*